A HISTORY OF THE DUTCH IN THE FAR EAST

By *ALBERT HYMA*

PROFESSOR OF HISTORY

UNIVERSITY OF MICHIGAN

GEORGE WAHR PUBLISHING CO.
Ann Arbor, Michigan
1953

Photographed & Lithoprinted by
BRAUN-BRUMFIELD, Inc.
Ann Arbor, Mich.

TABLE OF CONTENTS

INTRODUCTION

IN MARCH 1942 the present writer published a book
entitled, *The Dutch in the Far East* (Ann Arbor,
Mich.: George Wahr). At that time the Japanese were
steadily pushing their way into the great archipelago
known as the Dutch East Indies (or Netherlands East
Indies). Their invasion, occupation and subsequent defeat caused what an Indonesian scholar recently called
"the most unexpected consequences for Indonesia." He
spoke of the Japanese occupation as an oppression and
went on as follows: "The four years . . . upset the whole
nation and shook beyond recognition standards and values
which under Dutch colonial rule had seemed firm as a
rock. . . . Nothing and nobody remained untouched."
The Japanese government encouraged the whole population to rise in favor of its East-Asian imperialistic dreams.
The Indonesian youth plunged "enthusiastically and with
high ideals into the boiling sea of war which the Japanese
had calculatingly unleashed in Indonesia." [1]

Then followed years of disillusionment. Even peace
did not bring back the old days of order and meticulous
progress in nearly all directions. The revolution, which
began with slogans of liberty and prosperity, ended with
the liberty to destroy and to kill foreigners of all races.
Our Indonesian friend continues with these simple words:
"Out of this ferment emerged the tragedy and problems
of the Indonesian State and its peoples after their liberation. Indonesia, one of the richest countries of the world
and a nation with every possibility for advancement, became, as it were, swamped in a morass."

The history of Indonesia from 1942 to 1953 forms an
important chapter in the development of the Far Eastern
civilizations. Moreover, Dutch New Guinea has emerged

after World War II as a new field of exploitation for the Dutch people. It is high time that the truth be told about these matters, while many readers will welcome the account dealing with the great natural resources of Dutch New Guinea. Its oil reserves are more prolific than those of Bornea and Sumatra combined, while its nickel and coal supplies form storehouses of wealth for future use. Again, enormous areas of fertile clay soil in the southern region, favored by a perfect climate for the production of rice, will in the near future meet a need long felt by the half-starved peoples of the Far East.

The earlier work just mentioned was sold soon after publication, and for this reason its pages have been reproduced below, though revised to conform to present-day requirements. With the hauling down of the Dutch flag in Indonesia went other ancient ties which bound the natives to the so-called mother country in Europe. That term had rankled in the breasts of brave and ambitious young scholars who understood how long before there was a Dutch nation Java had been the center of a great empire. Nevertheless, European civilization had profoundly touched the hearts of the masses. No amount of scornful talking about colonialism could silence the demand for more of the good things that the Hollanders had imported and achieved. At the moment many currents of thought and feeling produce strange actions and aspiratitons. It would seem that the Dutch merchants are not yet through with their work in the Far East.

CHAPTER I

THE SECRET OF THE DUTCH
COMMERCIAL POLICY

DURING the seventeenth century, it became the custom for many Englishmen, when they were surprised about a certain remarkable incident, to say, "That
beats the Dutch." So popular did this proverb become
among Englishmen that it was transmitted to the Americans, most of whom no longer have any conception of how
it originated. They have forgotten that in the time of the
Puritans and the Pilgrim Fathers the Dutch were unsurpassed in commercial and industrial enterprise.

One distinguished British scholar has thrown much
light on the nature of the successes achieved by the Hollanders in many fields of enterprise. He writes thus: "Contemporaries in England began to be aware very early in
the seventeenth century that in many branches of social
organization the Dutch were far ahead of them. Pamphlets
began to point out Dutch practices which the English
ought to imitate or Dutch gains which the English ought
to contest. Right up to the English coast the Dutch had
the rich sea-fisheries almost to themselves. One of the few
scraps of economic history which have become, in our
time, generally known is the fact that the Dutch were then
the common carriers of the world and, in particular, of the
English. They had the best-managed merchant marine of
the world; their ships were the cheapest to build, and the
best adapted for their various purposes. Their commercial
policy was well fitted to stimulate trade and to make their
country 'the pack-house of the world.' In the organization
of business they had no equals. It was not until well on in
the eighteenth century that the insurance of English ship-

ping came to be effected at home instead of in Amsterdam.
. . . For English economic writers it was a puzzle: they
groped uncertainly towards the truth, which it is now easy
to see, that this difference was a symptom and a result of
the backwardness of England and the superior development of Dutch resources. Happily for us our intercourse
with the Dutch people at this time was as intimate as any
we ever had with foreigners before the days of railways
and steam navigation. Once they had become aware of
their backwardness, the English began what led the late
Dr. Cunningham to call the middle and later period of
the seventeenth century in our economic history, that of
'conscious imitation of the Dutch.' They set themselves
to overtake the Dutch, and in so doing they transformed
their whole economic life."[1]

Illuminating also is the analysis of another of Britain's
most distinguished historians: "By taking to the sea, the
English fell under the influence of the Dutch. As friends
or as enemies, as partners or as rivals, men of the two nations were now in perpetual contact. Holland affected
every department of English life, more, perhaps, than any
other nation has ever done by the mere force of example.
The little republic, which from 1600 to 1650 maintained
its territory as a safe and prosperous oasis in the midst of
the wilderness of fire and destruction around, was during
those years the leader of mankind in most of the sciences
and arts. She was the school of scientific war, agriculture,
gardening, finance, and trade, and of numberless arts and
crafts; the academy of painting; the home of theology
whence Calvinist and Arminian alike drew their theories;
the asylum for philosophy and free speculation; and last,
but not least, the example to our merchants and our politicians of a community which had attained prosperity, en-
lightenment, and power by rebellion against a legitimate
Prince."[2]

It has been widely assumed by both historians. and economists that the Dutch Republic reached its greatest political and economic power about the year 1648, when the Peace of Westphalia was signed. After this date a steady and rather rapid decline is said to have set in. Much has often been made of the Navigation Act of Oliver Cromwell, which was passed in the year 1651, and which is alleged to have been the death-blow of the Dutch merchant marine. Moreover, a large number of writers, both in Great Britain and in the United States, have assumed that the government of the Dutch Republic was of such a nature as to prevent unity of action and efficiency of operation, especially in times of crisis. It has often been fashionable to compare England with Rome, and Holland with Carthage. Just as Rome destroyed Carthage, so England is said to have ruined Dutch commerce during the second half of the seventeenth century.[3]

But the amazing thing about Dutch commerce of the seventeenth century is that, instead of having declined during the second half of this century, it was considerably enhanced. Moreover, long after the year 1700 it continued to increase. It should be noted, for example, that between 1720 and 1729 exports from the Dutch Republic to France were, on an average, only about 60 per cent each year of what they were between 1769 and 1780. The same proportion may be seen in the exports from France to the Dutch Republic during those years.[4]

A recent article in *The Economic History Review* states correctly that "Dutch and English observers have commonly conspired to antedate the commercial decline of the Netherlands by attaching it to what appeared obvious or catastrophic—the British Navigation Acts or the Anglo-Dutch wars. Thus it was widely held that the peak of Dutch prosperity was reached about 1648 and that the British Navigation Acts spelt the beginning of economic decadence. The recent work of Dutch historians—Dr. van Dillen and Dr. van der Kooy in particular—has made it necessary to discard this theory, and has done a good deal to clarify the stages in the real decline of Holland by analysing the subtler change in her economic structure. It is now safe to assume that the practical monopoly of European transport and commerce which the Dutch established in the early seventeenth century by reason of their geographical position, their superior commercial organisation and technique, and the economic backwardness of their neighbours, stood intact until about 1730." [5]

The leading experts in economic history in Europe have at last come to the conclusion that both Great Britain and France, until about 1730, failed to become independent of the Dutch intermediary trade.[6] The Dutch Republic remained, as before, the greatest center of commerce in the western world. Until 1730, Amsterdam also was the greatest financial center of Europe.[7]

Inasmuch as the Dutch retained their enviable position in the fields of commerce and banking for more than seventy years after the first Navigation Act was passed (1651), and after the Peace of Westphalia was signed; and since a large number of pessimistic writers, who had predicted the extinction of the Dutch Republic in 1672, were completely mistaken in their forecast, it will be an interesting task to determine what were the factors involved in the expansion of Dutch sea power and commerce during the seventeenth century. Before analyzing the views of contemporary writers in Great Britain, France, Germany, and Italy, most of whom did not fully understand all the reasons why the Dutch merchants were able to surpass those of all other nations, we shall examine the results of the researches by leading historians, economists, and sociologists during the past twenty-five years.

Dutch sea power was making tremendous strides before the beginning of the seventeenth century. The textile industries in the province of Holland; the herring fishery, which had grown from humble beginnings in Zeeland about the year 1425 to enormous proportions by 1525; the proximity of Antwerp, Ghent, and Brussels; the growth of commerce with England and the Baltic Sea in the fifteenth century, accompanied by the destruction of the Hansa League; the shipbuilding industries, with their constant output of new ships seeking employment; the shifting of the great trade routes from the Mediterranean to the Atlantic seaboard; the unfortunate experiences of the provinces in the southern Netherlands, to be known for a time as the Spanish Netherlands, in losing the bulk of their trade and industries to Holland and England; the weakening of French competition in the eastern Mediterranean, owing to the civil and religious wars raging in France between 1562 and 1593; the decline of both French and Venetian sea power in the second half of the sixteenth century; and the annexation of Portugal in 1580 by the king of Spain—these and other factors not so easily recognized by scholars, combined to give the Dutch a decided advantage over their European neighbors. Then, as the seventeenth century opened, the English queen passed away, and for forty-six years England was ruled by two Stuart monarchs who were not interested sufficiently in the development of English trade and sea power. In short, in the period between 1500 and 1650 a number of fortuitous circumstances aided the Dutch in securing about one-half of the seaborne trade of Europe, more than one-half of the important fisheries in the North Sea, a large portion of the textile industries of the European countries, 50 per cent of all the merchant vessels in the western world, the bulk of the spice trade and the finest tropical colonies.

The factors just enumerated have long been known to historians in the United States as well as in Europe. Now it remains to examine those which are less concrete and more difficult to evaluate. First of all we are confronted with the problem as to whether Calvinism materially aided the expansion of Dutch commerce and industry during the seventeenth century. The thesis of Max Weber, claiming a close connection between these two factors, has never been popular among Dutch historians, but in Great Britain and the United States it used to be supported by a large number of teachers in the fields of the social sciences. For a time it also seemed as if the university in Amsterdam which is controlled by the orthodox Calvinists in the Netherlands and entitled The Free University would also adopt Weber's conclusions.[8] But one of the professors in this university, on April 13, 1939, published a lengthy review in the official organ (the *Standaard*) of the orthodox Calvinist political party (the Anti-Revolutionary Party), of a work by the present writer, entitled *Christianity, Capitalism and Communism*. This review represents the official opinion of the faculty in this university and of the political party in question. It accepts all the conclusions drawn regarding the relation between Calvinism and capitalism, especially in the Netherlands.[9]

In addition to the reluctance on the part of practically all well-known Dutch historians to accept the thesis of Max Weber,[10] there may be mentioned here two books which have been written in recent years by capable authorities in the field. The first of these was published in 1933 by W. R. Robertson, and is entitled *Aspects in the Rise of Economic Individualism: A Criticism of Max Weber and His School*.[11] Mr. Robertson has pointed out something that has escaped the attention of many recent historians and economists, namely, the phenomenal expansion of industry and commerce in the southern provinces of the Netherlands, where more than 80 per cent of the population is Roman Catholic. According to Max

Weber and his followers, the spirit of capitalism was fostered more successfully by Calvinism than by Roman Catholicism or Lutheranism. Consequently, Mr. Robertson has done scholarship a great service in showing that the Roman Catholics in the Netherlands provide an excellent refutation of this part of Max Weber's thesis. Unfortunately, however, Mr. Robertson has become a bit too enthusiastic in his praise of the Roman Catholics in the Netherlands. He is of the opinion that only in the province of Zeeland has the country remained predominantly Calvinistic. Then he adds these words: "And Zealand is the least progressive of the provinces, a province of fishermen and farmers." [12]

The other writer who has discussed the supposed connection between Calvinism and capitalism in the Dutch Republic is A. Fanfani, who has long been known as one of the outstanding experts in Europe in the field of economics.[13] Mr. Fanfani has a curious idea, however, about the nature of Dutch commerce during the sixteenth century. He argues that there is no need to study the relationship between Calvinism and capitalism in the Netherlands during the sixteenth century, because this region declined in that century. As proof he cites the fact that the Venetian galleys which used to sail to the Netherlands each year up to 1532, ceased going there after this year. The thought seems never to have occurred to Fanfani that the rapidly rising sea power of the Dutch and Flemings rendered the voyages of the Venetian merchants unprofitable.[14]

How important secular forces are in the growth of commerce and industry, may be seen in studying the history of the Baltic trade. From 1598 to 1613, when Puritanism was very powerful in England, at least in the field of religion and theology, an average of fewer than 250 English ships passed legitimately through the Sound each year. In the period from 1614 to 1640, the average was practically the same, although (or because?) the government of England was very hostile to the Puritans. From 1641 to 1657, when the Puritans and Independents controlled the government, the average was below one hundred; but from 1678 to 1688 it was over five hundred, despite the power of the Anglicans and the Restoration of 1660. From 1723 to 1740, it was about one thousand; and from 1751 to 1775 it was over fourteen hundred. England's merchant marine increased about as fast as Calvinism and Puritanism in England declined, although there is probably no connection between these two phenomena.

In the Dutch Republic, we also witness a remarkable process. Whereas the province of Holland controlled about one-half of the Baltic trade from 1497 to 1548, and from one-third to one-half from 1557 to 1686 (showing a relative loss in the total trade as Calvinism increased in the province, which is the reverse of what would be expected of Holland if the Weber thesis worked), the province of Zeeland, situated to the south of Holland, and therefore farther removed from the Baltic Sea, had to be satisfied with between 1 and 2 per cent of the total, and often with even less. Was this perhaps because Zeeland did not contain so many energetic Calvinists? No, the Calvinists in Zeeland were stronger proportionately than they were in Holland. The two northern provinces, on the other hand, enjoyed the control of more than 15 per cent of the Baltic trade, both before they became Calvinistic and afterward. In the eighteenth century, when orthodox Calvinism was well-nigh dead in the northern provinces, as far as the majority of the population was concerned, these two provinces gradually gained on Holland, and, by 1726, they surpassed it in number of ships they sent to the Baltic Sea.

Furthermore, the leading industries in the Dutch Republic during the period from 1581 to 1700, when orthodox Calvinism was far stronger in the northern provinces than in Holland, were nevertheless situated for the most part in Holland. It was also Holland which owned most of the shares in the East India Company and the West India Company; and it was Holland that possessed the leading bank and the only stock market. More money was to be found in Holland than in all the other six provinces put together. Nevertheless, Holland could boast of only one university in the republic out of a total of five. Holland, between 1611 and 1672, was not recognized as the leading center of orthodox Calvinist theology. It is true that the international Calvinist synod of Dordrecht (1618–1619) was held in the province of Holland, but its president had come from the extreme north. And, between 1636 and 1700, Utrecht surpassed Leyden as a center of orthodox Calvinist theology. Today, Calvinism is weakest in the most thriving hives of Dutch industry, as is not strange at all.

Dutch fishing and trade were doing very well before there were any Calvinists in the Netherlands. When, for example, in the year 1503, that is, six years before Calvin was born, 718 ships from the province of Holland sailed through the Sound out of a total of 1,222, it can hardly be said that Calvinism brought such a decided advantage to Dutch shipping.[15] And when, in the first quarter of the fifteenth century, the industrious fishermen in Zeeland developed their world-famous process of curing herring (which was kept a secret for more than two hundred years), no one dreamed then of ascribing this event to a change in religion or theology. The obligation to work hard was in the blood of the Dutch long before Calvin was ever heard of, and the frugality of their middle class was considered a virtue when Thomas à Kempis lived among them and wrote his *Imitation of Christ* (1415–1425).

Unfortunately, the great majority of writers who have discussed the influence of Calvinism upon the growth of

modern capitalism seem to have overlooked the remarkable misunderstanding of Calvinist theology revealed by
Max Weber himself on the question of predestination.
Weber argues that in Calvin's theology "the Father in
heaven of the New Testament, so human and understanding . . . is gone." Moreover, continues Weber, "in its extreme inhumanity this doctrine must above all have had
one consequence for the life of a generation which surrendered to its magnificent consistency." No one could
help the sinner, no priest, no sacraments, no church, and
finally, no God.[16]

Max Weber undoubtedly made too much of the doctrine of predestination, and in separating the Arminians
in the Netherlands from the orthodox Calvinists, he came
to the conclusion that the Arminians did not fall within
the scope of his survey, since they had rejected the Calvinistic doctrine of predestination. Nevertheless, they were
very active in business. They owned many of the shares
in the Dutch East India Company, and a large number of
them actively participated in the great stock exchange in
Amsterdam. The Arminians, as a rule, belonged to the
middle and upper classes, while in such cities as Amsterdam and Leyden the poorer classes were, for the most
part, devotedly attached to orthodox Calvinism.

It is of the utmost importance to study carefully what
the orthodox Calvinists in the Netherlands had to say about
the doctrine of predestination. Their opinion differed
considerably from that of Max Weber and his supporters.
They did not by any means think that no one could help
the sinner, not even any pastor, any sacraments, or church,
or God Himself. Such reasoning they would have called
blasphemy. One of their best definitions of predestination was expressed thus: "He, in the first place, presented
to them His only begotten Son, whose sufferings, although
sufficient for the expiation of all men's sins, nevertheless,

according to God's decree, served alone to the reconciliation of the elect. God caused the Gospel to be preached to
them, making the same, through the Holy Ghost, of
strength upon their minds; so that they not merely obtain
power to repent and believe, but also actually and volun-
tarily do repent and believe." [17]

In short, it was, for the most part, secular forces that
enabled the Dutch merchants of the seventeenth century
to gain many advantages over their competitors in foreign
lands. Once having achieved the lead, they tenaciously
clung to it, so that even in the century of decline, that is,
the eighteenth century, the Dutch merchants did not
nearly so rapidly lose their former ambition and enthusiasm as did the owners of industrial establishments, the
scholars in the five great state universities, the outstanding artists, the most eminent literary figures, and the political leaders. Since these merchants were exceptional,
living as they did in the midst of universal decline, lux-
urious surroundings, pessimism, and indolence, it will be
very much worth while to investigate the methods employed by them, for it must undoubtedly have been these
remarkable methods of theirs that permitted them, during
the opening years of the eighteenth century, to occupy a
place in the fields of commerce and sea power that was
altogether out of proportion to that held by the Dutch
Republic in the realm of politics. Although it has long
been fashionable to extol the Dutch merchants of the beginning of the seventeenth century and to describe the
terrible and swift decline of Dutch commerce about one
hundred years later, the original sources left by contemporary writers show that the Hollanders were as much admired in the year 1700 as they had been in the year 1600.
Several writers have pointed out how well Sir Walter
Raleigh understood the nature of Dutch commerce when,
during the first decade of the seventeenth century, he

addressed a treatise to King James I, in which he analyzed
the extraordinary success attained by the Dutch merchants. But as a rule modern interpreters overlook certain serious errors that are to be found in his treatise.
When they examine figures concerning Dutch fishing and
commerce a hundred years after Raleigh wrote his treatise,
they are struck by what seems to them a terrible decline,
whereas the amount of Dutch commerce was greater in
the later period than that in the earlier period. Even so,
Sir Walter Raleigh's careful deductions, coming from the
pen of a man who actually saw the Dutch merchants at
work in several Dutch ports, are not to be despised. We
shall examine his remarks in the light attained by Dutch
historical scholarship during the past fifty years.

Sir Walter Raleigh claimed that the Hollanders built
one thousand ships a year, although they did not have one
timber tree growing in their country, nor any commodities produced there with which to load one hundred ships,
and yet they had twenty thousand ships and vessels and all
employed. In his opinion, the Hollanders used 400,000
men in taking care of these vessels.[18] But the truth is, as
pointed out by Professor P. J. Blok, that the Dutch employed about three thousand vessels in their fishing industry, and engaged the services of forty thousand men. Mr.
Blok also indicates that the total of the other vessels in
their merchant marine was about ten thousand, of which
eight hundred were used in the Baltic trade, twelve hundred in the trade with Spain, four hundred in the commerce with Italy, and about six thousand in the coastal
trade, especially with England, Germany, and France.
The total number of men employed in the merchant marine was about one hundred thousand.[19]

Raleigh gives the following seven reasons to account
for the phenomenal success of the Dutch merchants in the
first two decades of the seventeenth century:

1. The merchant staplers which make all things in abundance, by reason of their storehouses continually replenished with all kind of commodities.

2. The liberty of free traffick for strangers to buy and sell in Holland, and other countries and states, as if they were freeborn, makes great intercourse.

3. The small duties levied upon merchants draws all nations to trade with them.

4. Their fashioned ships continually freighted before ours, by reason of their few mariners and great bulk, serving the merchant cheap.

5. Their forwardness to further all manner of trading.

6. Their wonderful employment of their busses for fishing, and the great returns they make.

7. Their giving free custom, inwards and outwards, for any new-erected trade; by means whereof they have gotten already almost the sole trade into their hands.[20]

Raleigh said that the Hollanders permitted the inhabitants of many other nations to live among them, which meant an increase in their population, and more ready access to the markets of those countries from which the people have come. Secondly, the Hollanders levied very low customs and convoy duties, which naturally promoted the expansion of commerce and industry. Furthermore, the Hollanders had a great abundance of precious metals and commodities of all sorts, which they stored in their great warehouses, ready to distribute them to other nations in times of want. Raleigh also noted how clever the Hollanders were in making various types of ships to suit the different kinds of trade in which they engaged. He wrote thus: "To bring this to pass, they have many advantages of us; the one is, by their fashioned ships called boyers, hoybarks, hoys, and others that are made to hold great bulk of merchandise, and to sail with a few men for profit. For example; though an English ship of two hun-

dred tons, and a Holland ship, or any other of the petty
States of the same burden be at Dantzic, or any other place
beyond the seas, or in England, they do serve the merchant
better cheap by one hundred pounds in his freight than
we can, by reason he hath but nine or ten mariners, and
we near thirty; thus he saveth twenty men's meat and
wages in a voyage; and so in all other their ships according
to their burden, by which means they are freighted,
wheresoever they come, to great profit, whilst our ships
lie still and decay, or go to Newcastle for coals." [21]

Raleigh continued in showing that an English ship
might be loading cargo at a French port, where there also
might be a Dutch ship doing the same thing. When the
English ship returned home, it would have to pay about
nine hundred pounds customs duties, whereas the Hollanders would have to pay about fifty pounds. It might be
argued, Raleigh said, that in this manner the Dutch government did not collect enough revenue, but the flow of
commerce was so enormous that, instead of hurting its
own interests, the Dutch government was greatly benefited by its enlightened policy. The Dutch government, as
a matter of fact, received twice as much as the English
government. Furthermore, only about 1 per cent of all
the commodities imported by the Dutch merchants was
consumed in the Dutch Republic, while all the rest was
sold again to other countries, thus enabling the merchants
of the Netherlands to buy and sell in great volume, and
to furnish employment for all the men on the ships. Consequently, so argued Raleigh, it was not his purpose to
diminish the revenues of the British king, but to increase
them, as was done by the Hollanders.

Raleigh also observed that the Dutch government was
vitally interested in promoting the welfare of its merchants wherever they might be engaged in commerce. The
government was exceedingly efficient in supervising all

imports and exports, and in negotiating with foreign governments who had molested the Dutch merchants.

According to Raleigh, about five or six hundred Dutch ships were sent to England each year with merchandise of various sorts, and they stored them in the warehouses in England until the prices should rise high enough to suit them. But the English, on the other hand, did not send more than fifty vessels a year to the Netherlands, to import merchandise there. Unless there should be a great scarcity in such a land as England, foreign merchants did not care to go there, because they disliked the high duties they had to pay in English ports. He also referred to the experiences of the merchants of Genoa in Italy, who used to be very prosperous, until the government suddenly decided to levy a 16 per cent customs duty on all foreign merchants importing goods to Genoa. "So," continued Raleigh, "at the present day we do not have more than three ships which go to Genoa each year, but on the contrary, the duke of Florence constructed the excellent port Leghorn (Livorno), where he levied a small customs duty, and thus enabled Florence to grow rich and powerful."

Raleigh had much to say about the enormous extent of Dutch fishing, most of his figures being correct, except as we observed, the size of the fishing fleet. He was also too enthusiastic in describing the manner in which the merchants of Amsterdam amassed grain and stored it in their warehouses, although, so he reasoned, no grain whatsoever is raised in the Dutch Republic itself. Such a statement is, of course, a gross exaggeration, because Dutch farming flourished together with Dutch industry and Dutch fishing. Nevertheless, a large number of writers since the time of Raleigh have copied all these figures of his without making the necessary corrections. But it remains true that his illuminating survey has thrown much light on the manner in which the Dutch merchants during the first two decades of the seventeenth century strove successfully to keep ahead of all their competitors in foreign lands.

It is useful to compare the comments of Sir Walter Raleigh with those made one hundred years later by Archbishop Huet, of Avranches, in France. This learned and sagacious clergyman wrote a treatise in the year 1700, which is not only more extensive than that by Sir Walter Raleigh, but also more penetrating and more valuable than his. It was promptly translated into the English language, and on the title page of the English edition it is stated that the contents are useful for every Englishman to know.[22]

We shall follow the second English edition of the year 1719 in analyzing the comments made by the French archbishop. The author states in his preface that he was anxious to write a treatise on the nature and extent of Dutch commerce at the end of the seventeenth century, because in his judgment nothing is so little understood in France as this subject of commerce. This is particularly true of persons employed in the highest posts of the government. He points out that both England and Holland have governments that take the greatest care to protect the commerce of their subjects. In the recent wars, he continues, the British and Dutch governments had in mind the protection of commercial interests. He even says that this was the principal motive that caused the last wars, in which opinion he is partly correct, though he exaggerates. He describes with admiration the work done by Queen Elizabeth for England, but he adds the observation that nothing can compare with what the Dutch have accomplished. He exclaims that it will always be a subject of astonishment and wonder that a handful of merchants who fled into a little country unable to produce enough to feed its own inhabitants, should defeat the greatest power on earth, and make the king of Spain sue for peace. But what is most wonderful, he continues, and what ought to surprise us the most is that the wars never interrupted their trade, and it was during the lengthy war against Spain, which lasted eighty years, that they laid the foundations of their great empire in the East Indies and along the coast of Africa. Perhaps even more astonishing was the fact that they actually traded with their own enemies, the Spaniards, even in the midst of their wars, and that they derived much of their wealth from this trade with their enemies.[23]

"We Frenchmen," said Huet, "have been reproached that the genius of our Nation was not proper for a foreign commerce." But he referred to Jacques Couer, who was Superintendent of the Finances in the reign of Charles VII. He was a grand businessman. Why could not others be like him? All that the French merchants needed was a great leader. The writer had lived among the ablest of Dutch merchants, whose views he was about to set forth. "One ought ever to look upon them as the true Oracles of Commerce."[24]

In the first chapter of the treatise the archbishop remarked that trade had no enemies so mortal as constraint, thus showing himself to be an enemy of mercantilism and one of the forerunners of the principle of free trade. In the same chapter he made the sagacious observation that commerce may flourish in a monarchy as well as in a free state, meaning a republic, for never did commerce and industry thrive so much as it did in the Low Countries under the four princes of the house of Burgundy, and two of the house of Austria. The writer said that he used to labor under the error that commerce required a republican form of government in order to expand freely, but after having consulted with the outstanding politicians of England and Holland, he came to another conclusion. He thought that even in France under an absolute monarchy both commerce and industry could thrive more than ever before, if only the principal ministers of the king would pay any attention to it.

In the second chapter the author mentioned the fact that the central government of the United provinces or the Dutch Republic, called the States-General, "omitted nothing all that time to increase their trade where it was already established, or to establish it where they never had established it before." He referred to the time between 1609 and 1621, when Spain and the Netherlands were not actively engaged in warfare, having concluded a truce in the year 1609, which will be discussed more fully by the present writer in another chapter. Huet also mentioned the treaty which the Dutch signed in 1612 with the Turks, adding that about the same time the Dutch through their astute diplomacy made favorable commercial treaties with the ruler of Morocco and the emperor of Japan. Moreover, from 1621 to 1697, in spite of numerous wars, the Dutch were able to extend their commerce over all parts of the world.

Excellent is the discussion of the fisheries and the industries. By importing vast amounts of raw materials and exporting manufactured goods, the Dutch showed that they perfectly understood the good points of mercantilism. In the field of the textile industries during the seventeenth century, as the writer pointed out, they led all nations. He compared Amsterdam with ancient Alexandria, of whom one classical writer said: "All its inhabitants followed some trade; that the lame and the gouty were employed, and even those that had the gout in their hands did not sit idle.[25]

There was little question concerning the superiority of the woolen goods manufactured in the Netherlands, but even the finished silks of the Dutch were preferred in Germany, the northern countries, Portugal, and other lands, where the French manufacturers could not compete with them, largely because the Dutch goods were from 15 to 20 per cent cheaper. Although the goods manufactured in France were superior in quality and in appearance, the Dutch pieces were larger, and as soon as the French had perfected a new design of material, the Dutch immediately imitated them and undersold them.

The lumber industry, shipbuilding, the manufacture of dairy products, the refineries for the production of salt, the soap factories, the printing establishments and many other industries were carefully analyzed and received the highest praise from this keen French observer.

One of the most important observations of Huet was that concerning the manufacture of ships. When foreigners placed orders for Dutch ships, they knew that the vessels were ready even before the order had been placed. The ships were less expensive than all others, and the Hollanders sent convoys with their merchant ships. "Besides, they are very just and faithful in giving a good account of all they are entrusted with. This trust considerably increases their navigation, and causes them to build a vast number of ships which gives constant employment to a prodigious number of seamen, who repair thither from all parts, and on their arrival are always sure of finding businesses." [26]

Very enlightening is his discussion of the trade with Russia, where the English used to be far ahead of the Dutch, but they did not take the proper pains to study the needs and moods of their customers. The writer wondered why the English had not exerted themselves to get a monopoly of the Russian trade, which they had almost secured in the previous century. But now, that is, about the year 1700, they sent only four or five ships to Russia a year, over against about forty by the Dutch. English cloths in Russia were not wanted any more, because they were more expensive than the Dutch. Although the Dutch cloth shrunk, the Russians said that was to be expected of new cloth, for they were attracted by the low price of these goods. Besides, the Dutch sent over a vast quantity of toys that sold even better than cloths. The Dutch were much more numerous in Russia than the English, they had much more money at their disposal, they educated the Russians in getting the most for their money, and they gave them presents. (This, as we shall see, is exactly the way in which they were able to secure a monopoly of the European trade with Japan.)

Near the end of the fourth chapter the writer showed that the Dutch had more trade with Norway than all other nations together. Although the Norwegians did not even have money with which to buy goods, the Dutch supplied them with the money with which they bought their timber. For the protection of the trade with Norway and Denmark, the Dutch government had signed treaties with the king of Denmark, notably those of 1645 and of 1669.

Another important point observed by the writer was that the people of Poland and other countries to the south of the Baltic Sea insisted upon getting Dutch coins, and in many cases would take no others. Consequently, the Hollanders had obtained a decided advantage over competitors from other countries.[27]

Huet was struck by the fact that the Dutch government left no stone unturned to prevent the countries in the north from dealing directly with those of the west and south. Being situated between the north and south, the Dutch took advantage of their favorable position.[27]

In order to increase their trade with the Germans, the Dutch had always been careful to preserve the liberties of the city of Cologne, and the navigation of the Rhine. "They have, in like manner, frequently protected the liberties of Hamburg against the attempts of the king of Denmark, and those of Bremen against the Swedes. It should be noted in particular, said the author, that the Dutch had always had a particular care not to suffer any new customs or imposts to be laid on the navigation of the five great rivers of Germany, "by means of which they derive such an advantageous trade, and render themselves formidable." Even in the Spanish Netherlands they were masters of the trade from all parts. They trade there with the greatest of liberty, authority, and ease imaginable, "by reason of their bordering on these provinces, and the advantages they have of the rivers and canals."

At the opening of the eighth chapter the author minimized the harmful results of the Navigation Act of Oliver Cromwell. The Dutch merchants, in order to placate the English, permitted the latter to import into the Netherlands a great variety of goods, even many that were not produced in England at all. The following words indicate how clearly the French archbishop understood the difficulties under which the Dutch merchants of the seventeenth century labored and how ably they overcame the said difficulties: "The absolute necessity that the Dutch have of the English ports on the Channel is one of the principal reasons that make them suffer that great inequality in the respected liberty of the trade between the two nations, and to suit themselves to the laws that the English have made in relation thereto."

The tariff war between Colbert and the government of the Dutch Republic was also excellently analyzed. The high tariff of 1667 was not maintained, because the Dutch were able in 1678, at the conclusion of their war with France, to have the lower tariff of 1664 restored. The writer observed that the Dutch were eminently successful in imitating all of the important French industries. He was also correct in his analysis of the causes of the war in 1689, which many historians have wrongly called the War of the League of Augsburg, but which Prof. G. N. Clark, of Oxford University, has properly named the War of the Dutch Alliance. The Dutch call it the Nine Years' War.

Since the Dutch and the Spaniards were friends from 1667 to the end of the seventeenth century, the trade between Spain and the Netherlands was very considerable at that time. The French had lost practically the whole of their export trade in luxuries with Spain. "It is true," said Huet, "that these rich stuffs at first were neither so well made nor so beautiful as those made in France, but they have now come to that perfection in Holland that there is but very little difference."

Even more remarkable is the manner in which the Dutch were able to secure trade with the Spanish West Indies. Here, as the writer correctly observed, foreigners were not permitted to trade on the pain of death. Nevertheless, even the Spaniards themselves assisted the Hollanders. The latter would employ certain Spaniards who occupied important positions in the government or in society, and they would entrust these men with their trade. They would sell goods for the Hollanders in the Spanish colonies. This indirect way of trading with America was widely practised in Spain, and it was very seldom known that a Spaniard betrayed his trust. The court of Madrid was not unacquainted with these facts, but it was good politics for the court to assist the Dutch. Moreover, the Dutch had found means to carry on secret trade with the Spanish West Indies by means of their own island called Curaçao.

The writer also showed that he was familiar with the tactics employed by the Dutch government and its merchants in securing the lion's share of the trade in the Mediterranean Sea. The government set up a board of directors called "Chamber of Direction," which body made proper arrangements for convoys and for the appointment of consuls in the important sea ports in the Near East. Thus the

Italians and the French lost practically the whole of their trade with the Levant.[28] The chief reason why the English and the Dutch had been able to seize from the French and Italians the valuable textile trade with the eastern countries was that the former had taken the greatest pains to maintain high standards of weight and quality. Another reason was the low prices asked by the Hollanders and the English for their goods.

Exactly one-half of Huet's treatise is devoted to the trade between Holland and the Dutch East Indies. Since this subject will be discussed in greater detail by the present writer, it will suffice to state here that Huet also treated this aspect of Dutch commerce with care.

Many other French writers were tremendously impressed by the commercial activity of the Dutch. Voltaire, the most famous literary figure of the eighteenth century, was struck by the curious fact that merchandise could be brought along the canals up to the doors of the customers and warehouses.[29] This mode of transportation was so economical that for decades foreigners were placed at a distinct disadvantage.

Another keen thinker among the French, the world-famous Montesquieu, was amazed to see how everybody worked so hard in Amsterdam. Men, women, and children were carrying heavy burdens, and he was forced to conclude that it seemed as if Jupiter had transformed ants into men.[30] It would appear, therefore, that about the middle of the eighteenth century the Dutch merchants still kept their people very busy.

Returning now to the seventeenth century, we meet the famous French philosopher and mathematician, Descartes, who composed most of his important works in the Dutch Republic. He wrote thus: "Everybody was so attentive to his own profit, that I might live my whole life without ever being seen by a single person.[31]

Other factors involved in the rise and expansion of Dutch commerce were the famous Bank of Amsterdam and the stock market. Both of these institutions were a tribute to the wealth of the Dutch Republic. Numerous French writers have left testimony concerning the liberality with which the Dutch banks lent money to the merchants, while almost every one of them was deeply impressed by the stock market.[32]

One of the best works left by French writers was that by Joseph Accarias de Sérionne, entitled, *The Wealth of Holland*. It was published in London in the year 1778.[33] In this work, composed about the year 1760, the writer covered nearly all aspects of Dutch trade and commerce. Especially interesting is his discussion of the carrying trade, or freight trade. He said that this had seldom merited proper attention in the past. One reason why the Dutch were so successful was because they constructed a type of vessel which could be navigated through shallow waters and which extended into considerable proportions directly beneath the water line. For this reason these vessels were called "the big bellies." Although they were relatively slow, they had this distinct advantage that they could carry more freight than any other kind and required fewer persons on board than any others. They were also propelled with great ease. In this manner the Dutch could undersell the merchants of all other nations.[34] It might be added here that the peculiarity of the structure of these vessels enabled the Dutch to go through the Sound into the Baltic Sea and pay lower fees to the Danish government than would the owners of other vessels, because so much of the bulk was below the surface of the water, and that was not subject to taxation.

The writer just mentioned regretted to observe that the French were never able to overcome the lead of the Dutch, and so they were compelled to surrender to the latter almost all of their seaborne commerce. Especially successful in the Dutch Republic were the Frisians.

Another important factor in the development of Dutch commerce was the founding of great insurance companies which enabled the merchants to rely upon a steady trade regardless of how many pirates infested the shores of foreign countries, or of how many storms might wreck their vessels abroad. One of the first writers in modern times to take up the subject as an expert in the field was the great Dutch statesman, John de Witt.[35] The insurance business in Amsterdam grew to such proportions that many foreigners took advantage of the low rates prevailing there and the size of the capital employed. As late as in 1767, many of the German merchants refused to insure their goods in Berlin, and insisted on insurance from either Amsterdam or Hamburg. About the year 1720, there were about one hundred insurance offices in Amsterdam, against about eighteen in Hamburg. The English preferred Dutch insurance to their own until the middle of the eighteenth century. Some of the largest companies were located in Rotterdam. One of them had a capital of 12,600,000 guilders. This company was widely copied abroad.[36]

Perhaps the sagacity of the Dutch merchants is illustrated most clearly by the policy which the government was compelled to adopt towards foreigners and heretics. Whereas the leaders in the state church, that is, the orthodox Calvinist Church, frowned upon religious toleration, the municipal government of the leading cities and the national government strongly disapproved of the attitude of the clergy. It seems that the question of religious toleration in the Dutch Republic has seldom been understood by American historians. It has often been assumed, for example, that religious toleration flourished in the colony of New Netherland, especially in the city of New

Amsterdam, which is now New York. But the truth is that the only church recognized in the Dutch colony was the Dutch Reformed Church. No other church was tolerated. Whenever a group of persons attempted to form another, the Reformed churches in Amsterdam took swift action, and continued to harass the directors of the West India Company until the latter prohibited the new church from organizing.[37]

It is a significant fact that the Calvinists in the Netherlands originally had imitated the churches in Geneva under Calvin and Beza by permitting the civil government to examine their church ordinances before they were ratified, to exercise a considerable measure of control over the choice of pastors, to be present in the synods, and to help the authorities in the Church in executing the decisions made by the ecclesiastical powers. The records of the synods held in 1568, 1571, 1574, 1578, 1581, and 1586 all reveal the subservient attitude displayed by the clergy toward the magistrates in the cities, the members of the various provincial estates, and the national body called the States-General.[38]

But in the first half of the seventeenth century the Calvinist clergy in the Dutch Republic developed various viewpoints on the relation between Church and State, some retaining, for the most part, the orthodox Calvinist opinions, while others went to an extreme which closely approximated that of the Anabaptists and the Baptists. The pamphlet literature of the time throws much light upon this remarkable development. One of the most important compositions was from the pen of the learned minister in The Hague, John Wtenbogardt, entitled, *Treatise of the Office and Authority of a Higher Christian Ruler in Ecclesiastical Matters,* which, in the Dutch edition of 1610, filled 139 pages. The author, who was a friend of Hugo Grotius, showed clearly that both Calvin and the recent synods in the Netherlands had favored the view that the civil powers should exercise authority over the Church. He also quoted from Beza and Professor William Perkins at Cambridge, showing that these scholars had approved the arrangement which had been inaugurated by Calvin at Geneva and by Queen Elizabeth in England. On the other hand, numerous Calvinists, led by Professor Sybrandus Lubbertus, attacked Wtenbogardt and Grotius on this point, asserting that the Church should be entirely independent of the State. In one of the most effective pamphlets, the opinions of Professor Francis Junius were set forth as he had presented them in a work dated 1581, when he was professor at Leyden.[39] Professor Lubbertus, in 1614, published a whole treatise on the subject.

At the very time that the French Calvinists were becoming very conservative, admitting that they had wrongly swerved from the path marked out for them by Calvin, many of their brethren in the Dutch Republic could no longer remain true to the great master. How is one to explain this remarkable phenomenon? That England, in 1610, set the example for the Dutch Calvinists seems contrary to the facts now known to us. As we have just observed, the English exponents of the doctrine of an independent church were not permitted to preach their viewpoints openly in their native country. One of them, named Thomas Helwys, after a sojourn in Amsterdam, returned to England in 1611, where he published a book, of which he sent a copy to King James I, together with a letter which is still preserved in the Bodleian Library. In this letter he wrote: "The king is a mortal man, and not God; therefore he has no power over the immortal souls of his subjects, to make laws and ordinances for them, and to set spiritual lords over them. If the king have authority to make spiritual lords and laws, then he is an immortal God, and not a mortal man."[40]

It would seem that the Baptists in the Dutch Republic strongly affected the political views of the Calvinists. Both in Holland and in England a real spirit of democracy began to spread, which spirit manifested itself first on Dutch soil before it became very powerful in England among the ranks of the so-called Levelers. The demand for universal manhood suffrage was one of the symptoms of the new thought. The realistic way of discussing the origin of royal power and prerogative was another symptom.

In short, one must not give the Dutch merchants too much credit for the maintenance of religious toleration in their republic, but they cannot be ignored. How shocked the pious Calvinistic clergy must have been when thousands of Jews were permitted to settle in the city of Amsterdam, and to purchase for a few dollars the rights of citizenship! The municipal government of Amsterdam was so careful to protect the Jews that they arrived in ever increasing numbers, with the result that at the opening of the nineteenth century Amsterdam had the largest Jewish population of any city in the world. The history of the Jews in Amsterdam has been admirably portrayed by a Jewish rabbi in this country, whose book on the economic activities of the Jews in Amsterdam during the seventeenth and eighteenth centuries merits serious study.[41]

This Jewish writer was the first to treat in any detail and with adequate knowledge this important subject. In his introduction he writes thus: "Amsterdam, with its growing prominence in the galaxy of commercial cities, welcomed the persecuted Jews, especially since they were traders, and traders who by long experience and wide international connections could bring wealth and influence to the city on the Amstel. The Jews realized the relative tolerance of the developing commercial city, and the advantages accruing from settlement in the northern metropolis. They went there because Amsterdam was the enemy of Spain and because its star was in the ascendant. It was displacing Antwerp as a commercial depot, and bade fair to become the staple market for all of Europe. It was extending its sphere of influence into the Indies and the Americas. Holland was to become the carrier of Europe by developing its merchant marine. The Dutch metropolis was centrally situated and, while it had few resources of its own, its manufacture and shipping were great because of its advantageous position in Europe. Since the wealth of Amsterdam was based on trade and not on natural resources, the Jew with his channels of commerce and credit well established, found an ideal field for his operations. It should be borne in mind, however, that Holland was the richest country north of the Alps long before the Marrano settlement."[42]

One of the most important deductions made by this Jewish writer is that, contrary to the opinions of famous European and American historians, the Jews did not materially increase the capitalistic spirit in the Dutch Republic. The same, as we saw, may be said of the Calvinists, and for a very good reason. It is the secular factors in the expansion of Dutch trade which must be studied very largely to the exclusion of religious factors.

The Jews from Portugal and Spain, like the Pilgrim Fathers of England, were attracted by the opportunity presented in the Dutch Republic to make there a living and to worship God in their own private manner. It is true that they were not permitted to compete publicly with the established state churches of the Calvinists. Nevertheless, they enjoyed a measure of toleration that was practically unknown in the western world during the first half of the seventeenth century. As one keen Dutch writer observed about the year 1660: "Next to the freedom to worship God comes freedom to make one's living for all inhabitants. Here [in Amsterdam] it is very necessary to

attract foreigners. And although this is of disadvantage to
some old residents who would like to keep the best solely
for themselves and pretend that a citizen should have pref-
erences above a stranger, the truth of the matter is that a
state which is not self-sufficient must constantly draw new
inhabitants to it or perish." [43]

So intent were the members of the municipal council
in Amsterdam upon the protection of Dutch commerce
that they even permitted pirates to operate upon the seas
and attack foreign competitors. Although the federal government often was compelled to check the daring exploita-
tions of its subjects, [44] it happened on numerous occasions
that secretly the Dutch pirates were encouraged. [45]

The freedom of the press in the Dutch Republic also
contributed materially to the expansion of Dutch commerce. It would appear that during the seventeenth century the Dutch printing presses produced more books
than all other European presses put together. From 1600
to 1624, there were 96 book printers in Amsterdam, from
1625 to 1649 there were 154, while from 1650 to 1674
there were 190, and in the closing quarter of the seventeenth century the number had risen to 273. [46]

Illuminating are these words from the pen of one He-
brew printer in Amsterdam, written about the year 1667:
"For several years I myself printed more than a million
Bibles for England and Scotland. There is no plow boy or
servant girl there without one." So tolerant was the central government of the Dutch Republic that it gave Athias
(for that was his name) a gold chain, and in 1670 it granted
him a monopoly, for fifteen years, of the printing and sale
of English Bibles. The document containing this grant
states that Joseph Athias has spent many thousands of
guilders for setting up the type for the whole of the English Bible. "In order to make pleasanter and more agree-
able for purchasers he added singing notes." He provided

for the English congregations musical notations for the
Book of Psalms in the Old Testament. This is exactly what
the orthodox Calvinists had also done in the Netherlands,
for in their opinion it was permitted to sing only psalms
and hymns that appeared in the Bible.[47] The States-General in the monopoly just mentioned went so far as to say
that Mr. Joseph Athias did not undertake his work in
order to make a profit for himself, but only to serve the
inhabitants of the Dutch Republic and other countries.
It was indeed very kind of a government in the seventeenth
century to say that about a Jew. Even in our so-called "enlightened" twentieth century there are governments of
great nations who possess but a small fraction of the spirit
of toleration shown thus by the Dutch government in 1670.

One of the leading Jews in Amsterdam finally persuaded Oliver Cromwell to grant to the Jews permission
to reside once more in England.[48] About seven years earlier, in 1648, during the debates at Whitehall, one of the
speakers had pointed out that the spirit of toleration prevailing in the Dutch Republic was of great benefit to the
people living there: "Witness the country next from us,
that hath all the marks of a flourishing state upon it—I
mean the Low Countries: they are not so against, or afraid
of, this toleration. And I am not so against (or afraid of it
as some) on the other side that are (wont) to fear some
(damage to religion by) suffering (it). That which I would
hint is, that now we are come here to settle something for
magistrates (we may settle something for the Church
too)."[49]

Two important factors remain for discussion, which
in the eyes of many commentators during the past fifty
years seemed to restrict the ready flow of Dutch commerce
in the course of the seventeenth and eighteenth centuries.
The first of these is the alleged weakness in the system of
government maintained in the Dutch Republic from 1579

to 1795. The second is the rivalry with the English, which was reflected by the Navigation Act of 1651, by three naval wars, and by numerous pamphlets which pointed out the manner in which England must seek to check, and in the end overcome, the lead of the Dutch. It is the opinion of the present writer that both of these factors have been greatly exaggerated by numerous critics for the reason that they were looking for catastrophic causes of the decline of Dutch commerce, whereas the decline assumed no serious proportions until the system of government of the Dutch Republic had resulted in national union and great powers had been concentrated in the hands of the executive; and when Dutch fisheries, commerce, and industries could no longer compete with those of the rising states of the eighteenth century, such as Great Britain, Prussia, Russia, and the American colonies.

The government of the Dutch Republic was complicated, as has been pointed out in the excellent description of it in the *History of Holland* by Professor George Edmundson.[50] The writer states that he has given a brief account of "one of the most strangely complicated systems of government the world has ever seen—especially strange because no one could ever say positively where or with whom the sovereignty really resided."[51] J. E. Barker quotes Cardinal Bentivoglio, who, in 1630, observed that the government of the Dutch Republic was too much in the power of some of the provinces which lorded over the rest. Consequently, so he concluded, there was no real and effective unity among the seven provinces. They merely maintained an outward appearance of such unity. But there were many diversities of interest and religious differences as well. There were so many different religious sects in the Republic that one wondered how they ever could be united to form a defense against the enemies of the Republic.[52] Mr. Barker also draws a comparison between the Dutch Republic and the United States of America, which was torn in a terrible civil war (1861–1865). But it might be argued, on the contrary, that the Holy Roman Empire had a much more complicated government than the Dutch Republic, and yet it was able to survive numerous wars and disasters between 962 and 1806. It would seem that the form of government in itself does not determine the measure of prosperity enjoyed by a certain nation. Some have flourished under a democratic form of government, others under an aristocratic form, and still others under an absolute monarchy. The most amazing success in the march of civilization was that attained by the small and numerous Greek city-states during the fifth century B.C. On the other hand, the Romans achieved many marked successes during the second and third centuries of our era, when their form of government was autocratic. The same may be said of the Egyptians and the ancient Babylonians.

Perhaps the majority of British and American commentators have not been thoroughly familiar with various aspects of the political institutions maintained during the history of the Dutch Republic. To begin with, the document called the Union of Utrecht, signed in 1579, was not regarded by the leaders in the Dutch government as binding in all its details. It was understood that various articles should be applied in accordance with changed conditions. For example, Article IX stated that in matters of war, peace, truce, and revenues contributed by the various provinces, a unanimous decision was necessary. Nevertheless, the truce signed with Spain in 1609 was opposed by the province of Zeeland, and the peace of 1648 was against the wishes of Zeeland and Utrecht. But many writers have ignored these details, seeing only the letter of the written constitution, and forgetting how it was applied in times of crisis. Article X stated that no province or city was permitted to negotiate with foreign governments. Occasionally this article was violated, especially by the province of Holland, but never in such manner as to enable critics to conclude that national unity was lacking. French diplomats during the second half of the seventeenth century frequently negotiated with various cities and provinces, but they realized all the time that only the national government could take the necessary action. Their aim merely was to exert influence upon important personages who might be able to persuade the representatives from the various provinces in the States-General to take action in favor of France.

Many historians have objected to the term "Dutch Republic." The official title or name of the country was "United Provinces," or "United Netherlands." From 1579 to 1588 the nation was regarded as a federal state, somewhat similar to the present United States of America. From 1588 to 1618 it was more like a union of independent states. But, after 1618, public opinion was divided between that of the party which favored a strong central government and that of the States' Rights Party.[53] It may seem strange that at the very time when the States' Rights Party controlled the foreign policy of the republic (1650 to 1672 and 1702 to 1747), commerce throve, while the greatest measure of decline occurred between 1747 and 1795, when all the provinces were ruled by the same executive, who finally received hereditary prerogatives.

What foreigners could not understand was the immense power of the so-called "regent" class in the cities. The regents belonged to the patricians, whose fathers or grand-fathers had risen from the ranks of the tanners, brewers, cloth buyers, or soap boilers. These regents dominated the federal government. Amsterdam at times exercised more power in the States-General than did the six provinces outside of Holland. Professor P. Geyl, of the

University of Utrecht, writes thus: "All things considered, this Holland regent class is not only the most important political factor, but also the most notable social phenomenon in the Netherlands throughout the seventeenth century and beyond. Certainly the most typical. Probably, for this reason, historical tradition has shown this class little favour. This intermixing of commerce and government, this concentration of political power in middle-class hands, made an unpleasant impression on many foreigners, as indeed did the whole sudden outburst of commercial capitalism in the Northern Netherlands." [54]

Perhaps it may be said that the position of the executive officer called the *Stadhouder* was peculiar, but it cannot be shown that his quarrels with the States-General or the Council of State precipitated the decline of Dutch commerce. As a rule the two northern provinces had a stadhouder of their own, who possessed very little power. The other five were governed first by William the Silent, of the House of Orange, then by his son Maurice, and later by the younger son, Frederick Henry. The latter, in turn, was succeeded by William II, who died in 1650. Then followed a period of twenty-two years in which there was no stadhouder in these five provinces. But when, in 1672, the Dutch Republic was attacked by Great Britain, France, and two German states, the people rose against the States' Rights Party, and compelled the leaders of this party to appoint William III as stadhouder. When he died, in 1702, without leaving any heir to succeed him, another long period of rule without a stadhouder followed for the five provinces in question. But by 1747 all of the seven provinces were united more firmly than ever before, since now for the first time they all had the same stadhouder. It was from 1747 to 1787 that the stadhouder wielded extraordinary powers, surpassing those of William III. During the rule of William IV, from 1747 to 1766, the stadhouder was more powerful than ever. But exactly during that period Dutch commerce began its real decline. This decline was accelerated during the reign of William V, whose rule was disturbed by the rise of the Democrotic Party, influenced by the French. But, although his government introduced many reforms in almost every direction, it was helpless in its attempt to restore the position once occupied by the Dutch merchants.[55]

Even when, in 1788, the stadhouder was restored to the position occupied by William IV, and although the office was made hereditary, it was now much too late to bring about a similar restoration of the declining commerce and industry. It is not surprising, therefore, that the leading experts in the field of economic history no longer seek the causes of the decline of Dutch commerce in the alleged weakening of the Dutch government, but rather in a variety of other factors, such as have been so admirably analyzed by C. H. Wilson in his article published in *The Economic History Review*.[56]

One might almost be justified in concluding that Dutch commerce declined during the eighteenth century in spite of the numerous measures which had been adopted for its benefit by the government. In the only satisfactory economic history of the Netherlands that has been published thus far[57] there appears a lengthy discussion of what the author calls the *Handelspolitik* of the Dutch. The writer points out that until the middle of the sixteenth century it was only in the trade with the Baltic Sea and its coastal regions that the northern Netherlands surpassed the southern Netherlands. He points out first of all the importance of the fall of Antwerp, which resulted in the removal of the leading bankers and merchants to Amsterdam. He discusses also the incompetent rule of Leicester, the defeat of the Spanish Armada, the immigration of thousands of foreigners, who brought with them immense amounts of capital, and the relation between the Dutch and the Hanseatic League.

The next subject taken up by the author is the commercial policy adopted by the Dutch government. He refers to the effort made to protect the enormous flow of commerce with the Baltic Sea through the Sound, and he mentions certain important treaties made by the Dutch government for the benefit of the merchants.

It is interesting to note that in the year 1780 only 2,021 Dutch ships passed through the Sound, as compared with 2,058 English ships. Five years later the number of Dutch ships had fallen to 1,571, while the English had risen to 2,535. In 1790, the number of Dutch vessels was 2,009, and the number of English vessels 5,788. In 1793, only 807 Dutch ships passed through the Sound, as against 3,478 English ships. In other words, when the power of the stadhouder was very considerable, and the national policy unified, Dutch commerce declined very rapidly.

Illuminating also is the discussion of the commercial relations between the Dutch Republic and the Holy Roman Empire, especially Germany. In this field, much work still remains to be done. But Mr. Baasch has made an excellent beginning. He points out the importance of the Rhine as an artery of commerce, especially for the Dutch. In order to prevent foreign merchants from making use of the Dutch streams, a relatively high tariff was levied on those streams. In this connection we may observe, as Mr. C. H. Wilson has pointed out, that, in 1667, the Dutch government in the Treaty of Breda was able to obtain important concessions from the British government, in that the Navigation Act of 1651 was relaxed, so as to permit the Hollanders to transport, in their own ships, goods from the Rhine provinces in Germany. For this country was correctly considered as the hinterland of the Dutch Republic.[58]

Immigrants from the Netherlands, both the northern and southern provinces, played an important part in the economic history of Germany during the sixteenth, seventeenth, and eighteenth centuries. They carried with them highly advanced economic principles and ideas, which were of great value to the backward Germans.[59]

But the commercial relations between the Dutch Republic, on the one hand, and such countries as France, Spain, and Italy, on the other have not yet been adequately treated. Much also remains to be done in the field of economic history of Russia. Thus far, too much attention has been paid to the Dutch merchants only, and not enough to the original documents left by the governments of the Ottoman Empire, Russia, the Scandinavian countries, and the Mediterranean area.

But the Anglo-Dutch commercial rivalry has been ably discussed from time to time by competent experts. They have analyzed the numerous treatises in which English merchants and statesmen discussed the notable successes attained by the Dutch merchants of the seventeenth century. One of these pamphlets has been analyzed above, namely, that by Sir Walter Raleigh. Douglas Campbell explained the importance of a letter addressed, in 1659, by Samuel Lamb, a merchant residing in London, to Oliver Cromwell.[60] Mr. Lamb mentioned four reasons which explained the success of the Dutch merchants. Firstly, the statesmen controlling the Dutch government were for the most part merchants themselves, who were bred to trade from their youth, and who improved their knowledge through foreign travel. Consequently, their laws and treaties were very beneficial to the Dutch merchants. Secondly, when a Dutch merchant died, his property was equally divided among his children, and the business was continued and expanded by them. In England, on the other hand, the property went to the eldest son, who frequently used it to buy estates in the country, where he spent his life in ease and hunting. Thirdly, the Hollanders were known for their honesty. Fourthly, the Dutch government levied tolls and duties for the benefit of the Dutch merchants, and the latter adjusted themselves very quickly to the change of conditions and needs of their customers.

J. E. Barker also studied important treatises by Englishmen, notably those of Misselden (1632), Lewes Roberts (1641), Sir John Keymer (1601), and Sir James Burroughs.[61]

Even in British India, the subject has attracted attention, and in an excellent work on the East India trade several other treatises have been mentioned, notably those by Captain Pring; Master Nathaniel Courthop; John Chamberlain, the author of *Trade's Increase;* Sir Walter Raleigh; Conway, in his work entitled *Early Voyages to Spitzbergen;* Selden; Sir John Boroughs; Thomas Mun; Malynes; Digges; Tobias gentleman; and especially Sir Josiah Childe, the governor of the English East India Company.[62]

Professor Charles M. Andrews, of Yale University, has devoted a whole chapter to the general Anglo-Dutch commercial rivalry in the fourth volume of his work entitled *The Colonial Period of American History,* published in 1938 by the Yale University Press. He mentions the following writers: Roger Coke (1670, 1671, 1675); William de Britaine (1672); Henry Stubbe, the author of *The English Ballance* (1672); Sir Josiah Childe (1668 and later editions); William Petyt (1680); Sir Francis Brewster (1695), the author of *The Naked Truth in an Essay on Trade* (1696); Defoe (1712); and John Withers, the author of *The Dutch Better Friends than the French* (1713).[63]

Professor Andrews states that in his opinion "the federal system of government had many disadvantages in ad-

ministering efficiently the affairs of the navy, because of
lack of coördination among the various local bodies." He
refers to Oliver Goldsmith, who, in 1762, pointed to a long
period of indolence, too much attention to trade and
money making, and too little attention to the art of warfare. But it must not be forgotten that the Dutch did not
reach the height of their naval power until 1672, and the
height of the military power until about 1710.[64]

Professor Andrews and Goldsmith correctly surmised
that the Dutch merchants were laboring under great difficulties. There were indeed serious weaknesses in the
system of government, while at least during the eighteenth
century the character of the average Hollander left much
to be desired. In a nation where indolence and selfish-
ness abound, no form of government will be in a position
to make up for lack of virtue and industry. We all recall
how, during the course of the year 1938 and 1939, many
statesmen in Russia, Germany, and Italy observed the
weaknesses in the governments of Great Britain, France,
and the United States. These statesmen argued that the
democratic countries were not efficiently governed, and
for that reason were bound to decline. One school of critics will argue that too much democracy hurts business,
while another school will advance the theory that too much
autocracy is a hindrance to business. Both of these schools
are correct up to a certain point.

The factors involved in the decline of the Dutch Republic during the eighteenth century remind us very much
of those that are said to have caused the decline of the Roman Empire. First there came along a group of historians
who claimed that the decline of Rome was very largely
external. They had much to say about the harmful results
of the barbarian invasions, the intermarrying of the two
races, the loss of the fertility of the soil, the spread of the
Christian religion and the institution of slavery. Later

another group of historians appeared, emphasizing what they called the internal factors, especially moral degeneration. As Professor Rostovtsev, of Yale University, observed in his monumental work on the social and economic history of the Roman Empire, the Romans of the third century of our era had "utterly lost their balance." Thus it was with the Hollanders during the second half of the eighteenth century. Although the system of government was practically the same as it had been in the seventeenth century, it suddenly seemed as if the defects had greatly increased. It also seemed as if the competitors in England, France, and Germany had become so aggressive that there was no hope left for the Hollanders. Nevertheless, so shrewd and industrious had the Dutch merchants of the seventeenth century been that when the Dutch Republic was about to give up its ghost about the year 1795, there was enough commerce left in that country to credit each Hollander with four times as much commerce as the average Englishman and seven times as much as the average Frenchman.[65] It was obvious that a country with an area of only about 10,000 square miles could not indefinitely control a greater volume of commerce than England, which was ten times as large, or as France, which was more than fifteen times as large.

Returning now to the competition offered by the English, recent scholars, as was observed above, have learned that the Navigation Act of 1651 not only hurt the Dutch merchants very little but was positively harmful to the English themselves. A learned scholar in the University of London has recently shown that this act caused further disorder in English commerce.[66] As one English writer stated in 1697, Parliament had passed the Navigation Acts and intended thereby to check the volume of Dutch trade and to increase the English trade, but both reacted quite to the contrary.[67]

Much has been written about the expansion of sea power under Oliver Cromwell, but the figures presented by contemporary and later writers indicate that British shipping was far from prosperous between 1649 and 1660. Major Burton wrote, about the year 1656, that the Hollanders were making fun of the English, saying that the English were asleep and that nearly seventy English vessels were lying at the ports without any convoy. In the summer of 1656, the same writer said that there were between three hundred and four hundred coal vessels on the seas, with scarcely any protection for them.[68]

Conditions in England seem to have been the worst between 1658 and 1660. It has been shown above, that, according to the official records of the Danish government, very few ships from England sailed through the Sound during the decade from 1651 to 1660. One English official reported that almost all English merchants were beginning to trade with Dutch ships.[69]

Professor Charles M. Andrews has even gone so far as to say that the Navigation Act of 1651 "injured England's commerce more than it did the commerce of Holland."[70] During the naval war between the two countries from 1651 to 1654, so continues Professor Andrews, the losses were perhaps evenly distributed, in which opinion he is no doubt correct. This observation on the part of Professor Andrews is significant, because both American and European writers were usually of the opinion that the Dutch emerged completely defeated and hopelessly outclassed. It has often been said that grass was growing in the streets of Amsterdam as the English emerged triumphantly. However, the English colonies in America continued to ignore the Navigation Act of 1651, and "they welcomed the Dutch as warmly as ever."[71]

Oliver Cromwell and his associates had favored a political union with the Hollanders, but the latter had insisted on an economic union rather than a political one.[72] The Dutch realized that, since England was much larger than Holland, the latter would be simply a satellite of the former. On the other hand, the English understood equally well that in the fields of commerce and industry the Dutch were so far ahead of the English that, as Mr. John More said to the British ambassador at The Hague, Ralph Winwood, in 1610: "In case of joining, it would be on equal terms, the art and industry of their people would wear out ours." Even as late as in 1661, Mr. Thurloe expressed similar sentiments, saying: "Least the English should be wholly eaten out by the people of the united Netherlands."

The second Anglo-Dutch war was followed by the treaty of Breda in 1667, which, as we saw above, permitted the Hollanders to ship goods from the Rhine Valley in Dutch vessels, instead of in German vessels, as before this date. This concession of the English was merely a symptom of their weariness after two years of hard fighting, during which both nations incurred heavy losses.[73]

The third Anglo-Dutch war broke out in 1672, when both France and England declared war against the Dutch Republic. This war was largely a result of a desire of King Charles II to support his cousin, King Louis XIV, of France, and partly to please the English merchants and industrialists who hoped to be able to cripple the Dutch this time.[74] But in the midst of the war, in 1673, a large number of members in the Parliament came to the conclusion that England should have declared war against France, her potential enemy, rather than against Holland, which was bound to decline in the near future.[75]

It must not be imagined, however, that the British merchants suddenly became attached to their Dutch competitors. Interesting are the arguments advanced in the year 1672 by an English writer, called Henry Stubbe, who

published two treatises to show that the English government was entirely justified in declaring war upon the
Dutch Republic.[76]

Stubbe had carefully studied a considerable number
of works written by the Hollanders about their commerce
and their system of government, as well as the history of
their country. What he has to say about the Dutch in Japan is worth careful consideration. He remarks that the
Dutch were shamefully subservient to the Japanese government, for they were willing to deliver to the Japanese
on their arrival in Japan, each time, all their religious
books, which may not be restored to them until their departure. They may express no public confession of the
Christian religion. They may not even give, verbally,
thanks to God for the food that they eat, nor may they
make any motion or gesture with their hands or eyes that
may seem like prayer to God. The Roman Catholics in
Japan were shamefully put to death at the instigation of
the Dutch, who cared for nothing except financial profit.[77]

Stubbe also shows considerable familiarity with the
system of government in the Dutch Republic. He correctly remarks that the province of Holland tries to domi-
nate all the other six provinces. He should have reflected,
however, on the fact that this province paid about 57 per
cent of all the revenues paid by the seven provinces to the
national government. Since the province had only one
out of seven votes in the States-General and but three out
of twelve votes in the Council of State, it was natural that
it felt entitled to more power than was represented in these
votes. Stubbe goes on to say that the decrees of the States-
General have little force in the various provinces. Each
mayor kept the keys to the gates of his respective city. The
soldiers of the national government were not permitted to
be quartered in the homes of private citizens, unless they
received permission from the provincial governments.

The nobility were excluded from all commands by the jealous followers "of that insolent son of a tallow-chandler, whose deportment made him no less insupportable at home than he was among foreign princes." [78]

Here Stubbe expressed an opinion that was shared by thousands of foreigners who did not understand how a son of a tanner, or a brewer, or a soap manufacturer, could ever have become an important figure in a great city or even in a province. The middle classes of the cities had actually usurped the power that formerly had been wielded by the nobles and clergymen. Many of the Hollanders treated the king of England with scant respect, being Republicans.

The writer was also correct in his analysis of the lack of democracy in the Dutch Republic. He wrote thus: "It is manifest that the Republic was no democracy, nor were the people free." What he meant was that the cities were controlled by closed corporations, and that the mayors were not elected by the people as a whole, but by a small group of aristocrats.

The Anglo-Dutch alliance of 1688, which was for the most part a repetition of that begun in 1674 and 1677, had important results in Europe and America, as well as in India. The Dutch were thus permitted to carry on their trade peacefully under the shelter of the huge British navy of the eighteenth century, while the English were in a position, with the support of the Dutch navy, to cripple effectively the French navy, and, in consequence, to deprive France of her foothold in Canada and India. Many competent British historians have looked upon William III as the most useful king that England has ever had. It was in his reign that the foundations of the British Empire were firmly laid. [79]

The first war that really struck a fatal blow to Dutch commerce was the fourth Anglo-Dutch war, which lasted from 1780–1784. As Mr. C. H. Wilson has pointed out, the financial relations between England and Holland had been excellent up until the year 1779.[80] But when the Hollanders observed during the course of 1788–89 that the British were being defeated by the French and the American rebels, they decided that it would be a good thing for them to join with the French and Americans. Before they could make up their minds, the British declared war on them. The Dutch Republic was entirely unprepared for such a contest against her powerful enemy across the North Sea. The period from 1780 to 1795 was indeed filled with scandal, corruption and humiliation.[81]

The financial relations between the Dutch Republic and England before the year 1702 have been admirably analyzed by Dr. J. F. Bense, the author of the interesting work entitled *Anglo-Dutch Relations from the Earliest Times to the Death of William the Third*.[82] Mr. Bense states that the English admired the system of taxation which was developed in the Dutch Republic during the seventeenth century. In 1643, Pym, a prominent Puritan leader, introduced an excise on a number of beverages; in 1644, he added another on a number of commonly used commodities. The tax was named after the Dutch one, and proved very satisfactory. In 1660, it was retained, notwithstanding the change in the government.

Mr. Bense also indicates how Sir William Petty, a noted English economist, after having studied in the two universities of Utrecht and Amsterdam, and after matriculating at Leyden in 1644, corresponded with Dutch scholars. He was one of the founders of the Royal Society. On February 28, 1663–64, Pepys wrote: "He showed me a discourse of his concerning the revenues of this and foreign States. That the Hollanders have the best manner of tax, which is only on the expense of the provisions, by an excise; and do conclude that no other tax is proper for

England but a pound-rate, or excise upon the expense of the provisions."

The government of the Dutch Republic was praised by many foreigners, as we saw, because of its enlightened system of taxation. Import and export duties were very low, as compared with those of other countries. A twofold tax was levied on commerce, namely, that which was called the convoys and the other which was called the licences. There can be no doubt that the sagacious policy adopted by the government of the Dutch Republic was very beneficial to the merchants of the time.[83]

Before concluding the present chapter, we must note briefly what the Hollanders had to say about the English during the course of the seventeenth century. In December, 1627, the association of merchants in the Netherlands who bought cloths from the English for the purpose of dyeing them and re-selling them, addressed a document to the States-General in which they discussed eight points concerning the freedom of trade on the part of the English in the Netherlands and the difficulties experienced by the Dutch merchants in England. In the first place, the English merchants, called the Merchant Adventurers, possessed a house of their own in the city of Delft which was said to be entirely free of charge to them. Here the English did not have to pay any excises on wine or beer, and they also paid no import duties on the cloths which they imported from England. Moreover, they were exempt from jurisdiction in criminal and civil affairs in the Dutch courts, and also in other respects they enjoyed privileges above those granted to the inhabitants of the Dutch Republic. On the other hand, the merchants of the Dutch Republic did not enjoy such privileges in England, for they had to pay import duties to the king of England for everything that they took to that country. The rate was 4 per cent more than the English themselves paid.

In the second place, when the English sent goods from the Dutch Republic in exchange for others, they enjoyed the same liberties that the inhabitants of the Dutch Republic had received, and paid no more duties than the Dutch merchants themselves. In shipping these goods they also did not have to pay any more convoy duties than the inhabitants of the Dutch Republic. On the contrary, the Hollanders in England, when they exchanged goods, could buy these freely in the market halls in England, but had to have them bought by a free English citizen in London, who derived his profits from the said purchase. Then, when these goods were exported from England, the Hollanders had to pay almost twice as much as the English did.

In the third place, the English in the Dutch Republic might employ all their servants and associates and might trade with their own men, either wholesale or retail; they could also have their own stores where they traded publicly as the Hollanders did themselves. On the contrary, the Hollanders could not trade with each other in England, and they also could not have their own stores in England.

In the fourth place, the English could take along with them many products with which they might trade and derive profit therefrom. They enjoyed the same privileges as the inhabitants of the Dutch Republic. On the contrary, the Hollanders could not import into England, cottons, cotton thread, raw silk, drugs from the Levant, nor any other product of the Levant, no cod liver oil, nor any other oil, nor any products from whales, nor many other goods. The other four points need not be mentioned here in detail, since they are not important.[84]

Of a similar nature is a letter addressed by one of the leading Dutch officials operating for the Dutch government in the Near East. In November, 1644, he wrote to

the States-General that not only did the Dutch merchants
have to pay tolls and duties in the Ottoman Empire, but
the Dutch government had to give presents to the rulers.
He recommended that goods imported from the Near
East into the Netherlands by Dutch or other vessels should
be taxed with a 2 per cent import duty. He made no distinction, therefore, between the vessels used by Hollanders and those used by foreigners. The English, on the other
hand, levied an additional tax on products imported by
foreign merchants. The goods coming from the Near East
were so heavily taxed that it was impossible for the foreigners to transport them to England. The French followed the same method, charging foreigners in addition
to the ordinary toll and duties a 3 per cent import tax.[85]

Furthermore, the buyers of English cloths in the city
of Amsterdam, about the year 1616, addressed a letter to
the municipal council of the city in which they stated that
the Merchant Adventurers from England enjoyed far too
many privileges in Amsterdam: "The English bring vast
quantities of cloths from England into the Netherlands,
which they dye with their own men, and ship to Germany,
the Balkan countries, and Russia. In this way many Hollanders are deprived of an honest means of making a living. Such practices are impossible in France, Spain, and
Denmark, where the English are not permitted, unless
they propose to adjust themselves to the harsh conditions
existing there."[86]

Ever since the first half of the seventeenth century it
has been characteristic of the Dutch people to assume an
attitude such as is usually adopted by a merchant in a store
who wants to placate his customers in every way possible.
Foreigners residing in the Netherlands as a rule have been
treated with unusual courtesy and have been welcomed,
not as inferiors, but often as superiors. The example given
above could be multiplied indefinitely to indicate that

one important reason why Dutch commerce was so extensive during the sixteenth and seventeenth centuries is the
combination of low import and export duties (which
amounted to only 1 or 2 per cent), the exceptional advantages accorded to foreigners living in the Netherlands, and
the astute manner in which the Hollanders abroad cheer-
fully underwent humiliation after humiliation in order
to maintain commercial relations between their native
country and the country in which they were operating.
This attitude will explain why presents were given to the
rulers of the Ottoman Empire and Japan. It will also
throw light on the extraordinary experiences of the Dutch
merchants in Japan, which will be discussed below.

We are now in a position to evaluate the numerous
factors that caused the Dutch merchants of the seventeenth century to surpass in many respects all their competitors, no matter how hard the latter tried to keep up
with them. Notwithstanding the three wars declared and
fought by the English against the Dutch, the Navigation
Acts, and the antagonism of Louis XIV of France as expressed in the three wars he waged against the Dutch between 1672 and 1713—notwithstanding the great distance
that separated the Dutch Republic from the Mediterranean Sea and the Far East, the commercial and colonial
empire constructed by the intrepid Hollanders continued
to increase in size.

Commentators, during the period after 1700, strongly
emphasized what they considered the favorable location
of the Dutch Republic.[87] In their opinion this was the
most important factor, for it enabled the Dutch to become
the intermediaries between the inhabitants of northern
and southern Europe. The present writer, however, is of
the opinion that this factor was subordinate to others. Despite its location, in periods of decline as well as in times of
immense prosperity, during the seventeenth century the

merchants of Holland seized upon every opportunity offered them, while in later times they not seldom were less
aggressive and less ambitious. The question of physical
geography is always important, but it must be viewed in
its proper perspective. In the fourteenth century the
Venetians boldly appeared in Dutch ports, where they
snatched from the Hollanders commerce that was relatively easy to capture, but in the seventeenth century the
Dutch arrived in the Mediterranean Sea, where they
traded with Constantinople as well as with Venice and
Alexandria—all of that in spite of the geographical position of Holland. The Hollanders also sailed past the shores
of Portugal on their way to the East Indies and thus seized
from the Portuguese their valuable Spice Islands—that
and much more in disregard of the favorable location of
Portugal. Moreover, the Dutch sailed through English
waters to deliver European products to the English colonies in America—knowing very well their disadvantageous
situation to the east of the British Isles.

Much has also been said about the organization of
Dutch trade and industry. This is likewise natural and
proper, for a skillful manipulation of tools is required of
all persons engaged in commerce and industry. As has
been pointed out in this chapter, the Dutch merchants of
the seventeenth century were unsurpassed in their efforts
to reduce selling costs, to attract customers by lowering
the prices of their goods, to make the most of the vessels
they operated, to induce their government to assist in the
free flow of commerce, to combine buying and selling in
such manner that their ships would always have a cargo,
to acquire adequate funds of capital, to insure cargoes, to
improve harbor facilities, to facilitate exchange of foreign
accounts and currencies, to perfect, whenever possible, the
quality of their wares, and to cater to the whims and needs
of their foreign clients. However, that which we refer to

as the organization of Dutch trade is, strictly speaking, only a part of all the tactics jointly employed by the merchants of the Dutch Republic. Like the first factor we have just considered (the geographical position), this second factor is merely subordinated to something else that we shall analyze presently.[88]

Furthermore, racial characteristics and religious beliefs must also be evaluated in their proper setting. The Hollanders had not become a superior race, as may well be seen in their earlier history and in the period of their decline from 1750 to 1800. To credit Calvinism with an aptitude for assisting the rise of modern capitalism is misleading, for Scotland and Switzerland were Calvinistic countries during the seventeenth century, and yet they were far from successful in building up a commercial or colonial empire. When Germany was adopting Protestantism in the sixteenth century, she rapidly declined economically, but when Italy flourished most she was thoroughly Roman Catholic. The Byzantine Empire was, for seven centuries, the richest state in Europe at a time when the Greek Catholic faith reigned supreme in this nation. In Canada, the French region around Quebec and Montreal is the commercial heart of the country, although here the Catholics decidedly predominate. And Japan has recently risen to a position of great economic power entirely without the assistance of Calvinism or Puritanism.[89]

There is also no need of elaborating any further on the nature of the Dutch government during the seventeenth century. Whatever may have been its drawbacks in the field of politics, its enlightened policies as regards religious liberty (notwithstanding the uncompromising attitude of many leading members of the Calvinist clergy, who would have preferred persecution of heretics and foreign merchants to religious toleration), and the freedom of speech and the press more than made up for these drawbacks.

Moreover, excessive state supervision was carefully avoided, so that the Dutch Republic in the age of mercantilism was an oasis of free enterprise and competition.

Finally, the fortuitous circumstances alluded to above, such as the economic disasters in the southern Netherlands, the decline of Germany and Italy, the stupid policies of the Stuart monarchs in England, and the warlike propensities of Louis XIV of France—these are also of secondary importance. It takes more than negative factors to raise a nation of 10,000 square miles (one-fifth the size of Michigan) with one and one-half million inhabitants to an empire of one million square miles embracing the most valuable colonial regions in the world, with the largest merchant marine, the most powerful corporation, the first great modern public bank, and the first stock market of early modern times. To understand how this little republic was able to monopolize all the European trade with Japan from 1642 to 1859 requires more than a discussion of physical geography and other obvious factors that have so often been analyzed before.

The rise of the Dutch Republic, so ably described by one of our leading historians,[90] is indeed one of the most remarkable phenomena in the history of civilization. But unfortunately, the economic phase of this tremendous manifestation of human energy has been rarely discussed in recent literature. It can only be properly appreciated when it is taken up as a portion of the whole development. At a certain period in the history of mankind the forces that control the progress of the human race saw fit to enable the Dutch people to outstrip all their neighbors. The Hollanders were suddenly endowed with talents that seem to belong only to supermen. They founded five state universities; operated magnificent commercial establishments; offered freedom of religion to Jews, Anabaptists, Puritans, and Lutherans; built a highly efficient navy;

possessed a famous school of painting; led the world in
scientific research; experimented with advanced political
and social theories; and developed important theological
and legal viewpoints. Their merchants, like their theo-
logians and scientists, shared in this marvelous outburst
of activity, with the result that even foreigners, like Spi-
noza and Descartes, basked in the glory reflected by Dutch
civilization. As one American professor of history has so
eloquently said, the Dutch Republic became the first sea-
power and the first money-power of the seventeenth century. "Her material and spiritual power, her tolerance
and freedom, became the envy of the world." [91]

CHAPTER II

THE BEGINNINGS OF DUTCH SEA POWER IN THE FAR EAST

COMPARED with the Portuguese and the English, the navigators of the Dutch Republic were very slow in establishing direct trading contacts with the Far East. This hesitation on the part of the Dutch is all the more remarkable when one considers how powerful they were upon the sea long before the end of the sixteenth century. For example, as early as 1503, out of a total of 1,222 ships that passed legitimately through the Sound into the Baltic Sea, 718 came from the province of Holland and 46 from Friesland. This was a clear indication of the supremacy of the Dutch merchants in the Baltic Sea when there were no Englishmen trading in the Far East and when the Portuguese had barely started their operations on the coast of India and in the Malay Archipelago. From 1497 to 1548 the province of Holland alone controlled one-half of all the trade, and between 1557 and 1686 this same province was in control of from one-third to one-half of the shipping in the Baltic Sea. But between 1598 and 1613, an average of fewer than 250 English ships passed through the Sound each year. In the period from 1614 to 1640 the average was practically the same.

The rise of Dutch sea power in the Far East is a subject of great importance, but it was not until 1935 that the historians in the Netherlands paid as much attention to it as it deserved. Furthermore, the Dutch generally were also not aware of the fact that the English, under Queen Elizabeth, had so greatly weakened the Spaniards and the Portuguese that indirectly they made it possible for the Dutch to seize the valuable colonies of the Portuguese in the

Malay Archipelago. Until 1939, only one comprehensive history of the rise of the Dutch sea power in the Far East was published.[1]

Before the Dutch actually sailed around Africa, they tried, on three different occasions, to reach the Far East by way of the Arctic Ocean. When they finally realized that it was entirely impossible, they had to follow in the footsteps of the Portuguese and the English. Now the question arises once more: Why did the Dutch wait so long before they sailed to the Malay Archipelago by way of the African coast? Since, at an early date, they had secured a large share of the trade in the Baltic Sea, and since their fishing fleet was the largest in the world during the course of the sixteenth century, why could they not conceive the idea of preceding the Portuguese and the Spaniards and the English in the Far East? The products from the Far East used to be carried through the Near East and thence through Venice, Genoa, and other Italian and Spanish ports. From the Mediterranean ports, these goods were brought to central and western Europe by way of the Alpine passes, the Rhone valley, and the road that stretched north of the Alps to the North Sea and the Baltic Sea. The Hollanders were engaged in the role of intermediaries. They used to go to Lisbon, where they exchanged the grain, the fish, and the wood of northern Europe for the wine, the oil, and the fruits of southern Europe. The ships supplied by the English and the Dutch were very small, and did not permit the crew to carry along enough food for trips that extended beyond Lisbon or Cadiz. Before the Dutch could venture on longer voyages, they first had to invent a new type of ship, which finally made its appearance in 1594. Until 1594, therefore, the Hollanders were not known so much as merchants as they were considered freight carriers. At first they did not even carry the goods to their own ports, but to Bruges and later to Antwerp, which two ports were located to the south of the Dutch provinces. From Venice and Lisbon the Dutch fetched the goods that had come from the Far East. Venice and Lisbon were the last stations in the long trade route from central and southern Asia to western Europe. As long as the ports of Constantinople and Alexandria were open to the traffic engaged in by the Christians of the West, all was well, and the Dutch did not care to disturb the old routes of commerce. But the fall of Constantinople in 1453, and the capture of Alexandria by the Turks in 1517, profoundly altered the course of world commerce. As Dr. Colenbrander says, the Italians sought the solution of the problem in driving the Turks out of the Near East. In this vain and hopeless attempt the Italians wasted much of their energy. Individual Italian merchants and sailors placed themselves at the disposal of foreigners. The Italian commercial companies did not seem to be able to conceive a plan whereby they might make themselves independent of the routes to the Near East. And thus it happened that while the Italians were disputing the exact means of recapturing their former trade, the Portuguese and other nations in the west took swift action and altered the course of world commerce between the Far East and western Europe.

The reader will recall that King Philip II, of Spain, in 1580 annexed Portugal and thus secured control of the great port of Lisbon. For several years, the Dutch continued to trade in Lisbon, although they were engaged in a war with the king of Spain. Philip II needed the trade of the Dutch as freight carriers, and although occasionally the Dutch sailors who came to Lisbon were molested and sometimes were deprived of their cargoes, the desire for financial gain was so strong among the Dutch that they continued to trade with Lisbon as long as it was feasible and practical. At the same time, however, the thought occurred many times to leading Dutch merchants, just as it had occurred to the Portuguese a century earlier, that it would be advantageous to secure the spices and other Oriental luxuries at the very places where they were produced. So it naturally followed that soon after the new type of ship, called the flute ship, had been invented, in 1594, the first trip to the Far East was undertaken by Dutch merchants.

In 1594, a number of ambitious and adventurous Dutch merchants founded the Company of the Far Regions. It was their intention to equip two expeditions to the Malay Archipelago. They were not primarily interested in inflicting damage upon the interests of the Portuguese, but to establish commercial relations with certain regions that had not yet been visited by the Portuguese. In this manner perhaps the great emporium of the spice trade might be removed from Lisbon to Amsterdam. The instructions which were subsequently given to the navigators in the service of this company show clearly that they were not permitted to combine piracy with peaceful trading pursuits. They were not to imitate the English Captain James Lancaster. Portugal was to be regarded as a neutral power, not a hostile state.[2]

However, it did not seem possible to maintain a neutral policy against the Portuguese. For that reason, in 1603, the managers of the Company of the Far Regions, which in 1602 had become a part of the Dutch East India Company, gave instructions to the commander of the large fleet about to sail to the Far East to drop the passive attitude toward the Portuguese and to attack them whenever necessary. As a matter of fact, as early as 1602 an active state of war had broken out between the Portuguese and the Dutch. It was at this time that the distinguished Dutch scholar Hugo Grotius was urged to write a treatise in defense of the actions contemplated by the Dutch. So well did Hugo Grotius perform his task that, according to James Brown Scott and Professor Robert Fruin, his commentary entitled *De Jure Praedae* is the greatest work he ever wrote. He was a very precocious person, and after 1605 his mental equipment and moral standards gradually deteriorated. The purpose of this commentary, as will be explained more fully below, was to show that the Portuguese had no right to exclude other Europeans from the lucrative spice trade in the Far East. Grotius insisted on the freedom of the seas, and a few years later he published part of one chapter taken from the commentary, and entitled it *Mare Liberum,* or *On the Freedom of the Seas.* It was widely read in the seventeenth century.

The most important events that occurred between 1598 and 1603 have been brilliantly described by Professor R. Fruin, who wrote these illuminating passages:

"The trade of the Dutch with the East Indies really dates only from 1598, one year after the first Dutch fleet which had discovered and opened the way to the Archipelago had returned to the port of Amsterdam. The first voyage had brought the shipowners little or no profit, but proved to all Dutch merchants the certainty that the power of the Portuguese, who posed as lords and masters of India, was by no means so formidable as had been thought and that it was possible to rival them there without running great risks. These joyous tidings were not ignored. In a single year, 1598, no fewer than twenty-two ships equipped by five Holland and Zeeland companies sailed to profit by the wealth of India and the impotence of the Portuguese. The profit, however, was not very considerable on the whole. One shipping company was more fortunate than the others, but the combined profits, after deducting the expenses, did not yield high interest on the capital invested. This was chiefly caused by the necessity of increasing the crews and armaments for protection against the Portuguese and, in spite of these defensive measures, by the loss suffered without chance of indemnity through the cunning and violence of their rivals. In dispatching the first fleets, the shipowners and the government had wisely decided that it was undesirable to transfer the war, which was being waged against the Spaniards on the seas of Europe, to the Indian Sea and there continue it against the Portuguese. Consequently, the shipmasters had been explicitly ordered to use their guns and ammunition, with which they were well provided, only in self-defense and 'to attack or damage no ship, to whatever nation it might belong, on the voyage out or when homeward bound.'

"But in the eyes of the Portuguese, the trade with the Indies and traffic with the natives, however peacefully conducted, in itself amounted to an injustice to them, and was an encroachment upon their vested rights which they opposed at first by cunning and then by main force. They considered the Dutch merchants and masters, as soon as they appeared in the Indies, as pirates and treated them accordingly. The Dutch defended themselves as well as they could; but in warfare mere warding off violence without aggressive action cannot be adhered to long. Consequently, the Dutch sailors now and then, forced by necessity, transgressed their instructions and as allies, as was said, of independent Indian princes attacked the enemy. In this way they had their vengeance, but in so doing they did not make up for the losses which their property and trade constantly suffered. The treasures of the Portuguese merchants were conveyed in large, unwieldy vessels, which, far from committing acts of hostility, evaded all fighting and were bent on nothing but safely reaching the port whither they were bound. To attack and capture these would have been contrary to the explicit orders given our shipmasters and, however they might long to seize these desirable prizes, they let the caracks sail by unmolested.

"Thus things remained for some years. Every ship that came back home brought new tidings of ill-usage. The rancor against the Portuguese rapidly increased in this country and silenced considerations of immediate self-interest. At the same time people began to see that real self-interest demanded that violence be answered with violence and damage with damage. A few powerless ship-owners, however, were unable to effect this; it required the union of all forces. This was understood by the government and especially by the Advocate of Holland. Out of the several small companies they formed one united company to which they gave an exclusive patent for trading with the Indies, for founding Dutch colonies there, for constructing fortresses, recruiting soldiers, and concluding treaties with Indian princes. In the charter, it was true, no mention was made, as yet, of other prizes than those that might be captured in warding off the enemy's violence. But it was in the nature of things that matters could not remain thus. The government confessed afterward that in founding the company it aimed especially at the weakening of the Spanish power. How could it, then, have prohibited the most effective means to this end, namely, the seizing of the enemy's treasures?"[3]

It was by no means a coincidence that in 1595 and 1596 one of the Dutch sailors who had been employed by the Portuguese issued two important books in which he described the activities of the Portuguese in the Malay Archipelago and the surrounding regions. He also added a description of the geography of those countries. This was J. H. Van Linschoten, author of the *Reysgeschrift* of 1595 and the *Itinerario* of 1596. As early as 1598 translations of the *Itinerario* appeared both in English and in German. The English in particular made excellent use of it.

Two Latin translations followed in 1599, and a French one in 1610, which was reprinted in 1619 and 1638.[4]

The first voyage of the Dutch to the Malay Archipelago was led by Cornelis de Houtman, who had previously been sent to Lisbon to obtain secret information about the trade with the Far East. Four ships took part in this trip with a combined crew of 248 men. The commercial company in Amsterdam, which had equipped a fleet, was, as we saw, the Company of the Far Regions. Its first trip was by no means a success. On June 23, 1596, the ships arrived at the port of Bantam, where first they were well treated and began to take in cargoes of pepper. A little later a Portuguese agent appeared on the scene, and promised the natives a large sum of money if they would deliver to the Portuguese the ships of the unwanted foreigners. When Mr. Houtman heard of this, he lost his head and captured two Javanese vessels. After leaving Bantam, he purchased further supplies in other ports of Java, but everywhere news of his privateering had preceded him, and he was not permitted to trade there any more. Furthermore, his crew refused to go with him to the Spice Islands, and he was forced to return to the Netherlands.[5]

Although the financial gain of the first voyage was very small, and although Houtman had not been very tactful, nevertheless the fact that the Dutch had been able to establish direct contacts with the Malay Archipelago caused tremendous enthusiasm in the Netherlands. A second company was founded immediately, and began to equip new fleets. It was called the "new" company, in contrast to the other called the "old company." In order to avoid competition between the two companies, the older company decided to buy the second company. This was accomplished and the combined companies were called the "Old Company." They equipped a fleet which left for the Far East on May 1, 1598.[6]

Altogether twenty-two ships were sent by the Dutch
to the Far East in the year 1598. Three of these ships were
dispatched by a company recently founded in the province
of Zeeland. When these ships arrived in the Malay Archipelago, they found that all the pepper had been purchased
by the fleet that had been sent from Amsterdam. So they
had to remain there for eight months before they could
find any pepper for themselves. In Rotterdam also a new
company was founded, which in 1598 sent out five ships.
Still another company in Rotterdam equipped four ships
of its own.[7]

It is not to be imagined, however, that all of these fleets
were combined in an effort to trade directly with the Malay
Archipelago. One of the fleets went around the Cape of
Good Hope. Three of the vessels sailed under the command of Admiral Van Neck and left the Netherlands on
November 25, 1598; five others belonging to the same
fleet were dispatched under the direction of Admiral Van
Warwijck. Another fleet crossed the southern Atlantic,
the Straight of Magellan, and the southern Pacific; it belonged to the so-called Magellan Company, and was directed by Admiral Van Noort.[8]

In 1599 a number of merchants in Amsterdam founded
a new company intended to trade with the Far East, and
named it the Brabant Company, because most of these
merchants had come from the Province of Brabant. They
had joined that large group of fugitives from the South
who had fled before the soldiers of Spain, particularly after
the fall of Antwerp in 1585, which caused an enormous
influx of Antwerp merchants to Amsterdam. In this manner, Amsterdam became the world's foremost port, taking
over the role formerly played by Antwerp.[9]

Before the Dutch East India Company was finally
founded, in order to avoid further competition among the
various Dutch companies, fourteen fleets made up of sixty-

five ships had departed for the Malay Archipelago. Eleven of those sixty-five ships did not return to the Netherlands. Much money and many lives were wasted in the fruitless attempt to secure greater advantages than those of the companies belonging to other Hollanders. It also was perfectly obvious that separate fleets were not strong enough to fight independently against the Portuguese and the Spaniards. Furthermore, in 1600 the English merchants had founded the English East India Company, and in the same year this company sent out its own fleet. Now the Dutch would have to compete not only with their own countrymen, they would have to fight not only against the Spaniards and the Portuguese, but they would also have to reckon with the English. It should be noted besides that the energetic Dutch had not confined themselves to trade with the Malay Archipelago, but they had made voyages to the mainland of India, Siam, China, Japan, and Ceylon. Even in the little towns of Delft, Hoorn, and Enkhuizen two expeditions were being prepared.

Fortunately for the Dutch merchants, the central government was led by a diplomat of the first rank, called Oldenbarnevelt who, unlike Hugo Grotius, was a man of heroic qualities. He was not a mere patriot, but had a vision that extended beyond the provincial frontiers of Holland. He insisted that the various companies should be amalgamated, and form one united national company. This was a matter of national interest, he argued. If the Dutch did not take such action, he averred that the English would soon surpass them and would take away from them their recently fortified trading posts in the Far East.

Oldenbarnevelt, the able Advocate of Holland, invited the representatives of all these commercial companies to come together in The Hague. Here they held their meetings under his leadership. Three months of heated arguments were required before Oldenbarnevelt was able to complete the delicate negotiations. In March, 1602, the States-General of the Dutch Republic finally granted the united company its charter.

This document provided that the company would receive a monopoly of the trade between the Cape of Good Hope and the Strait of Magellan. The charter would be valid for twenty-one years, and could be renewed at the end of that period. The company would be permitted to declare war and to maintain armed forces in the regions specified in the terms of the charter. It could fortify its trading posts and it could arm its vessels. Naturally, it also would have the privilege of equipping its own armies. It could occupy whatever stretch of land it deemed valuable and erect there factories and fortifications.[10]

The company was divided into six units called chambers, namely, those of the city of Amsterdam, the province of Zeeland, and the chambers located respectively in the cities of Delft, Hoorn, Rotterdam, and Enkhuizen. The Chamber of Amsterdam was to subscribe for one-half of the total capitalization, Zeeland was to provide for one-fourth, and each of the remaining chambers one-sixteenth. The executive council of the company was to be made up of seventeen persons, of which number Amsterdam would have eight, Zeeland four, and each of the remaining chambers one. The seventeenth member was to be chosen by one of the smaller chambers. This council was henceforth known as the College of Seventeen.[11]

All of the directors of the companies which were united to form the Dutch East India Company retained their officers as directors. These offices they kept for life. Since there were seventy-six of them,[12] this was the number with which the company began its existence. But the charter stated that in the future the total number would be sixty. The chamber of Amsterdam was to be represented by twenty, that of Zeeland by twelve, and that of each of the others by seven. When new directors were to be appointed, the existing officials would nominate three persons, from which the provincial government would select one. This would be the new director. Once in every decade the accounts of the company would be examined, and each subscriber would have the privilege of exchanging his stock for cash.[13]

All inhabitants of the republic had the right to buy shares in the company. In case more money was offered than could be used, those who had subscribed for more than thirty thousand guilders would be obliged to reduce their subscriptions so that other persons with more modest means would be able to purchase shares in proportion to their means.[14] It is interesting to observe that among the subscribers there were two Jews, who were of Portuguese descent; one subscribed for eighteen hundred guilders, the other for three thousand guilders.[15]

Equally remarkable was the fact that a German was permitted to buy shares valued at thirty thousand guilders. The largest single amount paid by any individual was sixty thousand guilders, subscribed by a merchant in Amsterdam, while the next largest amount was fifty-five thousand guilders by a wealthy person from Leeuwarden, the provincial capital of Friesland. However, the well-known Lemaire surpassed even these, because on August 5, 1602, he subscribed for twelve thousand guilders, on August 14 for twelve thousand guilders more, while later in the same day he spent the same amount again, and on August 30 he bought shares for thirty thousand guilders, making a total of ninety-seven thousand guilders. Furthermore, he also bought subscriptions for his wife, and for most of his twenty-two children. It was also fashionable for some of the rich merchants and statesmen to buy stock for their maids and other servants. For example, the mayor of Amsterdam gave to one of his maids stock which cost him fifty guilders. But most of the subscriptions were for stock that cost between óne thousand and ten thousand guilders.[16]

Whereas the former Dutch companies had been loosely governed, and whereas in each case the capital had been subscribed for each particular voyage, the united company was a real modern joint-stock company. It had been Oldenbarnevelt's aim to found a truly national company, in which any citizen could participate, if he had the means with which to do so.[17]

How well the affairs of the Dutch East India Company were managed may be seen in the following list of dividends declared by the company during the period from 1602 to 1702.

1610	125	percent in spices and 7½ percent in money
1612	30	percent in notes.
1612	87½	percent in cash.
1613	42½	percent in cash.
1618	62½	percent in cash.
1620	57½	percent in cash.
1623	25	percent in spices.
1625	20	percent in cash.
1627	12½	percent in cash.
1629	25	percent in cash.
1631	17½	percent in cash.
1633	32½	percent in cash.
1635	45	percent in spices.
1636	37½	percent in spices.
1637	40	percent in spices.
1638	10	percent in spices, 25 percent in cash.
1640	15	percent in spices and 25 percent in cash.
1641	40	percent in spices.

1642	. . . . .	50	percent in cash.
1643	. . . . .	15	percent in spices.
1644	. . . . .	25	percent in spices and 20 percent in cash.
1646	. . . . .	47½	percent in cash.
1648	. . . . .	25	percent in cash.
1649	. . . . .	30	percent in cash.
1650	. . . . .	20	percent in cash.
1651	. . . . .	15	percent in cash.
1652	. . . . .	25	percent in cash.
1653	. . . . .	12½	percent in cash.
1654	. . . . .	15	percent in cash.
1655	. . . . .	12½	percent in cash.
1656	. . . . .	27½	percent in cash.
1658	. . . . .	40	percent in cash.
1659	. . . . .	12½	percent in cash.
1660	. . . . .	40	percent in cash.
1661	. . . . .	25	percent in cash.
1663	. . . . .	30	percent in cash.
1665	. . . . .	27½	percent in cash.
1668	. . . . .	12½	percent in cash.
1669	. . . . .	12½	percent in cash.
1670	. . . . .	40	percent in cash.
1671	. . . . .	60	percent in cash.
1672	. . . . .	15	percent in cash.
1673	. . . . .	33⅓	percent in government notes.
1676	. . . . .	25	percent in cash.
1679	. . . . .	12½	percent in notes.
1681	. . . . .	22½	percent in notes.
1682	. . . . .	33⅓	percent in notes.
1685	. . . . .	40	percent in cash.
1686	. . . . .	12½	percent in cash.
1687	. . . . .	20	percent in cash.
1688	. . . . .	33⅓	percent in cash.
1689	. . . . .	33⅓	percent in cash.

1690	40	percent in cash.
1691	20	percent in cash.
1692	25	percent in cash.
1693	20	percent in cash.
1694	20	percent in cash.
1695	25	percent in cash.
1696	15	percent in receipts payable by each respective chamber.
1697	15	percent in similar receipts.
1698	15	percent in similar receipts and 15 percent in cash.
1699	15	percent in cash.
1700	25	percent in cash.
1701	20	percent in cash.
1702	20	percent in cash.[18]

From this list it appears that in the period from 1651 to 1654, when the Dutch were carrying on a naval and a commercial war with the English, the Dutch East India Company was still able each year to pay out handsome dividends to its stockholders. It has been generally assumed that the Dutch were unable during the course of this period to maintain their profitable trade with the Malay Archipelago. But the figures indicated above show that this popular conception must be erroneous.

Contrasted with the earlier Dutch companies, the united Dutch East India Company originally gave instructions that only one fleet at a time was permitted to go to the Malay Archipelago. Thus it happened in 1602 that a fleet of fifteen ships sailed for the Far East. This fleet was commanded by the Admiral Warwijck, who had a new stone factory erected in Bantam.[19] In the island of Borneo he started a trade in diamonds. He also went to China, and there he signed a contract with the Chinese authorities for a regular trade in silks, which Chinese vessels were to

transport to Bantam. At this port they were to be received
by officials of the East India Company.[20]

In 1603, a fleet of twelve ships sailed to the Malay
Archipelago, where, in 1605, the admiral of the Dutch
fleet seized an important Portuguese port.[21] One of the
Dutch vessels visited the Coromandel coast in India, and
founded there the first Dutch factory. Another vessel discovered the south coast of New Guinea and the north coast
of Australia. However, little was written about it, so that
as late as the eighteenth century when Cook visited the
same region, he was surprised to note that New Guinea
did not belong to the mainland of Australia.[22]

No fleet was sent in 1604, but in 1605 eleven ships
sailed under the command of Matelieff. The admiral was
able to seize Ambon, where he left orders to convert the
natives to the Calvinist faith. On the island of Ternate he
had a fort erected, and after that he visited China.[23]

A fleet sent out in 1606 and made up of eleven vessels,
was not successful. Like the earlier ones, this particular
one was also unable to drive the Spaniards out of the valuable Spice Islands. As the reader will recall, the Spaniards
had occupied the Philippines during the sixteenth century, and from those islands as a base of operations, they
had extended their sway over the Spice Islands between
the Philippines and the great islands of Borneo and Java.
This being the case, the Dutch government decided in
1606 to blockade the Spanish coast in Europe. As a result,
a Dutch fleet under Admiral Jacob Van Heemskerck not
only prevented the Spanish fleet from leaving its port, but
he completely destroyed it at Gibraltar (April 25, 1607).[24]
This expedition had also been supported by the Dutch
East India Company. Its own fleet, which in 1607 went to
the Far East under the command of Verhoeff, failed to seize
the city of Goa in India, but was notable in this respect that
it established commercial relations with Japan.[25]

On March 29, 1608, the directors of the Dutch East India Company sent a message to Admiral Verhoeff, which included the following words: "The islands of Banda and Moluccas are the principal aims that we are shooting at." They explained that here the most valuable spices were grown, and that it was absolutely necessary to secure those islands before September 1, 1609, and to equip them with fortifications and armed forces. Admiral Verhoeff immediately carried out these orders, and tried to erect a fortress on the island of Banda. But the natives refused to permit this, and when he tried to execute his plans against their wishes, he and fifty of his men were attacked and murdered.[26]

At that time there lay before the island of Banda a ship of the English East India Company commanded by Keeling, who had encouraged the natives in their opposition to Verhoeff. However, the vice-admiral Hoen employed all the forces at his command, drove away the English under Keeling, and declared the island of Banda the property of the States-General and of the Dutch East India Company. Now he erected the fort called Nassau, and thus there was established in the heart of the Spice Islands the Dutch supremacy. A little later a second English ship appeared there, commanded by Middleton, who persuaded the natives to hand over to him their spices, instead of to the Dutch who were still in Nassau. He paid the natives with arms, both lead and powder, so that each Hollander was certain to be shot to death if he ventured beyond his fortification.[27]

Thus far five expeditions had been sent by the new East India Company, and apparently each had been a partial failure. Not only had it been impossible to occupy the most important places held by the Portuguese, but the Spaniards had not yet been driven out of the Moluccas, and even Banda had not yet been properly occupied. Furthermore, the English had arrived and showed themselves to be treacherous competitors. It now became absolutely necessary to do in the Far East what the Dutch had done at home, namely, to concentrate all their efforts on a few places, and using them as bases for operations, to extend their power over adjoining regions. For that reason, on November 27, 1609, the Dutch East India Company appointed a governor-general for the whole of the Malay Archipelago.[28] The directors of the company also decided to appoint a council of five men, of whom they appointed the governor-general as a member together with two other members. They added that these three were to decide who the other two should be. Pieter Both was the first governor-general. In 1610, he was sent to the Far East in command of eight ships, and received orders to found a European colony there.[29] Preachers and craftsmen, as well as thirty-six women, were sent along with the regular crews. Both determined to found the colony near the present site of Batavia, which, during the past three hundred years, has been the capital of the Dutch colonies in the Far East.[30]

CHAPTER III

THE VOYAGE OF HENRY HUDSON
AND THE FOUNDING OF
NEW NETHERLAND

THE year 1609 marks the end of the first period in the history of the Dutch East India Company and of the rise of Dutch sea power in the Far East. Since it was generally expected that in this year the Dutch and the Spaniards would agree on at least a truce, if not a real peace, the directors of the Dutch East India Company tried with all the means at their disposal to obtain as much colonial territory in the Far East as possible, reasoning that the right of occupation and of conquest would no doubt determine the extent of the territory to be held by the Dutch outside of Europe. At about the same time, as we have just seen, Dutch statesmen and merchants determined to centralize the government of the occupied lands in the Far East. They finally appointed a governor-general, and prepared themselves for active competition with the English and the French.

The negotiations with the representatives of the Spanish government concerning the terms of a truce or peace to be determined upon, lasted for many months. It was very difficult to agree upon the privileges to be enjoyed by the Dutch merchants and sailors outside of European territory. The Spaniards were quite willing to acknowledge that the Dutch had obtained the status of a free and independent state in Europe. But they were extremely reluctant to permit the Dutch to trade in the Far East. They reasoned that divine laws and papal bulls had determined who should trade in the region between the Cape of Good

Hope on the west and the Strait of Magellan on the east. The Dutch were to be excluded from the trade in the Indian and the Pacific Oceans. But would the Dutch merchants agree to such terms?

The directors of the Dutch East India Company immediately published pamphlets addressed to the States-General, to the ministers and ambassadors in foreign countries, and to the public in general. They argued that the demands of the Spanish government were entirely unreasonable and unjust. Since the Dutch government represented a free and independent state, it followed naturally that whatever conquests it had obtained in foreign lands were the possessions of an independent government. The principle of free trade outside of Europe should be maintained. For had not the Dutch company, with enormous expense, with great energy, and in the midst of grave dangers, organized its fleets, built its factories, and erected its fortifications? If all this commerce were to be abandoned, if all the blood which had been shed counted for nothing, then it would be better to continue the war with Spain. The Dutch merchants also pointed out that they had signed contracts and treaties with Indian princes. They were obliged to maintain those treaties and contracts. It was their duty to defend the natives against the Spaniards and the Portuguese. Why should the Netherlands desert those princes and deliver them to the revenge of their former masters? It was also pointed out that the Dutch East India Company had received a charter from the States-General, and that it was necessary to maintain all the terms of this charter.

One reason why the leading merchants in the Netherlands were so anxious for the continuation of war, was that a state of active war permitted them to seize prizes. For that reason Hugo Grotius had written his learned commentary on the subject of the right of taking prizes.

Nor was it a coincidence that in this same year 1609 Hugo
Grotius published part of one chapter of this great treatise
under the title of *Mare Liberum,* or *Of the Freedom of
the Seas.* He never published any other portion of his
commentary. But his *Mare Liberum* was not only published in the original Latin, and often reprinted in that
version, but, in 1614, a Dutch translation appeared in
Leyden.[1]

In the years 1608 and 1609 the Dutch fought against
the medieval principle of monopoly and exclusive rights
which were being maintained by the government of Spain.
As a result of the activities thus carried on by the Dutch,
the law of nations in modern times has taken over many
of the principles thus propounded by the learned Dutch
writers and statesmen of the time. Not only did the Dutch,
in maintaining their terrific struggle with Spanish absolut-
ism, prepare the way for the rise of modern democracy
and representative government, but also in the field of
international law they made great contributions. But for
the present the king of Spain continued on his course. He
insisted that the Dutch should cease their trading with the
Malay Archipelago. No one except the Spanish government, so he argued, had the right to trade in that region.
For this reason the negotiations for peace that had been
carried on in the city of The Hague, were suddenly terminated on August 28, 1608. It seemed as if there were to
be no further negotiations for peace.[2]

As a result of the threats from the French and the English governments, the Dutch finally were willing to resume
negotiations for peace or a truce, which were concluded
on April 9, 1609, in the city of Antwerp. Here it was determined that a truce would interrupt the state of war for
a period of twelve years.[3]

Articles IV and V of the twelve years' truce signed respectively by representatives of the Spanish and Dutch

governments state: "The States-General and their subjects may not carry on commerce or traffic in the harbors
or places where the king of Spain ruled outside of the lim-
its of Europe, without direct permit of the king. But
they may carry on such commerce and traffic in the lands
of all other princes, potentates, and peoples outside of
Europe, which permit this trade, without that the king
or his officers are permitted to prevent such trade and
traffic. Outside of Europe the truce is to commence one
year after the signing of the treaty."

However, the Spanish officials were so reluctant to
carry out the contents of Articles IV and V of the Truce
that they refused to send a messenger to their possessions
in the Far East in order to acquaint the officials in that
region with the contents of the truce. Moreover, the officials in the Spanish colonies in the Far East, seeing that
they had received no instructions from their government
in Spain, declared that hostilities were to be continued in
the Malay Archipelago and adjoining regions. Apparently
it was the aim of those officials to destroy the newly founded
colonies of the Dutch in the Malay Archipelago and on
the mainland of India. By maintaining peace in Europe,
the Spaniards would be able to concentrate all their efforts
on the destruction of the Dutch possessions outside of Europe. But the sea power of the Dutch had by this time
become so extensive that it proved impossible for the
Spaniards and the Portuguese to check the rising might
of the Dutch Republic in the Indian and Pacific oceans.

Shortly before the first voyage of the Dutch to the
Malay Archipelago by way of the Cape of Good Hope, two
Dutch navigators, J. H. van Linschoten and Willem Barentsz, attempted to reach the same region by sailing
round the north coast of Asia (1594). They made another
attempt in the next year, while, in 1596, a third trip was
undertaken, this time under the leadership of Willem

Barentsz, Jacob van Heemskerck and Jan Cornelisz. Rijp. The intrepid sailors were compelled to spend the winter on the island of Nova Zembla, but, although they acquired some fame through their discovery of Spitzbergen, which they claimed for the Dutch government, they failed in their principal objective.[4]

After the first expedition to the Indian Ocean had been completed by Dutch navigators in 1597, it seemed for a time less advisable to seek a passage through the Arctic Ocean. But, as was just pointed out, when others were actively interested in finding such a passage and thereby threatening to usurp a part of the lucrative trade in spices, the directors of the Dutch East India Company immediately took steps to prevent this action on the part of their competitors. Henry Hudson, who had already been engaged in two voyages of considerable note,[5] offered his services to the Dutch East India Company, which signed a contract with him on January 8, 1609.[6]

In this contract it was stated that Hudson was to sail about April 1st in a vessel belonging to the Dutch East India Company, well equipped with men and provisions. He was to travel to the north of Nova Zembla and to remain at about the same latitude until the coast turned southward to a latitude of 60 degrees. There he was to take note of the land in as short a time as possible, after which work he should return at once, in order to report to the directors of the company what he had learned. His journals, maps and notes would become the property of the company, on condition that he receive the sum of eight hundred guilders, and if he should not return within one year, the company would give his wife or widow two hundred guilders. But if he returned after the expiration of one year, or within the year and having failed to find a good passage, the company would recompense him for his expense and efforts. In the meantime he should make his home in the Dutch Republic, and consider himself at the disposal of the company.

Hudson's own journal seems to be no longer extant, but we fortunately possess that written by Robert Juet, who accompanied Hudson on his third voyage.[7] According to Pieter van Dam, in his extensive history of the Dutch East India Company,[8] Hudson found too much ice in the vicinity of Nova Zembla, and for that reason he disregarded his instructions by sailing westward to North America. But he appears to have entertained plans of seeking a westward passage even when he was negotiating with the Dutch company.[9] At any rate, the directors of the Dutch East India Company were now thoroughly satisfied with their adherence to the old route around Africa. Nevertheless, explorations along the north coast of Asia continued for many decades.

Since the directors of the Dutch East India Company showed so little interest in the discovery of a passage by way of the north coast of Asia, it is not surprising that they also paid slight attention to the exploration of the coasts of America. Although Hudson had discovered the mouth of the river that was afterward named after him, which happened to be the most valuable region in America from a strategic point of view, the directors in Amsterdam made no effort to follow up the work done in this region by him.

The Dutch people as a whole had always displayed a similar attitude. When Christopher Columbus discovered America, the news of his discovery caused little stir in the Netherlands. Throughout the sixteenth century, when Spain was building a new Spain, when France was founding a new France, and when England was sending thousands of colonists to New England, the Dutch continued to expand in an eastward direction. They concentrated their efforts upon the Baltic shores, upon the carrying trade with Spain, France, Italy, and the northern countries of Europe, and upon the establishment of commercial contacts with the countries of the Far East. Since America did not produce the spices which the Dutch could so easily obtain in the Spice Islands, and also did not provide Europeans with an abundance of cotton cloths, such as northwestern India manufactured, nor with silks such as China produced, the Dutch for a time continued to look upon America as an obstacle in the path to the Far East, rather than a continent that promised a lucrative commercial development.

The question has often been asked why Henry Hudson did not return to the Netherlands, seeing that he had signed a contract with the directors of the Dutch East India Company, and had been promised eight hundred guilders if he would return within one year. It seems that he was afraid of his mutinous crew, who had at various times threatened him. Some of these men reasoned no doubt that if Hudson would present his report to the government of the Netherlands, he would mention their mutiny, and probably they would be hanged. Hudson was well aware of their thoughts, and for that reason he deemed it advisable not to bring back his vessel, the *Half-Moon,* to Dutch shores, but rather to those of Great Britain. In this way he saved his own life as well as the vessel. Although Hudson and his crew had intended to go to Ireland, they finally landed at the port of Dartmouth, in England.

From Dartmouth, Hudson communicated with the directors of the Dutch East India Company. He and his men proposed that they should be sent out on another voyage in search of the northwest passage. Hudson wanted six or seven of his men exchanged for others, and he proposed that the total number should be raised to twenty. But the directors of the Dutch Company ordered that the vessel be returned at once to the Netherlands. The English government, however, reasoned that Henry Hudson, being an Englishman, did not have the right to explore the coasts of America in a region that belonged to England, while he was in the service of a Dutch commercial company. For that reason the English government prohibited him from leaving his country.

An American author who wrote an excellent and interesting biography of Henry Hudson, made the following statement about the result of Hudson's voyage to America as considered by contemporary Hollanders: "No Dutch writer for several years after Hudson's voyage, either based any claim of territorial right upon it, or indeed thought the enterprise deserving of more than mere cursory mention. The explorer's body had long been tossed by the arctic waters in which he met his death, before the countrymen of Olden Barneveld thought it worth while to exploit his so-called discovery in order to strengthen their own title to New Netherland."[10]

Another American biographer reasoned that the maritime rivalry between England and Holland was at this time "too keenly felt to allow so famous and able a navigator as Henry Hudson to be retained in the Dutch service." This writer continued as follows: "Hudson belonged to England; hence, the Muscovy Company of London once more took him into their employ. Little was said about his exploration of the Great River on the American coast. That noble stream, the fur-producing forests at its source, the harbor at its mouth, the Island of Manhattan, with its possibilities in the way of a profitable traffic in peltries and green tobacco; all these belonged to the Virginia Company. If anything was to be done, let the Company furnish the men and ships to establish a trading post there. As for the Dutch, so long as they did not interfere with the rights of Great Britain they could do what they would with Hudson's discovery."[11]

The same writer devotes a whole chapter in his biography of Henry Hudson to the result of Hudson's third voyage, when he discovered the mouth and the course of the Hudson River from what is now Albany to New York City. After having discussed Henry Hudson's last voyage and his tragic death in the frozen waters of the North, and after having pointed out how, almost immediately upon his death, his name seems to have been forgotten by his contemporaries, he indicates the importance of his discoveries. After forty years of fighting against the greatest monarchy on the face of the earth, the Dutch Republic had become one of the leading states of Europe. Perhaps the most important year in the history of the young republic was the year 1609, when Henry Hudson discovered the river that was named after him. In that same year, as has been discussed here, the Twelve Years' Truce was signed with Spain. Gold and silver had been found by Spanish explorers in Central and South America. Although it could not be expected that precious metals would be found on the banks of the Hudson River, nevertheless there was something which could be turned into gold or silver. The Dutch merchants could buy enormous quantities of furs which could be sold again in Europe at a handsome profit. The Hollanders could build a New Netherland between New England and New Spain. There was little time to lose, and for that reason a number of merchants in Amsterdam dispatched another ship to the western hemisphere. It was sent in 1610 and the merchants of Amsterdam who had equipped the vessel were satisfied with the fair profits derived from the voyage. In 1614, a number of merchants in Amsterdam finally decided to found a company of their own, which was called the Company of New Netherland.

This company received from the Dutch government a charter of its own, but the charter stated that it would give

the merchants exclusive trading rights in New Netherland for the period of only three years. And when the
charter expired in 1617, the States-General refused to re-
new it. Four years of comparative inactivity followed, until, in 1621, the Dutch West India Company was founded.

As the name of the new company implied, its purpose
was not primarily to develop the colony of New Netherland, but to confine its operations very largely to the
tropical regions in America. During the sixteenth and
seventeenth centuries it was the consensus of opinion
among the leading merchants and statesmen in Europe
that colonies in tropical countries were much more valuable than those in the more temperate zones. The Dutch
East India Company had not engaged the services of Henry
Hudson in order to establish commercial contacts with the
Hudson Valley, but to find a shorter passage to the Far
East. Neither Henry Hudson nor his employers realized
how important the present site of New York City would
some day become. Nor were they particularly interested
in the abundance of furs that could be obtained in the
region to the east and to the west of the Hudson River.
Their aim continued to be to purchase spices, silks, and
cotton goods in the Malay Archipelago, India, and China.
In their opinion, the trade with Japan was more important
than that with North America. For that reason it is not
surprising that the Dutch, after the successful termination
of the second trade war with England, in the year 1667,
exchanged what they had called New Netherland for
English Guiana, on the mainland of South America. When
we compare the economic importance of the whole of
Guiana with the little island of Manhattan, we must smile
a bit at the ignorance of the Dutch merchants during the
seventeenth century so far as the future of North America
was concerned.

CHAPTER IV

THE ANGLO-DUTCH STRUGGLE FOR THE FREEDOM OF THE SEAS

IN the opening years of the seventeenth century, as we saw, the Dutch East India Company made extraordinarily rapid progress in conquering from the Portuguese their trading-posts in the East Indian Archipelago. Endowed originally with a capital eighteen times as large as that of its rival, the English East India Company, it continued to forge ahead, making contracts with the natives for securing the highly prized spices and erecting fortified places at points of great strategic advantage. Obviously, competition between the two companies with resultant ill-feeling could not long be avoided.

As soon as King James VI of Scotland had become King James I of England, in the year 1603, and had made peace with Spain, thus reversing the foreign policy of his predecessor, Queen Elizabeth, friction between the English and the Dutch ensued. In 1604, the English East India Company sent its second fleet, which was commanded by Henry Middleton, to the Malay Archipelago. This was the only voyage of the English East India Company during the seventeenth century to which a whole contemporary narrative was devoted. It was printed in London in 1606, and was entitled *The Last East-Indian Voyage*. In 1855, it was published again by the Hakluyt Society, under the title of *The Voyage of Sir Henry Middleton to Bantam and the Moluccan Islands; being the Second Voyage Sent forth by the Governor and Company of Merchants of London Trading to the East Indies*. This important treatise throws much light on the coming struggle between the English and the Dutch in the Malay Archipelago. Its writer re-

lated that on December 22, 1604, while the English fleet
was lying before the port of Bantam, the British ships were
visited by the vice-admiral of the Dutch fleet, which happened to be in the vicinity at the time. He offered refresh-
ments, and he said that he would be very glad to render
any assistance required by the English. The writer admitted that the Dutch were very courteous, which the
English appreciated, since their weakness "was so great."

From Bantam the English proceeded to the island of
Amboina, which at that time belonged to the Portuguese.
Since the English had just made peace with Spain, they
were permitted to trade with this island. The English
journal states that the natives of the island and other islands in the vicinity were enemies of the Portuguese, and
had sent a message to the Hollanders in Bantam asking for
aid in expelling the Portuguese from their islands. "If
this could be accomplished," so continues the journal,
"they would become subject to them, and sell none of their
cloves to any other nation but them." The Hollanders
would buy all the spices and would not permit any other
European nation to buy them. The journal continued as
follows: "This I know to be true, for the parties who were
sent to Bantam, I have often spoken withal."

In other words, before the close of 1604, it had become
apparent to the English that they would have to face stiff
competition from the Dutch. The intention of the Dutch
was to exclude all other nations from the spice trade in
the Moluccas. As it turned out, the Dutch afterwards
did conquer Amboina, and prohibited the English from
trading there. The latter left and removed to the island of
Ternate, whose sultan was the successor of the native
prince with whom Sir Francis Drake had carried on commercial relations.

Notwithstanding the activities of Sir Francis Drake,
who had actually traded with the natives, the latter had

become friends of the Dutch. When the English asked the king of Ternate whether he would permit them to establish a factory, he replied that the English should come back the next day to find out if he could grant his permission or not. Then the English appealed to the Dutch and told them that the king of Ternate was willing to let them have a factory. The Dutch replied that in their opinion the king of Ternate should not forget "himself so much as to grant us a factory, considering he had written to his Excellency [that is, the ruler of the Dutch Republic], and likewise promised him that they would trade with no nation but with them." Then the journal continues as follows: "Our general said that he had no reason to cross him for leaving a factory there, so that Sir Francis Drake had traded in Ternate before the names of the Hollanders were known in those parts of the world." This means that the English saw no reason why the Dutch would prevent the English from getting a factory on the island of Ternate, since they had preceded the Dutch there. The English then felt themselves obliged to leave, and "to take their best advantage for their adventurers." These "adventurers" were the Merchant Adventurers, the subscribers who advanced the money with which to equip the merchant-ship or the fleet of merchant-ships, as they were called. In 1604, the English East India Company was not yet a full-fledged joint-stock company, or a corporation.

Afterwards the English began to deal directly with the king of Ternate. The journal reports that one day he came down with a great company of his nobles and had a tent erected, asking the leader of the English to come ashore, which he did. "The king caused him to sit down by him, excusing himself that they left not a factory there, alleging that the Hollanders had forced him to the contrary; he and his subjects owe them much, which he hoped to pay the next harvest; and that then he would take another

order with them: which being done, he caused a letter to
be read by his secretary openly, the contents whereof follow at the end of the book." Then he asked the general to
come back in the near future, and he would be welcome.
But the English leader answered that it was in vain for
the English to return there, so long as the Hollanders were
in control of the situation, "holding it a disparagement to
his nation to give place to them, being so far their inferiors."

At the end of this journal there appears a remarkable
letter addressed by the king of Ternate to King James I of
England. The king referred to the former visit of Sir Francis Drake to his island, and told how his predecessor had
sent a ring to Queen Elizabeth of England. He added that
his father had looked in vain for the return of the great
English captain. The king himself, after the death of his
father, had cherished the same hope until he was the father
of eleven children. In the meantime he was informed that
the English were of such a bad disposition that they did not
come any more as peaceable merchants but to rob the natives of their country. But he had found out that this information was absolutely false, which made him very
happy. In the course of time, certain ships arrived, which
the king of Ternate hoped were English. When he came
to the conclusion that no more English ships would be
forthcoming, he was compelled to write to the prince of
Holland, and ask for aid against his ancient enemies, the
Portuguese. The prince of Holland replied by sending his
armed forces, which drove all the Portuguese out of Amboina and Tidore.

Captain Henry Middleton desired to leave a factory
on the island, and the king of Ternate was very willing,
but the captain of the Hollanders refused to let him do
this. The Hollanders argued that, since they had enabled
the natives to free themselves from the Portuguese, they

need not permit any other foreign power to trade with them. "So that we were forced against our will to yield to the Hollanders, whereof we crave pardon of your Highness. If any of your nation come hereafter, they shall be welcome. And whereas the chief captain of the Hollanders does solicit us, that we shall not hold any friendship with your nation, nor give a hearing to your Highness's letters, yet for all that, if you please to send your men here again they shall be welcome. And in token of our friendship, which we desire of your Majesty, we have sent you a small remembrance in the form of cloves, our country being poor and yielding not better commodity, which we pray your Highness will accept in good part."

There can be no question about the determined manner in which the Hollanders attempted to prevent the English competitors from obtaining spices in the Malay Archipelago. After 1610, they became more and more rude and forceful. As a result of their apparent aim to establish a monopoly of the commerce with all of the islands in the Malay Archipelago,[1] the men who were in the service of the English East India Company were compelled to notify their directors in London.

In the month of November, 1611, the "Merchants of London Trading the East Indies"[2] addressed a letter of complaint to Robert Cecil, Earl of Salisbury, Lord High Treasurer of England. The enraged merchants stated that "after having long and patiently endured sundry notorious wrongs and injurious courses at the hands of the Hollanders," they were "enforced at last to break silence." They showed that the Dutch merchants had secured possession of valuable regions, in which they followed the same tactics previously employed by the Portuguese, debarring other European powers from trading there. They claimed that the English had that right before any other nation except the Portuguese, for Sir Francis Drake had at

one time "made a contract with the king of Ternata for
the trade of cloves in that island." In the southern part of
Java, so continues the petition, the English had long enjoyed the right to purchase pepper, while Captain Lancaster sailed as far as Sumatra and bought a cargo of
pepper. Afterward the Hollanders arrived with English
pilots and came to Bantam, thus building up a lucrative
trade. Gradually they usurped the trade in the Moluccas,
trying to keep all English merchants away. Consequently,
the English merchants humbly requested the lord treasurer, who was the principal minister of King James I, to
render them honorable assistance and obtain mediation
through negotiation with the States-General of the Dutch
Republic.[3]

It may be doubted, however, that the English at this
time had just cause for complaint, for their commanders
had played a questionable role in Banda, where the Dutch
admiral, Verhoeff, had been murdered by the natives. Pre-
posterous, certainly, was the allegation that the Dutch had
found their way to the East Indies only with the aid of the
English merchants and pilots.

King James nevertheless permitted the letters of complaint to be sent by his minister in The Hague, Sir Ralph
Winwood, to the States-General, which was in session as
usual in the same city. The English minister addressed the
Dutch statesmen in the French language, and, on January
31, 1613, he sent a copy of his speech to the Earl of Salisbury. He remarked that Sir Francis Drake and Sir Thomas
Cavendish had traded in the East Indies before the Dutch,
and that the latter "had been conducted thither by the
pilots of England" and "the merchants of England had
cordially welcomed the Dutch over there, providing them
with all necessities." He continued as follows: "When
your men became more powerful both in numbers and in
ships, they not only forgot the favors extended to them

previously when they were far removed from their native land, but they also forgot, it seems to me, in their rude comportment toward our men that there is a friendly relationship between the realm of Great Britain and the United Provinces ... In short, your men wish to secure a monopoly of the trade and to exclude the English entirely. ... The liberty of commerce depends upon the law of nations, which is not limited by space nor time." In this manner Hugo Grotius had argued not long ago in his *Mare Liberum,* and Sir Ralph Winwood was fully justified in using the same arguments, now that the English found themselves in exactly the same situation in which Grotius had seen the Dutch when faced by superior numbers of the Portuguese. It was very well, admitted Winwood, however, for the Dutch to "correct the insolence of the Spaniards," for until very recently the English and the Dutch had been fighting a common war against Spain. But he insisted that the English deserved a better treatment.

In the same letter Sir Ralph Winwood reports that Mr. Barnevelt (Oldenbarnevelt) made the following reply. He said that this was the first time that he had ever heard of any cause for complaint on the part of the English, and he requested Winwood to present his message in writing, which the latter had promptly done. He regretted that Salisbury had not been able to secure redress earlier, that is before the fleet of fourteen ships sailed from Amsterdam in the beginning of this month of January to the East Indies. He did not doubt that the States-General would write a conciliatory letter, for the Dutch government wished to promote friendly feeling with the English. However, he feared that the Dutch merchants would not yield sufficiently.[4]

The Dutch Government requested of the English minister that he prove the complaints of the English East India Company by furnishing concrete particulars. Winwood, however, replied at first that the King, his master, did not insist upon indemnification; but that he had merely instructed him to request of the States-General friendly treatment and a "free traffic" for his subjects in India. The answer to this note was couched in equally general terms. The States-General referred the English minister to the monopoly given to the Dutch company in its charter, as a means of protection in Indian waters against enemies and friendly competitors, and they reminded him of the fact that much blood had been shed there and heavy expenditures incurred, which the Dutch had to incur in order to secure for themselves fortifications and well-protected trading posts in the Moluccas. These fortifications were intended to ward off attacks by Spaniards and Portuguese alike. The representation of the state of affairs made by the English company, was not, however, refuted.[5]

Several other documents were presented to the English government, in which the Dutch explained the beginnings and the development of their navigation in Indian waters and the rights which the Dutch company believed it possessed there. Winwood wrote the king that in the Netherlands there were to be found many persons who were of the belief that the best way to overcome the resistance of the Spaniards and the Portuguese was a union of the English and Dutch forces in India.[6] However, when neither King James nor the English company was satisfied with these explanations and arguments, both companies, after conferences with their respective governments, decided to have their commissioners meet in a conference. After the English company had shown itself unwilling to take the first step, the Dutch company appointed commissioners for a trip to England.

The Dutch East India Company first appointed as its commissioners Reinier Pauw, former mayor of the city of

Amsterdam; Jacob Boreel, former mayor of the city of Middelburg; and Dirk Meerman, alderman of the city of Delft.[7] Shortly afterward Hugo Grotius was added to the committee, not only because of the services formerly rendered by him to the Dutch East India Company but also because he was expected to inform King James I about religious and ecclesiastical conditions in the Netherlands.[8]

Among the important papers once preserved by Hugo Grotius which are now a part of the Colonial Acquisitions of the General Government Archives in The Hague[9] there is a copy of an original document, dated The Hague, March 23, 1613. The superscription reads: "To Ambassador N. Caron." This was Noel Caron, the Dutch ambassador in England, who was naturally expected to present to King James I the viewpoints of the Dutch merchants. He is informed in the dispatch that "the United East India Company of these lands have decided, in order to promote friendly feeling and good neighborly relations between the subjects of His Majesty the King of England and the inhabitants of these lands, and also in the East Indies, to send to His Majesty a committee." The commissioners are to act with authority from the Dutch East India Company and from the States-General as well. They must seek to further the best interests of the government and the company, and use discretion, reason and common sense. They will not only treat with the king but also with the Privy Council (called Secret Council). We recall that the Dutch East India Company had secured from the States-General a charter in which very great powers had been delegated to the company. This is the reason why the negotiations in England were to break down. The Dutch government was conciliatory but the East India Company was not.

It is interesting to note that Mr. Boreel had been intimately acquainted with Grotius for years. Grotius and

Boreel's son (John) had been fellow-students in the University of Leyden, both in 1608 had married Zeeland girls, and both had rendered valuable services to the Dutch East India Company. Young Boreel's father had been a member of the Dutch East India Company since its foundation in 1602, and he was now a director in the board of Zeeland.

The original source material shows that Grotius was sent to England to represent both the Dutch East India Company and the States-General of the Dutch Republic. We possess the original copy of the report by Grotius, of the work performed in England by his commission. It was naturally drawn up in the Dutch language, and it was published from the original manuscript by Molhuysen in the appendix of the first volume of Grotius' Correspondence, as was stated above.

Hugo Grotius ranks among the first three or four most famous Hollanders. He was not only an expert in the field of international law, so that many scholars have referred to him as the "father of international law," but he was also an outstanding historian, a famous theologian and an authority on the classics. In order to understand his relationships with various Dutch merchants in general, and with the Dutch East India Company in particular, it is absolutely necessary to bear in mind both the scholarly attainments of Hugo Grotius and his family connections. Much indeed has been written about him that is erroneous or entirely misleading, because many writers have ignored the influence exerted upon him by his relatives and the friends of his youth.

Judging from the contacts that Grotius had made with various officials in the East India Company, it would seem that when he was sent to England in 1613 to represent the company, he did not set forth views which he himself had originated, but rather those of the directors of the East India Company, who told him in advance what to say.

This appears from the letter which Jacob Boreel addressed to Grotius on January 31, 1613. Mr. Boreel instructed Grotius as to what he should do with the information at his disposal. When Grotius arrives in England, he says, it will become clear to him that the English, contrary to the law of nations, are not to be permitted to trade in the East Indies as freely and as cheaply as the Dutch, who have with their blood and money conquered or built the places where they carry on their trade. "When I made this observation," so continued Boreel, "I did not think it advisable to argue about the right of occupation, the expenses incurred or the blood shed, or about the right of rulers who, like other rulers, enforce wherever they can their laws and ways of commerce." Boreel preferred to talk about the practices followed by the English in Virginia and the Davis' Strait. They wanted to charge every foreigner sailing through this strait the sum of five hundred dollars, for they argued that they had to spend much money in finding the passage. This would enable the Hollanders to compare what they were doing with what the English had done or wanted to do.

In the preliminary negotiations between the English and the Dutch, the former complained about the tactics of their rivals, who, so argued the English, followed the example set by the Portuguese in trying to obtain a monopoly of the trade in the East Indies. Robert Cecil, the Earl of Salisbury, who was the principal minister of James I, and Lord Treasurer, informed Sir Ralph Winwood, the English ambassador at The Hague, what sort of arguments were to be followed in negotiating with the Dutch. They were not to ask for indemnities to pay for the wrongs which had been inflicted upon the English merchants in the East Indies. But they should insist on changed tactics on the part of the Dutch, who were no longer to deprive the English of their proper share in the trade. The English would merely ask for the enforcement of natural law and the law of nations, according to which the seas and commerce were free to all nations.[10] It is curious that Salisbury, in his letter to Winwood, used almost exactly the same words as had Boreel in his letter of January 31, 1613, which was written to Grotius. Salisbury wrote: "Contrary to that general law of nations which admits a communion and liberty of commerce," the Dutch wanted to exclude the English from trading in the East Indies. This line of argument the English representatives in the Anglo-Dutch conference of 1613 continued to the very end.[11]

It may seem strange that Hugo Grotius was appointed to be the principal spokesman for the Dutch East India Company in the Anglo-Dutch Conference of 1613. For had he not defended the principle of the free sea in his *Mare Liberum,* which had been published in 1609? Would he perhaps have to withdraw some of his claims made four years earlier, in his *De Jure Praedae?* Some of the scholars who are familiar with these works and with the negotiations of 1613 have indeed been of the opinion that Grotius contradicted several statements to be found in his *Mare Liberum* when he defended the Dutch East India Company in London.

But this was not the opinion of Grotius' friends in Amsterdam and Middelburg. They realized that he did not have to retract anything he had previously stated in his *Mare Liberum,* though this could not be said for the whole of the *De Jure Praedae.* Few merchants in Amsterdam were embarrassed when *Mare Liberum* went through new editions in 1618, 1633 (three editions), and 1663; or when in 1614, an edition appeared in the Dutch language.

Much was expected of Grotius by his friends. His keen mind and his vast learning could not fail to impress some of his adversaries. The Board of Seventeen, that is, the smaller council which directed the affairs of the Dutch East India Company, had followed his career with much interest. On September 16, 1610, its members had deliberated on the question whether they "ought to have the trade with the East Indies described historically by the fiscal Grotius, or by some other learned person, in order to increase the honor and reputation of the company and the country."

Although the Board of Seventeen did not actually request Grotius or any other scholar to write this historical work, the directors continued to follow Grotius' career with much interest. This they clearly revealed in 1613, when they asked Grotius to represent them during the Anglo-Dutch conference in London. They would do so again in 1615, when negotiations were resumed, this time at The Hague, as will appear.

King James' attitude from the beginning was sympathetic toward the cause of the Dutch East India Company. He was of the opinion that the Hollanders should be permitted to fortify certain areas, while the English merchants had the right to share in the trade thus established and protected with the use of arms and fortifications. Matelief went so far as to write to Grotius that the English wanted to "use the leg of the Hollanders, in order to pull the chestnuts out of the fire for them." James resembled Prime Minister Neville Chamberlain, who in the year 1938 tried to check Hitler with his policy of appeasement. But, just as Hitler went ahead after the Munich Accord of 1938 and annexed regions which he had promised not to invade and occupy, so the Dutch merchants in the East Indies made agreements through their commissioners, and within a few years were to abrogate them. The English relied on words and promises, the Dutch on actions.

In his last message the king stated that after the negotiations had come to an end, it was felt by both commissions that the differences between the respective points of view could easily be removed. So he proposed that in the near future another conference should be held, this time in the Netherlands, where the Dutch representatives would no doubt receive greater authority and freedom of action than they had enjoyed in the previous negotiations. The king was quite right in making this statement, for thus far no agreements had been possible between the representatives of the two East India companies. All that the commissioners had been able to do was to argue back and forth, and to state the views entertained by the directors of the two great companies. For that reason it can be readily understood that the next conference would be of greater importance. We shall see that when the two commissions met in The Hague in the course of the year 1615, the English drew up an agreement which was made up of five points or articles.

It must not be imagined, however, that the conference of 1613 was devoid of important results. It enabled the merchants in the service of both companies to understand better the viewpoints of their competitors. It also prepared the way for the treaty that was finally signed between the governments of England and the Dutch Republic in the year 1619, as will appear. The English arguments were lucidly set forth in the first brief which they presented to the Dutch commissioners April 18, 1613. They expressed their views in the following words: "Before we treat concerning reform and amity we should reach an agreement about the facts, although meanwhile, indeed, in accordance with the law of nations there ought to exist the free right to all nations to travel to any portion whatsoever of the East Indies and to exercise commerce there.[12] *And moreover, before those regions were known to you we stood legally approved by their leaders and peoples, in pacts and agreements, as we can easily prove,[13]* lest you believe, through the reasons and allegations brought forward by you to the contrary, that relying only on conquests and agreements any prejudice to our right so firmly established could arise so that we could not, and ought not, to employ and enjoy free commerce in any region whatsoever of the East Indies. If we should at the present time in this matter be impeded in any fashion or on any pretext by you Dutch, with whom we have up to this time been joined in the closest friendship, we could neither think that this had been done by you without injustice, nor could we admit it without emotion. But we hope for and expect juster things from you in your prudence, and relying on this—your responses, acts, declarations hither transmitted notwithstanding—we do not hesitate to exercise free commerce in every region of the East Indies."

Of considerable importance is the third reply of the Dutch, which was dated May thirteenth, and answered the arguments presented by the English in their document dated May ninth. The Dutch stated their position thus: *"As far as the question is involved Your Majesty's subjects rely on the freedom of the law of nations, we on a sale already made and on the sanctity of treaties.* The question is, which ought to yield. The liberty which they themselves confess is circumscribed in many ways, or in the faith of agreements, which always ought to prevail wherever one promises a thing which he can fulfill. The Indians, who are the people in question, *can* promise us the handing over of all the spices, as Your Majesty's subjects confess, and they have promised they would, therefore they ought to. *And how great a crime it would be if the Indians were allowed, after they had drawn us into expenses otherwise unendurable on the reliance of those treaties, to withdraw from the treaties when our expenses were not restored! Freedom of the law of nations prevails up to the contract, not after the contract,* for by the contract the freedom of the contracting powers, and in the contracted matters, is extinguished. The individual has the right of deciding what he pleases about his affairs once, not oftener. Therefore, no kind of 'freedom' can cause what has been sold to one person to be sold to another. Certain negotiators say these agreements are shameful and unfair; *to us, on the contrary, it seems a most honorable course to defend oppressed nations and in return for the defense to accept what is least irksome to them.*"

It should be noted here that the English commissioners had referred to the *Mare Liberum* of Grotius, which was published anonymously in the year 1609. In their first document, as we saw, they had quoted from a chapter of this treatise. They also referred to this work in their third document. For that reason the Dutch retorted with the observation that the freedom of the law of nations prevails up to the signing of the contract, not after the contract had been signed. The freedom of the contracting powers is extinguished as soon as their contract has been signed. The Dutch continued thus:

"Moreover, it seems less honorable and less in conformity with justice to bring about, under the undefined color of some law, the occasion for violating faith and sworn oath, or to seek a harvest from another's sowing, and to transcribe the burdens to others, the profits to themselves. Nor does 'the assertor of the free sea' dissent from this, *everywhere asserting that* liberty is guaranteed before consent and so shows from a response of Ulpian[14] that even in those things which by nature are open to all one requires good faith so that the law of the contract be preserved even though contrary to freedom; indeed, if contracts of this kind prevail, neither poverty nor too great an expensiveness of goods follows—no more than follows in the case of the laws of some kingdoms which do not allow owners to sell their things abroad, so that those who desire to own them *must buy them from certain merchants;* nevertheless, they who so immoderately proclaim that freedom ·do not find fault with *those* laws. In addition, there are other regions which our commerce does not touch from which spices can be sought, and indeed safely enough as long as we detain the Spaniards elsewhere. Moreover, indeed, our struggle with Portugal and the divided possession (for that holds for Tidore and part of Ternate, spice-bearing places) would never permit too many rewards of spices for the guardianship. What is more, it has always been possible by sale of goods to obtain whatever was just from us, indebted as we are to the kindness of Your Majesty. We do not owe Spain the same debt, and we should not conceal that whatever is added to their power takes away from the security of Europe."

Not only King James but also Oldenbarnevelt and other influential statesmen in the Netherlands, earnestly desired from the very beginning to come to a peaceful solution of the disputes. They viewed the matter from a higher standpoint than the commanders of the English and the Dutch companies. Their interests were broader and their horizon was wider. They foresaw that the disputes which had arisen and the mutual antagonisms would, in the end, result in a breach of the peace between the two nations, which nations were not only closely knit together by treaties but also by a unity of religious principles, and they seemed destined jointly to represent in Europe a very positive system of statecraft. The Dutch and English statesmen were actually able a few years later to bring about a friendly conciliation between the two companies. But it was only done on paper and their attempts soon proved futile, for they did not succeed in uniting the interests of the two nations in the navigation and trade in the East Indies through an indissoluble bond or a complete union.

If at that time the sagacity of the statesmen had proved
victorious over the more limited insight and the selfish-
ness of the commanders of the two companies, Dutch sea
power in the Indies would have developed in an entirely
different fashion, and the vicissitudes of the Republic of
the United Netherlands would have followed a very different course. As a result, the relation between the Dutch
Republic and the government of Cromwell would also
have been different; for the commercial rivalry with the
Netherlands was the principal feature of Cromwell's foreign policy, and that policy was in complete accordance
with the views of the middle classes in England, which,
after the Revolution, had displaced the royal court and the
nobility.

The colonial policy, and even the whole foreign policy
of the Dutch Republic in relation to England from 1611
to 1619 followed a very dangerous course, and it is therefore all the more surprising that before 1939 not one
Dutch historian ever produced an accurate or complete
account of the very important negotiations which during
those years were carried on between the two governments.

The zeal of the diplomats, but especially the influence
of the King of England, who also from a Protestant standpoint was desirous of an intimate union between the English and Dutch interests in the Indies, finally brought it
about that the commanders of the English East India Company withdrew their passive resistance and, although with
great reluctance, agreed to one more attempt to bring
about a peaceful solution, for which purpose they were to
send their commissioners to Holland. Active negotiations
were not resumed until 1615, when the second Anglo-
Dutch conference was held.

How unwilling the directors of the Dutch East India
Company were to grant concessions may be seen in a letter
written by them on November 21, 1614, and addressed to

Jan Pietersz. Coen, the new Director-General of the East Indies. They wrote: "The trade of the English in the Moluccas must, as heretofore, be prevented with all possible means, without that recourse be had to maltreatment of them." [15]

Coen was quite ready for action. His reply was as follows: "If by night and day proud thieves broke into your house who were not ashamed of any robbery or other offense, how would you defend your property against them without having recourse to 'maltreatment?' This is what the English are doing against you in the Moluccas. Consequently, we are surprised to receive instructions not to do them bodily harm. If the English have this privilege above all other nations, it must be nice to be an Englishman." [16]

The letters of Coen and Grotius show clearly that the directors and employees of the Dutch East India Company had definite views on the rights which they had secured through conquests and fortifications in the Malay Archipelago. As Grotius had said in his *Mare Liberum,* when a person or a company or a nation acquires a piece of land by erecting on it certain buildings, this land is absolutely the property of the party which owns the building or buildings. This was in keeping with the law of nations and with all the expressions used by Grotius in his *Mare Liberum.* Grotius, in his letter to Winwood, revealed that, in his opinion, the English should change their mind somewhat as to the right that they expected to derive from merely appearing before the ports occupied by the Dutch. Land, buildings, and written contracts were regarded by the Dutch as real property, which could not be expected to be shared with others, unless the latter were willing to compensate the former for expenditures that they had incurred.

At the end of the year 1614, the English government appointed the following men to represent the East India

Company in the conference to be held early the next year in the city of The Hague: Sir Henry Wotton, the English ambassador in The Hague; Clement Edmondes, a clerk in the Privy Council; Robert Middleton, and Maurice (Morris) Abbott, merchants of the East India Company in London. They received their official instructions from their government as dated Jan. 2, 1614, that is, 1615, since the year in England did not begin until March twenty-fifth.[17]

According to the message sent by the States-General of the Dutch Republic to the English government, dated Feb. 14, 1615, the following persons had been appointed to represent the interests of the Dutch East India Company: Dirk Bass, mayor of Amsterdam; Albert Joachimi, a deputy in the States-General; Hugo Grotius; Jacob Boreel; Dirk Gerritsz; Dirk Meerman; Albert Fransz; and Dirk van Osse.[18] Oldenbarnevelt also frequently took part in the negotiations, which began in the closing days of January, 1615.[19]

The English commissioners arrived at Rotterdam on January 18 (28), 1615, and they were immediately received by the mayor of Rotterdam and by the pensionary, Hugo Grotius. Two days later Grotius introduced Admiral Matelief to them, who accompanied them to Delft. From there they went to The Hague.[20] After a few days the English had an audience with the States-General, and shortly afterwards they had a long discussion with Oldenbarnevelt, who repeatedly pointed out to the English that the East Indies would yield treasures just as great as those which the West Indies had given to Spain, if they would only unite with the Dutch in order to carry on with full force the war against the Spaniards and the Portuguese in India. In this way Oldenbarnevelt sought to conduct the negotiations to the advantage of the Dutch interests. He reasoned that if besides the Dutch company, which had to carry on an active warfare, another nation would trade peacefully in India, the Dutch would not long be able to endure such competition. Not only did Oldenbarnevelt entertain this fear, but it had arisen even before the signing of the truce in 1609. The Dutch commissioners continually harped upon the same point: offensive war of both companies with Spain and the exclusion of every competitor that might make his appearance. But this is exactly the point that the English wished to evade, and when finally they were called upon to give a direct answer, they flatly declared that they had received no instructions to discuss this question. The English preferred to have the negotiations, which were conducted almost entirely in writing, cover the field of natural law and the law of nations, from which they deduced that free trade upon all seas and in all lands was everywhere a natural right of all nations, and that the archipelago of the Spice Islands should be as accessible to the English as to the Dutch.[21]

In the report sent by the English commissioners to James I, dated April 10, 1615, they began with these words: "Upon meeting in conference with the deputies of the States touching the business of the East Indies, we first insisted, according to the instructions, upon free trade and merchandizing to all parts and places of the world, and particularly to the Moluccas *Jure Gentium.*" Free trade, they continued, was the right of every man by nature; it was one's birthright.[22]

This thesis was correct in the abstract, but it certainly was bold on the part of the British to advance it at the very time that they maintained the opposite thesis with relation to the fisheries in the northern seas, and that they had requested William Welwood to propound the thesis of the *mare clausum.* Hugo Grotius, who also during these negotiations was the chief writer on the side of the Dutch,[23] must have felt somewhat embarrassed to be called upon to refute this thesis at the very moment that he put together his *Mare Liberum* on behalf of the fisheries in the northern seas.

The refutation of the Dutch company turned by preference to a more practical field. It pointed out that the opening of the Moluccas was neither reasonable nor just nor possible. It was not reasonable, because the British would reap the advantages and the profits of those activities on the part of the Dutch which had meant for them excessive expenditures, injuries, and dangers. It was not just, because, if the English were freely admitted in the Moluccas, the contracts in which the natives had conceded the exclusive sale of spices to the Dutch East India Company would be rendered null and void, in spite of the fact that the company had obtained them after having incurred great risks and heavy expenditures. The law of nations could not give to the English the right to buy merchandise which had been purchased by the Dutch for a definite period and under a binding contract, while the products were to be delivered at stated times. Finally, the opening of the Moluccas was impossible without resulting in the total decline of the English and the Dutch trade and the restoration of the Spanish and Portuguese power in the Indies.[24]

During a period of three months these arguments were treated and maltreated in all sorts of ways, as may be seen in the written remonstrances and counter-remonstrances. This manner of negotiations produced, as the Dutch commanders correctly observed, nothing more than "frivolous and futile cavilings." The Dutch insisted upon their conditions, namely, that no union was possible and thinkable without the amalgamation of capitalization, of monopoly, and of armed forces, with which they would jointly carry on offensive war against Spain. The English, on the other hand, did not wish to relinquish their thesis, namely, that trade is free in all regions.

It is interesting to note, however, that the English for a time acted as if they favored the idea of the amalgamation as outlined by some of the Dutch. A remarkable proposal was drafted in the French language, a copy of which is to be found in the Public Record Office in London. The document stated that the joint capital was to be from 1,200,000 to 1,500,000 pounds sterling. Each year an amount of spices, silk, and porcelain was to be purchased for about 500,000 to 600,000 pounds. This would be the maximum quantity that western Europe would be able to consume annually. One-third of the total capital would thus be invested in the purchase of these oriental wares. The union of the companies would insure steady prices and a reasonable profit. The separation of the companies, on the other hand, would result in irregularities and needless competition. The united company would derive an annual profit of 20 or 25 per cent, which would be sufficient for carrying on a war against Spain, and, besides, for a handsome dividend on the shares. The new company would also be able to force the native kings to reduce the dues paid at Bantam and other places. At present they were being raised from day to day.

Moreover, trade with China will thus become a reality, and the West Indies will yield additional profits to the merchants of England and Holland. Various unknown regions will also be exploited. Discipline among the sailors employed will be improved, because the tension of rivalry and warfare between the English and the Dutch will have been obviated. The point is emphasized especially that the Spaniards have not kept the terms of the Twelve Years' Truce, which was to have left the Hollanders in possession of that share in the East Indian trade that they had acquired before April, 1609.[25]

So much did the English commissioners seem interested in this plan of united capitalization that they requested to inspect the books of the Dutch East India Company. Their request was granted, for it was felt by the directors that the avoidance of warfare was to be recommended. The Dutch had enough fighting to do against the Spanish empire. However, nothing came of this attempt to unite the two companies until the year 1619, when the governments of England and the United Netherlands agreed to amalgamate the two companies, though without the joint capitalization.

Near the end of the negotiations, in 1615, the English presented the following five propositions:

I. The only true bond of friendship and unity ought to consist in a mutually friendly treatment and reception in all places (hence also in the Moluccas).

II. Through mutual protection and assistance against everyone who should attack the allied parties or their respective friends.

III. "In making way for trade with the Chinese or any other Indian people that shall refuse to trade with either of us."

IV. In fortifying for the assurance (protection) of the common trade in such places as the two companies shall find convenient and where the king of Spain is not in actual possession.

V. In maintaining the colonies in the Moluccas, but a tax is to be levied upon the commodities produced there that will be the same for all persons who will buy spices in those regions.[26]

These articles were rejected by the Dutch, who reasoned that their acceptance would not only have implied the reversal of their whole system of trade and navigation, but that it would also have resulted in peace with Spain and the exclusion by Spain of the Dutch merchants in the

Malay Archipelago, and, consequently, the downfall of Dutch sea power in the East Indies.

There was nothing left for the English commissioners to do but to return to England, without having accomplished anything worth while. However, they had learned much about the organization of the Dutch company. Their rivals had also gathered considerable information. James I and Oldenbarnevelt continued to hope for better days. For had not Oldenbarnevelt, in his capacity as the leading Dutch statesman, brought the directors of those companies to The Hague in 1602, who amalgamated all their respective companies under his leadership? He might take such a step again.

In the meantime Hugo Grotius became increasingly involved in local politics and religious dissensions. During the months of March and April, 1615, his name ceases to stand out in the English dispatches. Oldenbarnevelt had taken his place. But he had instructed both the great statesman and the directors of the East India Company. His learning had been of considerable use to them when they had to meet the English with evidence drawn from the law of nations and from both classical and Christian writers of note. The closing days of the second Anglo-Dutch conference, which was held at The Hague from January to May, 1613, witnessed his withdrawal from the arena of East Indian affairs. By supporting the religious party that was defeated by Prince Maurice, the *stadhouder* of the Dutch Republic, he went down to defeat. His friend, Oldenbarnevelt, was executed in 1619, while Grotius was condemned to perpetual imprisonment. But Dutch sea power in the Far East continued to expand by leaps and bounds.

CHAPTER V

THE OCCUPATION OF THE MALAY ARCHIPELAGO

THE struggle which the Dutch, from 1610 to 1623, carried on in the Far East against the English, the Spaniards, and the Portuguese, resulted in the loss of the Spanish and Portuguese colonies in the East Indies and the failure on the part of the English to maintain their trade in that same region. At the end of this period, in 1623, the English also deserted their factory in Japan, owing to the fact that they were unable to derive a profit from the Japanese trade. The year 1623 marked the end of the first stage in the Anglo-Dutch rivalry for sea power and commerce in the Far East.

The Dutch, as we saw, were not particularly interested in discussions and negotiations with their competitors, but they relied entirely on action, that is, on fortifications, strong garrisons, and a large number of ships. Whereas the English East India Company, between 1600 and 1609, dispatched only twelve ships to the Malay Archipelago, the Dutch company sent fifty-five vessels. As one distinguished Dutch historian has recently stated, it was the tremendously powerful fleet of the Dutch in the Far East that had prepared the way for the English commerce in that region. The Dutch had enabled the English to carry on a peaceful trade in the Malay Archipelago, for the Dutch fortifications protected the trade there for both the English and the Dutch merchants. This Dutch authority continues that it was only natural for the Dutch to refuse to let the English share in the profits of the trade that they themselves had established at great expense. Notwithstanding the continued profession of friendship expressed in numerous letters and other documents, the Dutch merchants in the Malay Archipelago did not hesitate to seize islands and ports regardless of the question whether the English were present and objected to their action, or whether they had not yet arrived and expressed no interest in such places.[1]

Anglo-Dutch rivalry in the Malay Archipelago became more intense when, in 1612, the English company was reorganized, and now could compete more effectively with the Dutch rivals.[2] Although the leading merchants and statesmen in the Dutch Republic realized perfectly that a maintenance of the monopoly of the spice trade in the East Indies would result in hostilities between the English and the Dutch merchants in that region, the directors of the Dutch East India Company frequently issued orders to their employees in the East Indies to be as friendly and polite as possible to the English, while at the same time seizing as much property as they could get. The reason why these directors were compelled to follow such a confusing course of action was that they had received their charter from the States-General and they could not carry on their operations without the permission of the national government. This government was controlled by far-sighted statesmen, who wanted to maintain friendly relations with their allies, the English and the French. For example, the French document which was mentioned at the end of the preceding chapter, and in which it was proposed that the two great companies of England and Holland should amalgamate their capitalization, stated repeatedly that it was of the utmost importance to combine against the Spaniards in the Far East.

The English, on the other hand, were not too anxious to antagonize the Spaniards or the Portuguese, nor to take great risks in attacking them. It is well known that King James I, between 1613 and 1621, was trying to arrange a marriage alliance for his son with the Spanish king. His daughter, Elizabeth, had married Frederick, count of the Palatinate in Germany. When, in 1618, the Thirty-Years' War broke out in Germany, and when, a few years later, Frederick was in serious danger of losing his county in Germany, King James I was of the opinion that by courting the friendship of the Spanish government, he would be able to persuade this government to refrain from occupying the Palatinate with armed forces. The king, who was not a great diplomat, was continually duped by the Spanish diplomats.[3] But while he was hoping to establish a firm alliance with the Spaniards, he could not very well join the Dutch in open warfare against the Spaniards. Nevertheless, he continued to consider himself the ally of the Dutch. He often reminded the Dutch, owing to the assistance which his predecessor, Queen Elizabeth, had rendered them in the period from 1585 to 1603, and owing largely to his friendship in 1609, when the Twelve Years' Truce was made possible, that they should show their gratitude to him. They should be willing to do for his subjects in the East Indies what he had done for their subjects in the Dutch Republic.

After the English commissioners, in 1615, had been unable to secure any advantageous terms from the Dutch, and had returned to England in a rather gloomy mood, the English took desperate action in order to gain for themselves certain valuable regions at the expense of the Dutch. In 1616, Captain Samuel Castleton arrived with four vessels in the Moluccas. First he tried to seize one of the islands in the Banda group, but he was compelled by the Dutch to remove his vessels from its vicinity. Then he visited several other islands, and in 1617 he took possession of Poelo Run. But once more he was faced with stern Dutch resistance, with the result that on February 12 the Dutch seized his vessel, the *Swan,* while a few weeks later they captured another of his vessels, the *Defense.* The

Dutch governor-general, Reael, was a rather kindhearted person, and decided not to molest the English on the island of Poelo Run. He gave orders to his subordinates to treat both natives and Englishmen with forbearance, and to maintain friendly relations with native rebels and foreign competitors alike. Reael was a scholar, and he did not relish the thought of bloodshed and warfare. The directors of the Dutch East India Company, on the other hand, were of an entirely different mind. After they had spent millions of florins in order to build up their commercial contacts in the Malay Archipelago, they could not appreciate words of justice and kindness. On April 30, 1615, they sent instructions to Governor-General Gerard Reynst and Director Jan Pietersz. Coen, stating that "something on a large scale must be done against the enemies, the inhabitants of Banda must be subjugated, their leaders must be killed or driven out of the land, and if necessary the country must be turned into a desert, by uprooting the trees and shrubs."[4]

When, in October, 1617, Reael appeared at Bantam on the island of Java, he found the relations between the English and the Dutch on the one hand and between the Dutch and the natives on the other hand of such an unsatisfactory and perilous nature that he feared for the worst. While, in the two mother countries of England and the Dutch Republic, negotiations had been carried on for some time with the object in view of finding a satisfactory solution to the difficulties presented in the East Indies, the employees of the two great companies operating in those regions became increasingly hostile to each other. Very serious also was the situation in the town of Jacatra, which was located a short distance from Bantam. Here numerous fights broke out in the streets, and when a number of Spanish and Portuguese prisoners had escaped from the Dutch officials, they found a refuge in the ships of the

English. One of the Dutch officials now requested of the English that they return the prisoners, but they answered with words of scorn, flatly refusing his request. Then for a few weeks all was quiet again. However, the situation was not to remain that way, for soon one of the former Spanish prisoners appeared on the streets of Bantam, was captured by the Dutch officials and shut up in a warehouse. As soon as this became known, the English arrived with arms, and with the assistance of some of the natives, they robbed one of the warehouses of the Dutch, killing some of the Dutch and Javanese soldiers, and wounding some others. The English gained the upper hand but also lost some men in the fight. The most serious aspect of this quarrel had been the attack by the English on the Dutch factory. As soon as the governor-general and his council heard of this, they immediately gave orders to have a large fleet assembled before the port of Bantam, in order to make the English and the natives come to terms with them. The colonial government of the Dutch issued a proclamation stating that hereafter the English were to be excluded from the trade with Banda, Amboina, and the Moluccas. If the English should refuse to abide by the terms of this edict, they would be faced with stern measures on the part of the Dutch.[5] The person who had prevailed upon the governor-general and his council to take more severe measures against the English was the new director-general, Jan Pietersz. Coen, who was to become governor-general himself, and in due course of time make possible for the Dutch the conquest of the whole of the Malay Archipelago.[6] He was, in many respects, the greatest administrator the Dutch have ever had in this rich and valuable region. Coen sent a message to the directors of the Dutch East India Company in Amsterdam, in which he wrote as follows: "It is impossible for us to remain at friendly terms with the English. We had better declare war, because it is scandalous the way in which we murder each other at the present time, without the intervention on the part of either government. For some time now the English have sworn that they will have me hanged or stabbed, and now four of our men, who have served the company for a period of from ten to fifteen years, have been killed, while three Javanese soldiers, who saved the lives of the other Hollanders, also lost their lives." [7]

After having encountered many threats from the English and the natives, Coen now decided to fortify the town of Jacatra, and to maintain there a regular garrison of soldiers. Gradually he came to the conclusion that this town should be made the headquarters of all the Dutch settlements in the Malay Archipelago. It was not without reason that he had become afraid of English competition, for, in 1617, the capital of the English East India Company had been considerably enlarged, and the English were more determined than ever to secure for themselves a proper share of the trade with the East Indies. By November, 1618, a considerable number of English vessels lay before the port of Bantam. They were reinforced on December 8, 1618, by five newly arrived ships under the command of Thomas Dale and William Parker. Now the English possessed fifteen vessels in the waters before Bantam. Encouraged by this reinforcement, they became bolder than ever. They threatened the Dutch and said that they would drive them out of Amboina, Banda, and the Moluccas. They would seize for themselves the whole of the East Indies, and they would secure the body of Coen, whether dead or alive. The Hollanders afterward asserted that Thomas Dale had received a commission from King James I, in which he was instructed to attack the Dutch and to drive them out of the East Indies. But the Hollanders were entirely mistaken. James I still was of the opinion that peace should be maintained between his companies and those of the Dutch government. But he had worded his instructions to Thomas Dale in such fashion that it was difficult for Dale to discover actually what his duties were.[8]

The English, anxious for immediate action, on December 14, 1618, seized one of the Dutch vessels, the *Zwarte Leeuw,* which contained a rich cargo. Another vessel, the *Oude Zon,* had just arrived from Japan with a cargo worth half a million florins,[9] and barely evaded capture, while still another vessel also had difficulty in escaping the English.

It was in the middle of the night that Coen heard of this action. Immediately he sent a messenger to Jacatra, instructing him to find out from the English commander in that town what were the reasons for this attack on the Dutch vessels. The answer Coen received was oral and offensive. The messenger had been rudely treated by Thomas Dale, who said that he had purposely seized the ship and that he had placed his ships in the Sunda Strait, in order to seize all Dutch vessels. Before long he would appear before the town of Jacatra, where he would defeat the Dutch and seize General Coen, dead or alive. Never before had Coen been so rudely treated, but also never before had he shown himself so resourceful as now. He had expected that the great battle between the English and the Dutch would break out in the Moluccas, and he had not looked for this sudden attack on his forces upon the coast of Java. He had concentrated his naval strength in the Moluccas, where thus far the Dutch East India Company had had its headquarters and its most powerful fortifications, as well as its strongest garrisons. Here had been the center of the spice trade with the Far East. Here were the celebrated Spice Islands.

Only a short time before he had dispatched a number of vessels with proper ammunition to the Spice Islands.

He had only seven ships left under his own command. Two of these were filled with precious cargoes, and the other five were far from fully armed. To make matters worse, when the natives discovered the superior strength of the English, they determined to assist the latter, for they reasoned that it would be useless to side with the Dutch and submit to punishments to be meted out by the enraged Englishmen. On December 22, 1618, Coen saw that the town was surrounded by English and Javanese enemies. And on the morning of the next day he observed that the natives who had been in his service had all disappeared in the night. During the course of the day he was informed by spies that the enemies were preparing a secret attack upon the Hollanders with a force of seven thousand men.[10]

The Dutch were the first to open fire, for they decided that quick action alone would save them. They were successful in capturing some of the positions held by the English, but, owing to the lack of ammunition, they were forced to change their tactics. Furthermore, on December 29, Coen received news that the English fleet which had lain before Bantam, had departed and gone to Jacatra, in order to enlarge the English forces that were attacking the Dutch, to destroy the fort, and then to sail to the Moluccas, where they would overwhelm the Hollanders. The time had come, they believed, to drive the Dutch out of the whole Malay Archipelago.

Early in the morning of December 30, 1618, Coen called the members of his council together, and said to them that he could hardly believe that the English would be so bold as to attack the Dutch and to try to seize the strongly fortified town of Jacatra. It would not do to leave the town without some show of defense, although he realized that it would be impossible to hold it very long. Presently eleven English ships arrived before the port of

Jacatra. It was decided to attack these eleven ships with the seven Dutch ships. The defense of the fort at Jacatra was entrusted to Pieter van den Broek, while Coen took charge of the naval attack on the English. On January 1, 1619, a fierce battle was fought, but no decisive results were obtained by either side. The next morning the English received further reinforcements, and now they had at their disposal the total of fourteen vessels. The Dutch, who did not have much powder left, now determined to sail with their ships to the Moluccas, and there to obtain more vessels and more ammunition. Consequently, Coen and his sailors went at once to the island of Amboina, while he also notified the commander of the fort at Jacatra of what had taken place. Very important is the message he now sent to the directors of the Dutch East India Company. He wrote: "Now you will see how you have neglected your commerce with the East Indies. We have told you many times before that it was necessary for you to send us more ships, more men, and more ammunition. We have asked for twenty-five large vessels and ten boats each year. This would have been to the greatest possible advantage. Even if you had sent one hundred ships a year, we would have been able to use them to your great profit. So do not deceive yourselves any longer. Now the whole company is subjected to a thousand perils, and the profits will be reduced each year by two or three million florins, that is, you will receive that much less than you would have received if you had listened to our advice. You claim that it is impossible to maintain factories on an island like Java, which has so many inhabitants, as you say. We reply that according to the Portuguese and the Spaniards, a few Christians can do a great deal against hundreds of thousands of natives. Are we weaker than they? I admit that the beginning of the war will not result in immediate profits for the company, and that with small forces we cannot occupy the most important regions. But without war you can nowhere in this world arrive at secure peace. Nature teaches that war creates peace, and that where one does not sow, there one cannot reap. If your administration should become so great and noble that it will secure for the company all that it needs, who shall refuse to honor the United Netherlands and seek protection under its wings? Who shall dare to rise against us? I swear by the Almighty God that the United Company has no enemies that can do it more harm than ignorance and lack of preparation."[11]

During the absence of Coen and his fleet, the commander of the port at Jacatra faced the combined attacks of the English and the natives. It used to be believed by many Dutch historians that only supreme heroism on the part of the Dutch forces saved the town. But latest research has shown that it was not the courage of the Dutch but a number of fortuitous circumstances which prevented the English from seizing the town. A short time after the arrival of the English, under Sir Thomas Dale, and his ships before Bantam, Dale signed a secret offensive alliance with the king of Bantam against the Dutch. The English were to receive permission to build a factory on a piece of property which would be held strictly in their own possession. They were to be permitted to buy without duty all the products raised in the vicinity, except pepper, on which they were to pay a 5 per cent duty, and other spices, on which the duty was to be 3 per cent. The king of Bantam was not to sign any treaty of peace, of war, or of commerce with the Hollanders, nor was he to permit the Hollanders to live in any port of his dominions, or to erect fortifications, except with the permission of the English. The king was to unite his armed forces with those of the English, in order to take the Dutch fortification at Jacatra.[12]

After the signing of this contract, several thousand armed inhabitants of Bantam went over to Jacatra, while the English admiral removed from Bantam to Jacatra with his fleet. We have already seen that Coen, just before his departure for Amboina, had offered battle with the English, but seeing the superior strength of the English fleet, had withdrawn his forces to the Moluccas.

On January 31, 1619, the threat of the English and of the native forces who supported them was such that the Dutch commander had to surrender the town and the fortification to them. It was agreed that the fortification with its garrison and the Christian population, together with the ammunition on hand would go to the English Admiral Dale, while the money, the merchandise, and the jewels would be surrendered to the regent at Jacatra. The prisoners on both sides were to be set free, and the fort was to be evacuated one day after the signature of the capitulation. The garrison and the Christians, together with the Javanese soldiers, were to be dispatched on a vessel, to be provided for by the English, and they were to be transported to Coromandel on the mainland of India. But before this agreement could be carried out, the English began to quarrel with the natives, and as a result the town and fort of Jacatra were saved for the Dutch.

During the night of February 2, 1619, a sad drama was enacted in the native quarter of Jacatra. The unhappy regent, who for such a long time had been the willing tool of the Dutch and who had, on several occasions, deceived the English, now received his punishment. At the order of the king of Bantam the regent of Jacatra was ejected from his house and property, was driven to the mountains, and the town of Jacatra was made a part of Bantam. In the meantime, the English admiral, when he realized that there was no more profit to be derived for his company at Jacatra, removed with his fleet to Bantam, where he did not consider his money and his merchandise as being safe any more. The king of Bantam now informed the Dutch in the fortification at Jacatra that he would no longer support the English, but that, on the other hand, he also insisted on the dismantling of the fortification at Jacatra. After the fort had been abandoned and destroyed, the Dutch would be permitted to remain in the town of Jacatra, at least until the return of the Dutch fleet. The soldiers of Bantam would protect the Hollanders. But at the same time the news was spread that the English once more tried to seek friendly relations with the king of Bantam, in order to attack with their united forces the Dutch fort at Jacatra. The chief council in command of the Dutch fortification now came to the conclusion that nowhere could they find safety and protection. They saw that it was useless to look for protection of life and property from enemies or hypocritical friends. On February 27, 1619, the council determined to continue the defense of this fortification. New walls were erected, holes in the old walls were repaired, and everything in the power of the garrison was done to maintain it until the return of Coen.

Now that the enemies had vanished, the Dutch decided to hold some kind of a ceremony, to celebrate their delivery. On March 12, one of the Dutch captains called the population together. While flags were raised, and the bells were rung, and while the wine flowed freely, the fortress of Jacatra was renamed "Batavia." The four bulwarks received respectively the names of four Dutch provinces in the mother country. Conditions remained about the same during the next two months. But in the meantime about one hundred Hollanders were kept prisoners in Bantam, among them the former commander of the Dutch fort, Pieter van den Broeck. What would be the fate of these men? Suddenly on May 10, 1619, a small vessel appeared before the town of Jacatra, in order to notify the garrison that Coen was about to arrive with his whole fleet. A few days later he came with sixteen ships. Now the fort was truly relieved, but now also followed the hour of vengeance. Both the enemies of the Dutch and the unfaithful servants of the Dutch East India Company were severely punished. On May 30, 1619, Coen placed himself at the head of 1,000 armed men, who, accompanied by the sound of trumpets and by flying banners, leaped over the bulwarks, stormed the native quarters of the city and the Javanese garrison which numbered three thousand men, and drove them ahead of them as fast as they could run. The whole city was burned to the ground, and when evening fell there was nothing left of it.

Triumphantly Coen wrote the following words to the directors in the Netherlands: "In this manner we have driven the men of Bantam out of Jacatra, and have obtained possession of the land of Java. The honor and the reputation of the Dutch nation will through this deed be greatly enhanced, and now everyone will seek to be our friend. The foundation of the long wished-for dominion of the Malay Archipelago has now been laid, and a large part of the fertile country and the rich sea of India is yours. Now see and consider what good courage may accomplish!"

Immediately after the destruction of Jacatra, Coen sent a message to the king of Bantam, informing him of the destruction of this town, and adding that before long he would appear with his fleet before the city of Bantam. The news electrified both king and subjects. Their fears were increased when the native soldiers of Jacatra came running from that town and sought refuge in Bantam. Now everyone believed that Bantam would receive the same fate that had befallen Jacatra. Some of the soldiers were instructed to fortify the place, and arm themselves properly. On June 7, Coen appeared before Bantam as he had previously foretold. But it was not his intention either to take or destroy the city. Two days later he requested the rulers of Bantam that the Dutch prisoners should be set free within twenty-four hours, lest he should have to take such measures as he would deem fitting. Before the twenty-four hours were passed, the Dutch captives were delivered on board of the Dutch vessels.[13]

Owing to the hostile attitude adopted by the ruler of Bantam, Coen finally decided to remove the center of the spice trade from Bantam to the former site of Jacatra. Here he constructed a new town, which ever since that time has been called Batavia. Today it is still the capital of the Dutch East Indies.[14]

Now the question arose, What had happened to the English fleet that had tried to seize the Dutch fort at Jacatra? Among the first of the Hollanders to discover the whereabouts of this fleet was the captain of the Dutch ship, called the *Oranjeboom*. He had just arrived from the Netherlands with a number of vessels, and about four hundred miles from the coast of Sumatra, he encountered one of the English ships which had fled before Coen's fleet. The commander of the Dutch vessel was not aware of the war that had broken out between the English and the Dutch in the Malay Archipelago. So he went, accompanied by some of his men, on board the English ship and sat down in the cabin of the English captain. While he was being entertained in the cabin, the Hollanders were attacked by the English sailors. When the Dutch captain heard the noise above his head, he suddenly freed himself from the hands of the English, who also were going to seize him, and ran up the stairs, shouting, as he ran, to the Hollanders on the Dutch vessel: "You must get ready your guns and fire on the Englishmen!" Now the English captain, reluctant to start a fight, quickly let the Dutch captain go to his vessel.

In the meantime the Dutch fleet which had been stationed before the port of Bantam began to separate into smaller units. Three of the vessels were sent to the Gulf of Siam, and six others were dispatched to the pepper ports of Sumatra. The Dutch governor-general instructed them, in case they should meet English ships on the way, that they must not hesitate to seek revenge. The three ships which had been sent to the Gulf of Siam, found there two English vessels stationed before the port of Patani. They immediately started a fight with them, in which thirty-nine Englishmen and ten Hollanders lost their lives. Both English vessels were taken by the Hollanders. Among the English who fell was one of the greatest enemies of the Dutch in the East Indies, the captain and chief merchant of the English in the Far East, the courageous commander John Jordain.

The other fleet, which as we saw was made up of six ships and which had been dispatched to the west coast of Sumatra on October 11, 1619, encountered four English vessels. After a fierce struggle, the English once more yielded before the superior power of the Dutch. One of the English ships was set on fire, and before the evening fell, the others had been seized by the Dutch. Among the English who fell in this fight was also the captain. In this manner the Dutch, under the command of Coen, found their revenge upon the English. But still Coen was not satisfied. He wanted to start out on a new crusade, and drive the English from the coast of Sumatra and Coromandel. His letters continued to enumerate complaints against the English, against the French, against the Danes, and against all other competitors from Europe. But on March 27, 1620, there arrived in the East Indies the unexpected and unwished for news that the Dutch East India Company had signed a treaty with the English East India Company, stating that henceforth the two companies would be united, and that all fighting between the English and the Dutch must cease at once.

The treaty had been signed on July 17, 1619. It was the fruit of the third Anglo-Dutch conference, which had been held in the city of London. At last the English and the Dutch merchants had been able to come to some definite agreement. It is doubtful, however, that they themselves would ever have reached such an understanding if it had not been for the terrific pressure that had been put upon them by James I of England and Oldenbarnevelt of the Dutch Republic.[15] In the closing months of the year 1618, the two great companies finally agreed to send their commissioners to the conference. This time the Dutch commissioners were much more numerous than at the two earlier conferences, which were held respectively in 1613 and 1615. The Dutch commissioners were: Dirk Bas, mayor of Amsterdam; Jacob Boreel, former mayor of Middelburg; Arent Jacobss. Lodesteyn, counciler of the admiralty in Zeeland; Albert Franssen Sounck, former mayor of Hoorn and deputy in the Council of State of the Dutch Republic; Andries Ryckaerts, director in the Dutch East India Company; and Willem Boreel, attorney of the same company. These men were the representatives of both the States-General of the Dutch Republic and of the Dutch East India Company.

The Dutch commissioners had audience with King James I on December 20, 1618. They presented him with a document addressed to him by the States-General, dated November 27, which stated who the commissioners were and what their business was. After James had read this message, Willem Boreel delivered another in which he observed that according to Roman Law, which recognizes the law of nations, the person who repairs at his expense a house that is in a bad condition, takes over all obligations connected with the ownership of that piece of property.

The Dutch have acquired an extensive piece of property, inhabited by thousands of persons. They have spent immense sums of money on it, and for that reason they have refused thus far to let others have a share in it until they shall receive proper compensation.[16]

The king replied that the Dutch had brought up the most important factors in the issue that confronted the two companies. He was of the opinion that his subjects were in the right. As for the complaints made by the Dutch about their maltreatment by the English in the East Indies, they should have come to him; and he would have considered them. He would not have let his subjects fight in plain view of the Spaniards. He had reason to complain about that, and also about the offense the Dutch had given him personally and to his nation.

The king's attitude was very different from that displayed by him in 1613, when he had shown the Dutch commissioners a friendly disposition from beginning to end. But now the English were losing ground in the East Indies, and James was engaged in important negotiations with the king of Spain. The Spaniards had added their grievance against the Dutch to those of the East India Company. No wonder that the king acted so unpleasantly!

On January 24, the Dutch commissioners were asked by Clement Edmonds and Robert Bell to go to a building called Merchant Tailors' Hall, where they learned that the English commissioners were quite numerous. Six of them represented the English government: Sir John Digby, vice-chancellor; Sir Thomas Edmonds, treasurer; Sir Fulco Greville, chancellor of the exchequer; Sir Julius Caesar, master of the rolls; and Sir Edward Coke, chief justiciar. The English East India Company was represented by twelve men, including Sir Thomas Smith, the governor.

The English insisted on beginning with an examination of the complaints made by both nations against each other, especially the manner in which James I had been offended by slanderous tongues in the East Indies. On January 25, the Dutch presented their grievances in a lengthy document, drawn up in French. The English replied with a similar document, also in French, in which they demanded reparation to the amount of 200,000 pounds.

Then followed a discussion of all the complaints. This seems to have given both parties considerable satisfaction, and now they were in the mood to forget the past and draft a treaty. On February 9 they agreed upon the first article, which stated that hereafter the two nations would forgive the misdemeanors perpetrated thus far by their respective subjects. All prisoners were to be set free, and captured merchandise restored to its owners. But the reparations for ships that had been sunk would be considered later.

Next followed statements showing the capitalization of the two companies. The Dutch said their capital in the East Indies amounted to 12,503,496 florins, together with 4,000,000 florins cash in the Netherlands, and 3,000,000 florins in reserves. They gave no figures for the value of their new fleet of five ships; nor the fortifications in the East Indies, nor the ammunition and expenditures incurred in the past. The English claimed to have invested a total of 2,044,200 pounds sterling; in addition to the value of warehouses, provisions, etc. When the Dutch observed that the English claimed to have a larger capitalization than that of the Dutch, they asserted that the English had misrepresented the facts.

After lengthy negotiations on this point the Dutch declared that their company was worth three times as much as the other. This caused much surprise among the English, who said they did not see how each Hollander could be worth three times as much as each Englishman. It proved very difficult to come to an agreement on this point, and so the Dutch finally insisted on maintaining their separate capitalization. They also refused to let the English have one-half of the trade in the Malay Archipelago. Now the Dutch proposed an arrangement, made up of twenty-two articles, to which the English replied with one of twenty-five articles.

The Dutch commissioners proposed that trade should be free everywhere, except in the Moluccas, Amboina, and Banda, where the English were to receive a reasonable share. The English commissioners accepted the principle of separate capitalization, but insisted on one-half of the trade in the Spice Islands. It is not surprising that many weeks passed before the two commissions could arrive at a common ground. The Dutch could not forget all their past labors and expenditures, while the English, being a much larger nation, did not see why the Dutch should have more than half of the spice trade. At the end of April, the conference seemed to be getting nowhere,[17] but the national governments would not permit their merchants to wreck the negotiations, and at last, on July 17, a treaty was signed, comprising thirty articles.[18]

The first article had been agreed upon on February 9, and has been mentioned above. The second stated that the employees of both companies should live together as friends, neighbors, and allies. The third read: "Trade and traffic shall be free in the East Indies for both companies, so that each can use whatever capital it deems suitable." In Articles IV-VII it was stipulated that duties on East Indian products be reduced, and that prices be regulated. The eighth article stated that in the Spice Islands the English were to have one-third of the trade. Articles X-XVI provided for a Council of Defense in the East Indies. The presiding officer would alternately be English or Dutch. The council would have at its disposal twenty armed vessels. Articles XXIII–XXV discussed vaguely the manner of maintaining garrisons. The treaty was to be in force for twenty years.

The Dutch merchants were greatly displeased with these terms. The diplomats who had "perfected" them had not been aware of actual condition. Coen, on May 11, 1620 wrote in disgust to his directors: "The English are much obliged to you, for they had driven themselves out of the East Indies, and you have put them back." Nevertheless, Coen submitted himself to the terms of the treaty, although in his present capacity of governor-general he did have something to say about East Indian affairs.

The treaty of 1619 proved impossible to enforce. Coen wrote on July 31, 1620: "If the English were masters, the Hollanders would soon be driven out of the Indies. They are an unbearable nation. You are advised not to surrender to them a share of your rights, lands, forts, or places, especially where they intend to build their own forts. The Chinese are warning us against the inevitable conspiracies of the future." Coen was not too pessimistic, for in 1623 occurred the notorious Amboina massacre, when the infuriated Dutch officials had twelve Englishmen executed for alleged treason.

Under the leadership of Coen the Dutch succeeded in depriving the English of all but a small share in the trade in the Malay Archipelago.[19] The English were forced to abandon this area and sought better success on the mainland of India. Although afterward they could easily have resumed their former privileges in the East Indian waters, they were content with their own. For a brief period (1811–1815) they occupied and held the East Indies in their possession, when the Dutch, dominated by the French, were the enemies of Great Britain. But the British statesmen generously restored the whole of "Insulinde" to the Dutch at the Congress of Vienna (1815).

CHAPTER VI

THE CONQUEST OF FORMOSA AND
THE EUROPEAN TRADE
WITH JAPAN

LONG before the opening of the sixteenth century, the most enterprising commercial powers of Europe had cast covetous eyes upon the mysterious countries of China and Japan, for they were thought to be exceedingly wealthy. But, unfortunately for the Europeans, the rulers of China frowned upon their attempts to establish commercial contacts with the "Celestial Empire." Even the daring Portuguese had to content themselves with the use of but one port—Macao. The Dutch achieved still less, being told repeatedly that they must stay away from the Chinese mainland. Consequently, as we shall see, they endeavored to occupy a number of small islands near the coast, and when this enterprise was also prohibited by the Chinese, they seized the larger island of Formosa.

The situation in Japan, on the other hand, seemed very different from that in China, for the Portuguese not only founded thriving factories in several important Japanese cities but they also converted some 200,000 Japanese to the Christian faith. Furthermore, during the opening decades of the seventeenth century, both the English and the Dutch established factories of their own. But after 1640 the Japanese rulers reversed the policy adopted previously, so that afterward their country became more secluded than China. As a result, these two great oriental powers, to a considerable extent, remained out of touch with western civilization until the intrepid British and Americans forced them to "open their doors" about the middle of the nineteenth century.

The island of Formosa early attracted the attention of the Dutch traders in the Far East. Its position was extremely favorable, since it was easily accessible from China to the west, from the Philippines to the south, and from Japan to the north. Some parts of the island are rather mountainous, and in some sections there may be found lovely plains and excellent fields for pasture. The climate is suitable for the growing of semi-tropical vegetables and fruits, and when the Dutch appeared there for the first time, they found large quantities of sugar available for export trade, as well as excellent deer skins.[1]

In 1603, the Dutch East India Company resolved to send to the Far East a fleet of twelve ships, under Admiral Steven van der Hagen and an ambassador named John van Aertsen, who was to visit the emperor of China. His mission was to present gifts and letters from the States-General and the Prince of Orange, requesting the right of free trade in China, or if this were not permitted, at least that the Dutch might enjoy the use of some places along the sea coast, where they could secure sugar, silk, and other merchandise. He was to tell the native rulers of the excellent goods which were manufactured in Holland, such as blankets, sails, ropes, and all manner of textile goods for clothing. But if the Dutch merchants at Patani did not think it advisable for the men to proceed to the court of the Chinese emperor, the idea was to be given up.[2]

It so happened that the Chinese authorities were not permitted to let foreigners enter their country, and for that reason the Dutch, in order to save time and expense, decided to establish themselves first of all near the mainland on the little island of Pehoe in the group called Pescadores, or Fisherman's Islands. The first of the Hollanders to reach this island was Van Warwyck, who has been mentioned above. He departed from Patani on June 27, 1604, planning to sail directly to China, but being driven off his course by a storm, he arrived at Pehoe on August 7. On the western shore of this island he found an excellent bay, where, on August 29, another Dutch vessel joined his own. He waited in vain for permission to land on the Chinese coast, and he finally left the island on December 15 without having done any trading, because of the arrival upon the scene of some fifty junks owned by the Chinese.

In 1605, when Cornelis Matelief de Jonge sailed to the East Indies with a fleet of eleven ships, he took with him a letter for the Emperor of China which had been written by the Prince of Orange, and also one for the King of Siam, asking the latter for assistance in securing trade for the Dutch in China. It was also thought possible by the directors of the East India Company to secure trading rights in the islands of Lequeos and Formosa, which were located not far from those districts where the best silk was to be found.

The great desire for Chinese trade was due to the fact that there was a ready market for Chinese goods, and particularly silk, in Holland, where they were sold in large quantities and brought good profits. It may be noted here that the undamaged silk of the captured Portuguese carack, *St. Catherine*, mentioned by Hugo Grotius, produced greater profits than the spices did. The cargo was finally taken to Amsterdam, where it was sold at public auction. Hugo Grotius, good patriot as he was, took great care to defend the actions of his fellow-countrymen. In his brilliant work on the law of prizes he also described the auction itself. He said that an incredible multitude flocked from all the countries of Europe to the sale, which was held in August, 1604. The proceeds of the sale were awarded to the company of merchants in Amsterdam under whose order the fleet had sailed and had captured the *St. Catherine*. The admiral and the crew which had captured the ship also received a share in the booty.[3]

Although the capture of this carack had been made contrary to the orders of the provincial estates of Holland, the provincial government was not slow to praise the brave sailors who had participated in the capture. It was thought by the general public that, just as the Romans after the capture of Macedon had paid the expenses of the government out of the proceeds of their conquests; so the Dutch would henceforth defray the cost of war by what they captured from the enemy. At least, this is what Grotius reported in his commentary in question. Grotius himself praised the exploits of his heroes far beyond their real merit, and he called the captured prize "the finest and the true fruit of the trade with the Indies."[4] Financial gain was as popular then as it is now.

In 1609, the first Governor-General Both received instructions from the board of directors in Amsterdam to promote trade in fine white silk and other rareties which might be secured directly in China. But several years passed before anything fruitful was accomplished. As late as 1617, other instructions followed for opening up trade with China, but again little could be achieved. Shortly after the English and the Dutch had made peace with each other in the East Indies, and had agreed to join their two respective trading companies, they set up a Council of Defense, which, in 1620, decided to send a fleet of ten ships, five English and five Dutch, to sail north. Two of the ships should cruise between the Pescadores and Formosa, and two others should investigate what was going on at Macao to discover if any advantage could be derived there for the combined forces of the English and the Hollanders. The latter two ships should meet the first two between China and the Pescadores, and then sail in the vicinity until the first of August. But neither in that year nor in the next was anything concrete done for the promotion of trade with China itself.

Finally, in 1622, the great Governor-General Coen collected a fleet of fifteen Dutch and two English ships to drive the Portuguese from Macao. The fleet reached this city on June 22, 1622. The Dutch made a hasty landing, but some barrels of gunpowder blew up and caused considerable confusion among the Dutch as well as a lack of powder for offensive measures. Consequently, the siege was given up, and after this the Portuguese fortified the port. Having failed at Macao, the Hollanders continued on their way, and finally stopped at the Pescadores, which were considered of great value in that they lay on the route between China and Manila, the capital of the Philippines. The fleet was commanded by the capable Cornelis Reyerszoon, who ordered his soldiers to attack and seize the most valuable islands in the group, even though the English failed to make their appearance and assist the Hollanders. It was reasoned by the Dutch that the Pescadores would make a better trading post than Macao itself. From here they could seize the Chinese trade, or else attract it to the Pescadores. The Hollanders received instructions from their directors that in case the Chinese would give them no coöperation, they were to attack them and seize their junks; so that the emperor would hear about it and send messengers to find out the purpose of the Dutch. Through these messengers it would be made known to him that in case the Dutch prevented the Chinese from trading, there would be no lack of persons to trade with the Dutch, whether with or without the permission of the mandarin, since, especially in the province of Chincieu, the people could not do without trade, as their living depended entirely upon it.

In August, 1622, the Dutch began building fortifications on the most important islands in the Pescadores. But the Chinese objected to the presence of the foreigners, saying that these islands were their property. In the com-

paratively short space of two years the Chinese drove the
Dutch from the Pescadores, after which the latter moved
onward and made a settlement in Formosa.

At the same time it appears that the Chinese authorities assisted the Portuguese in fortifying the city of Macao,
which had never been done before. Moreover, the Chinese
resented the fact that the Hollanders had forced fifteen
hundred of their men to assist in putting up Dutch fortifications. The Dutch wanted peace with the Chinese, but
on their own terms. They asked for liberty of commerce
with China, and prohibition of all trade between the Chinese and the Spaniards at Manila. The Chinese authorities replied to the request of the Dutch by saying that the
latter must withdraw from the islands in the group of the
Pescadores, but they would have liberty to fortify themselves in Formosa.[5]

It is not surprising that in the journal kept at the castle
in Batavia we find the following note: "His Excellency
the General related that for more than twenty-two years
the Netherlanders had frequented the coast of China and
had attempted to establish trading contacts there, but that
they had been unable to receive an audience and had been
sent away without having accomplished their purpose."[6]

It was also well known among the English, even in
Japan, that the Hollanders were confronted with great
difficulties, not only in China, but also in the Pescadores.
The commander of the English factory in Japan wrote
thus: "The Hollanders have sent great stores of marines
and provisions to their fortification at the Pescadores,
thinking to get trade with the Chinese, by one means or
another; which I am persuaded will not fall out to their
expectation, except they take the Chinese junks which
trade with Formosa, and which is within sight of the
Pescadores."[7]

Finally, when the Dutch saw that the Chinese were

determined to drive them away, they agreed to move to
Formosa. The Chinese governor, in accordance with his
promise, had three junks fitted out and provided pilots
for the use of the Hollanders. After a long search they
could find no more suitable place than Tayowan, which
was a very small island lying on the southwest coast of
Formosa. Later this name was given to the whole of Formosa, probably because the great castle Zeelandia was
built upon the little island of Tayowan. Near the end of
1624, word was brought to Batavia from Governor Sonck
of Formosa concerning the departure from the Pescadores
and the arrival of the Hollanders in Formosa.[8]

When the Hollanders observed the large amount of
trade which the Japanese had established with Formosa,
and the great demand there was for deer skins which were
purchased in Formosa, they did not leave Pehoe with too
much regret, and quickly adjusted themselves to their new
environment. Each year the Chinese sent them four large
junks loaded with valuable silk and other commodities.[9]
Unfortunately, the harbor of Tayowan could only accom-
modate light ships of from twelve to fourteen feet draft;
gradually the bay filled up so that only ships with six or
eight feet draft could enter. However, Formosa was fertile, and it provided abundant food and an enormous
quantity of deerskins. Tayowan was inferior to Pehoe as a
war station because the occupants would be uncertain of
being able to leave the harbor at short notice, and because
of the greater distance from the Chinese coast. Moreover,
Pehoe controlled the channel on either side of the Pescadores, "and if it had continued in the hands of the Dutch,
the intercourse of the Portuguese at Macao with Japan
would have been carried on with a navigation eastward
of Formosa." But in commercial aspects Tayowan was
more important than Pehoe. After all, the difference in
distance from China to the two respective islands was re-

latively slight. Both were on the direct route from Batavia to Japan. Formosa was fruitful, while the Pescadores were practically nothing more than barren rocks. But as far as Chinese trade was concerned, neither one could compare with the city of Macao, held by the Portuguese.

On the south side of the bay of Tayowan, on a sandbar, a short distance from the mainland, the Dutch built a fort out of planks and sand, which was eleven rods, eight feet long; eight rods and three feet wide, and protected by a stone wall made from materials brought from Pehoe. The barracks were constructed from bamboo and straw. The fort Zeelandia was named after the ship *Zeelandia*, which brought the first Governor, Martin Sonck, to the island. A city of the same name grew up in the vicinity, and an excellent warehouse was built upon the same site. On the mainland, two fortified places were constructed, called respectively Province (Provintia) and Utrecht. During the first three years the main fort was called Orange, but in 1627 the name was changed to Zeelandia.[10] It was felt by the Hollanders that the capitalization of the Dutch East India Company would be strengthened by the settlement of Formosa, and that the Chinese would be attracted by this new settlement and divert trade from other places. In this way their enemies, namely, the Portuguese and the Spaniards, would be deprived of their contacts with China and all their trade would fall into the hands of the Hollanders.

A serious threat, however, was offered by the Spaniards, who were in no mood to see the trade between China and Manila disrupted. Soon rumors reached Japan, as well as Formosa, that the Spaniards in Manila were planning to send an expedition to Formosa. In 1626, they actually took possession of and fortified Kelang on the north coast of Formosa. Moreover, they sent a large fleet to the island, but that was destroyed by storm. A Portuguese attempt to occupy Formosa likewise failed. Nevertheless, it was not until 1642 that the Dutch finally made themselves masters of Kelang and the whole island.[11]

Contrasted with the feeble success attained by the Dutch in the islands near the Chinese coasts, was their extraordinary good fortune in Japan, where for 218 years they were the only Europeans permitted to trade. During that long period they provided the Japanese with various elements of western culture, and when, in 1859, the Japanese finally were forced to trade directly with the great powers of modern Europe, they relied upon their old friends, the Dutch, in building their navy and establishing diplomatic relations with the western nations. Their first warships were presented to them by the Dutch; their first use of modern ammunition was the result of Dutch training; their first acquaintance with the arts and sciences of the occidental world came through their Dutch teachers.

As was the case in the Malay Archipelago, the Portuguese preceded the Hollanders as traders. The first Hollander to visit Japan did so in the service of the Portuguese.[12] This was Dirck Gerritsz. Pomp, who was born in 1544 or in the opening months of 1545, and who, at the age of eleven, was sent to Lisbon. Two of his father's sisters had previously married certain well-established Dutch merchants in that city. About 1560, the relations between Portugal and the East Indies were so highly developed that the great Portuguese port became a notable school of training for young persons who wanted to study commerce and ship building. For five years Dirck attended school in Lisbon, where he learned the Portuguese language and afterwards served as interpreter on several Dutch ships. In 1568, he was a passenger on a Portuguese vessel which took him to Goa on the mainland of India. Here he ably served the Portuguese, but did not rise rapidly. However, by 1583 he was a constable. Some time before that he had made a trip to China and Japan, but the date of this voyage is not known.[13]

A second trip occurred in 1584, when, on board the *Santa Cruz,* he reached China and Japan. The Portuguese trade with these countries was carried on under a monopoly received from the king of Portugal. Each year a fleet left the city of Goa in the month of April, carrying various European products, such as velvet and woolen goods, mirrors, glassware, munitions, wine, and olive oil. The ships would first stop at Cochin, where they obtained pepper and ivory, then they visited Malacca, where spices and sandalwood were added to their cargo. Here they waited for favorable weather, and at the end of the year they would reach Macao. Since 1577, the imperial government of China had permitted the Portuguese to carry on commerce on the peninsula of Macao, where they traded with the city of Canton. At the great fair which was held twice a year for several months, the Portuguese ships destined for India and the Philippines or Japan, could obtain whatever wares their owners desired. One of the chief articles purchased from the Japanese was silk. On July 5, 1585, the *Santa Cruz* finally left Macao, and on July 31 arrived at the port of Nagasaki, in Japan.[14]

The Portuguese, unlike the Dutch, combined commercial gain with missionary efforts, in order to win converts for the Christian faith. By the year 1585, there were about 200,000 Christians in Japan alone. But this did not by any means please the officials in the Japanese government, who presently took steps to check the spread of the Christian religion. Dirck Gerritsz., who remained for eight months in this port of Nagasaki, observed very soon the attitude adopted by the Japanese toward the Christian missionaries. It was not until 1596 that the Christian martyrs were crucified, at which time twenty-six of them lost their lives in this city.[15]

Dirck Gerritsz. arrived with his companions at Goa in the year 1588. Finally, after many vicissitudes, he reached his native town of Enkhuizen in the Netherlands during the month of April, 1590.[16] Here he was welcomed as a remarkable personage, having visited both China and Japan, which was an unusual thing for a Hollander to accomplish at that time. His voyages were mentioned in various contemporary Dutch works. He himself also composed an account of his residence in India and his other voyages, entitled, *Of the Trade in the Indies, and of the Adventures that People Experience in These Countries: Written down as Dictated by Dirck Gerritsz, who has remained there for twenty-four years and has carried on trade over all the Indies.*[17] In this remarkable composition the author says: "In Japan there is a great deal of silver, which the inhabitants exchange for the silks of China. The Portuguese traders take the silver from Japan and change that for the gold of China. They also purchase silk and other luxuries in China. With these products they return to Goa. But in each of these places they have to remain for a period of about six months. As a result each trip takes about three years. Every year a number of vessels make the voyage from Goa to Lisbon.

"In the island of Japan live very pleasant people. But they worship idols, as do those of China. They also have images in their churches. But in the city of Nagasaki and the others in which the king of Portugal has subjects, there are the Jesuits, which they have driven away, some years ago, because they all wanted to be merchants. This island is as large as England. Beyond these islands the Portuguese merchants of India and Goa do not go. The inhabitants of China and Japan are large persons; they are broad, and most of them are white. But there are also some among them who are black; all of them are of the same size and general appearance."

Although this simple account of Dirck Gerritsz. has not had great historical value, nevertheless, owing to the fact that he was the first Hollander to visit China and Japan, he was consulted by numerous persons of importance, and eventually he exerted much influence upon those who finally determined to send Dutch vessels directly to these countries. He spoke so enthusiastically about the riches of China and Japan that, in 1599, the captain of a certain Dutch vessel, as we shall see, was induced to cross the Pacific Ocean and visit Japan.

Very important also is the description of Japan and the Japanese trade in the famous work by Linschoten, entitled *Itinerario*. Although Linschoten himself did not visit Japan, he had been to Goá, and he had learned a great deal about the Portuguese trade with Japan. He wrote thus: "Every year a Portuguese ship goes from Macao to Japan, taking silk along to Japan, and receiving in exchange for it a certain amount of silver. The Portuguese are established in Nagasaki, but they also are to be found in other places. The country extends from thirty degrees to thirty eight degrees latitude, and is situated at the distance of eighty miles from China, and it is three hundred miles from Macao in a northeastward direction. It is a cold country. The people live for the most part on rice; they drink no milk, but they use the flesh of wild animals and fish. They live in very good-looking houses, and they are dressed in silks, although they are more simple than the Chinese. They learn very rapidly, and they are very polite in their behavior . . . They are entirely different from other peoples, in their manners, in the way they prepare their food, and in their appreciation of the beauties of nature. There are rich silver mines. They attach great value to antiques, such as tea pots, small paintings, and arms. Sometimes they will pay for a single piece as much as four, five, and even fourteen thousand ducats." Linschoten

adds that the country is ruled by several absolute monarchs, who have delegated authority to officials of a lower
rank who also rule as absolute masters, while they in turn
have appointed subordinates.[18]

Linschoten indicated with a great degree of accuracy
the courses that had been followed by the Portuguese on
their way to China and Japan. He also showed by what
route the *Santa Cruz,* on which Dirck Gerritsz had sailed,
reached Japan. His map and that of Plancius[19] show all
the regions of Japan that were known to the Europeans at
that time. Tokyo was as yet unknown, but the region to
the south had frequently been visited by various Portuguese merchants and travelers.

There was to be found no better guide than Linschoten. As one Dutch authority has recently pointed out, the
first English navigator who visited Japan, John Saris, and
who arrived in that country in the year 1613, made such
good use of the directions of Linschoten that he declared:
"We found Jan van Linschoten's book very true."[20]

At this time Japan had a population of about fifteen
to twenty million inhabitants. The country was about as
thickly populated as Europe was at that time. Everywhere
the people were fairly prosperous, and they were anxious
to buy products from foreign countries; so that the merchants from these countries could obtain a very good price
for their wares. The only foreign merchants who had thus
far visited Japan regularly were the Portuguese. During
the course of the sixty years in which they had carried on
their trade at Nagasaki and elsewhere, they had made
great profit, but they were not in a position to fill the demand of the whole of Japan for foreign products. The
local ruler, later to become the shogun, at Nagasaki was
called Ijejasoe, or Ieyasu. He was extremely anxious to increase the foreign trade with Japan through the port of
Nagasaki. The large amount of precious metals, especially

silver, that had been heaped up by former rulers would enable the Japanese to purchase from foreign countries whatever their hearts desired. This is the reason why from the very beginning of the appearance of the Dutch and English at Nagasaki, he was so friendly to them, although he knew nothing about their nationality. He was not at all favorably inclined toward the Jesuits and other Christian missionaries, because they did not do enough to contribute to the increase of the foreign trade with Japan.[21]

As a result of the favorable publicity which Japan received from the two well-known Dutch writers, Dirck Gerritsz. Pomp and Linschoten, the national government promptly took steps to establish commercial contacts with this promising country. As early as 1595, the States-General gave instructions to the commander of the fleet which was to reach the Far East by way of the Arctic Ocean, to "proceed to the north of Russia, Moscovy, and Tartary to the kingdom of China and Japan." In the ninth article of these instructions he is ordered to investigate the government and the economic situation in Japan.[22]

In 1598, a company made up of local merchants in the city of Rotterdam[23] equipped a fleet of five vessels and sent it westward across the Atlantic Ocean, in order to sail through the Strait of Magellan, partly in order to attack the Spanish colonies in South America and partly to open up the trade with China and Japan. Of these five vessels only one reached Japan. This was the *Liefde,* which had formerly been called the *Erasmus.* Its captain was Jacob Quaeckernaeck, and its pilot was an Englishman named William Adams. When this ship arrived in Japan, it had on board five hundred guns, five thousand bullets of cast iron, five thousand pounds of powder, and various other forms of ammunition. The date of the arrival was April 19, 1600.[24] It was the first time a Dutch vessel had crossed the Pacific Ocean.

The place where the ship landed was the Bay of Beppoe on the northeast coast of the island of Kioesioe, which was never visited by European ships. It can easily be understood that the appearance of so strange a vessel caused considerable commotion among the natives. On the next day, a number of boats went up to the ship, among them one with two Jesuits on board. The latter were at first of the opinion that it must be a Spanish vessel that had drifted away from its course to Mexico, and they immediately notified the ruler of the island. When it was discovered that it was a Dutch ship, commanded by enemies of the king of Portugal and of Spain, the Jesuits naturally turned back before having visited the vessel. On April 21, a number of soldiers arrived with the aim of preventing the numerous natives from removing those articles that had not yet been taken away on the first day.

About the twenty-fifth of April the Dutch vessel was taken to the harbor of Boengo, or Bungo, where the sailors of the vessel were permitted to go on shore and to occupy a home of their own. A few days later, a Jesuit arrived from the city of Nagasaki with the order to take an inventory of the contents of the Dutch vessel. Presently the Hollanders were questioned as to the purpose of their voyage to Japan. They declared that they had come from the Netherlands and had sailed through the Strait of Magellan, in order to carry on a peaceful trade with Japan. The Jesuit, however, discovered that in the vessel there lay hidden cannon, bullets, axes, scythes, and spades, which seemed to furnish proof of their intention to make conquests in foreign lands and to found colonies there. Furthermore, they also did not look as prosperous as other merchants did. The Hollanders now feared that the Jesuit had turned the Japanese officials against them, and they expected to be crucified at once. Whatever the Japanese officials may have thought of the conclusion drawn by the

Jesuit who had taken the inventory, when they looked at the twenty-five weakened sailors that had been taken from the Dutch vessel, they could not see how such men could do them any harm. A message was sent to the "emperor" Ieyasu. On April 28, the news arrived that the pilot, William Adams, was invited to see the "emperor" at Osaka. Five boats appeared in order to conduct Adams to the ruler. On May 12, Adams appeared in the presence of Ieyasu, who not only was the local ruler of the island of Kioesioe, but claimed to be the emperor of the whole of Japan. He became shogun in 1603, but in 1600 his position was by no means secure. He was threatened on all sides by competitors, who almost precipitated a terrible civil war, but the Hollanders were not aware of this critical situation. Mr. Adams was accompanied by only one of the Hollanders, named Jan Joosten van Lodensteyn, who was the first Hollander to appear in the presence of the "emperor."

From the valuable account of Adams' extraordinary experiences in the imperial palace at Osaka we may repeat the following details. In 1598, he was hired chief pilot of the fleet of five ships which sailed from the port of Rotterdam. On April 6, 1599, the vessels passed the Strait of Magellan. Here they were forced to remain for the winter, and stayed there from April 6 to September 20, during which time most of their provisions were consumed. Presently the vessels dispersed, and the ship on which Adams was serving went to the coast of Chili. From Chili the crew took the ship to the island of Santa Maria. Then they crossed the Pacific Ocean, which took four months and twenty days. At the end of the voyage there were only seven men who could still stand on their feet, including Adams himself.[25] About his visit with the emperor he wrote thus: "The emperor, hearing of us, sent presently five frigates to us to bring me to the court where his majesty was . . . Now, when I came before him, he demanded of me from what country we were. So I answered him in all points: for there was nothing he demanded not, both concerning war and peace between country and country; the particulars whereof were too long to write. After this conference, I was commanded to prison, being well used, with one of our mariners that came with me to serve me."

Two days later, so continued Adams, the emperor called him again, demanding the reason why they had come from so far. He answered that they were a people who sought friendship with all nations, and they wanted to have trade in all countries, bringing such merchandise as their country had, and buying such merchandise in strange countries as their country desired. Through this trade both countries would be enriched. The emperor asked much concerning the wars between the Spanish and the Portuguese on the one hand and the Dutch on the other hand. He seems to have been very happy with the reply which Mr. Adams gave him. After the audience, as before, Mr. Adams was once more confined to prison, but this time his lodging was better than that in which he had been stationed before. Now he remained in prison for a period of thirty-nine days, during which time he heard no news either of the ship or of the captain. Every day he feared that he was to be crucified. This, he added, was the custom in Japan, just as hanging was in England.

Adams reported that during his imprisonment the Jesuits and the Portuguese presented a great deal of evidence against the Hollanders to the emperor, alleging that "we were thieves and robbers of all nations, and if we were suffered to live, it should be against the profit of his majesty and the country of Japan." No nation any longer would come to Japan without robbing. But if justice were administered, as the Hollanders deserved, it would terrify the rest of their nation; so that none of their sailors would ever dare to come to Japan any more. But Adams was of the opinion that God was merciful unto them all, and would not suffer the Japanese to do them any harm. So the emperor told the Jesuits and the Portuguese that thus far the Hollanders had done him no injury. Therefore, it was against reason to put these men to death, and if the Spaniards and the Hollanders chose to engage in war, that was also no cause for which to put the Hollanders to death.

On June 22, Adams appeared once more before the shogun Ieyasu. The latter, after having asked several more new questions, told him that he would be willing to have Adams get in touch with the other men who had been taken from the Dutch ship. This vessel, in the meantime, had been transported from the place where it had originally landed to Sakai, a town located about three miles from Osaka. It can readily be imagined how happy both Adams and the Hollanders were upon seeing each other again. But Adams was by no means pleased to observe that during his imprisonment the Japanese had taken away all the property from the ship. What Ieyasu had appreciated the most was the valuable ammunition which he was able to use in a great battle fought on October 21, 1600. In this battle he achieved a decisive victory over his leading competitors for the sole authority in the whole of Japan. Since that day his dynasty was master of the Japanese for a period of two and a half centuries. It is remarkable to observe that before the Dutch cannon and bullets arrived, Ieyasu was inactive, and watched with apparent lack of interest and concern the war-like preparations of his enemies. No sooner had the Dutch cannon appeared, than he began active fighting against his enemies. The Jesuits in Japan recorded that the Hollanders were used in this war for the purpose of manipulating the cannon for Ieyasu. There is no doubt that the Hollanders played an important role in

the establishment of the new Japanese empire.[26] It is also
worth noting that the Dutch enjoyed a favorable position
as long as this dynasty of Ieyasu ruled Japan. During the
two centuries after 1642, the Hollanders were in sole
charge of the European trade with Japan.

While the Hollanders were detained in Japan and
were enabled to find a means of making a respectable living, and while they married Japanese women, so that they
could carry on commerce on their own account, the Japanese government was made aware of the rising sea power
of the Dutch in the Far East. Early in the year 1601, it
happened on two different occasions that a Japanese vessel
returned from southern waters after having been in contact with a Dutch ship. On December 3, 1600, a Japanese
boat was captured by the Dutch on board the *Mauritius*
while they were in the vicinity of the city of Manila, in the
Philippines. But before long the Dutch set the Japanese
vessel free and gave the captain a banner and a passport in
the name of the stadhouder of the Dutch Republic. Another Japanese ship had encountered the same Dutch vessel, the *Mauritius,* on January 3, 1601, when both were
stationed near the coast of Borneo. The captain of the
Japanese ship was a Portuguese, who lived in Nagasaki
and who informed the Dutch captain of the arrival of a
ship in Japan manned by Hollanders. The Dutch captain,
who happened to be the admiral of the whole Dutch fleet,
Van Noort, presented to the Japanese vessel a Dutch flag
and a passport in the name of the stadhouder, Prince
Maurice. When the two Japanese captains and their respective crews brought the tidings of their adventures in
the East Indies to their government, the Japanese officials
began to reason that it would be an excellent policy to be
as friendly as possible to this great European power that
was able to equip so many vessels and to arm them so efficiently.

William Adams, although he was an Englishman, and had not been in command of the Dutch vessel, the *Liefde,* which had brought the crew to Japanese shores, was nevertheless regarded by the Japanese ruler as the most important person among all the sailors. The shogun commanded him to build a vessel for him. Adams also instructed Ieyasu in geometry and trigonometry. It was in 1605 that Adams constructed the first ship for the Japanese ruler, a vessel of about eighty tons, with which Adams made a number of trips along the shores of the various Japanese islands. In 1613, Adams had learned so much about the physical geography of Japan that he was able to draw a valuable map of all the important coasts, of which two copies were sent to the Hollanders in the Malay Archipelago. One went to the town of Bantam, and the other to the governor-general of the Dutch East Indies. Mr. Adams also built a second vessel, in which task he was aided by some of the Hollanders. Since Adams himself knew very little about the art of ship building, there can be no doubt that he was assisted by the Dutch carpenter Pieter Jansz. of Rotterdam.[27]

Owing to the valuable services which Adams thus rendered to the Japanese ruler, he was rewarded by the latter with the highest honors that could be bestowed on a foreigner residing in Japan. For example, when in 1618 an important group of officials came from Korea to visit the shogun, Adams was present during the audience. He also served as intermediary between the English and the Dutch on the one hand and the Japanese ruler on the other hand. For about two or three years he actually was in the service of the Dutch East India Company, while from 1613 to 1615 he was employed by the English East India Company, which paid him one hundred pounds sterling a year. But, after 1615, he resumed his independent commercial activities. He played an important role in the establishment of Dutch trade in Japan, while he did even more for the English East India Company in Japan.

It should be observed that among the Hollanders there were also able men who prepared the way for the Dutch merchants in the great ports of Japan. Most important of these was the man who had first accompanied Adams to the court of the Japanese shogun. This, as we saw above, was Jan Joosten van Lodensteyn. His ability and his industry were such that he finally procured a vessel of his own, with which he carried on commerce with Siam and other regions. He also established valuable contacts with the employees of the Dutch East India Company, and he traded with Englishmen, Spaniards, and Portuguese, as well as with the Japanese. The Dutch East India Company owed a great deal to him and to his associates, because these men, after having lived for several years in Japan, supplied the newcomers with valuable information and provided for them all manner of contacts which would have taken the officials in the employment of the Dutch East India Company years to collect and procure independently.

The Dutch were rather slow to follow up their advantageous position in Japan. They felt that they had so much to do in the Malay Archipelago that they should not extend their commercial activities to the coasts of Japan before they were quite ready with the defenses in the East Indies. As we have seen, the federal government of the Dutch Republic appeared more interested in opening direct commercial relations with Japan than were the directors of the Dutch East India Company. It was not until May 12, 1605, that a fleet of the Dutch East India Company arrived in the Malay Archipelago with instructions to visit China and Japan. The separate companies which preceded the founding of the Dutch East India Company had intended to do this work earlier, and in December, 1599, Vice-

Admiral Jacob Wilkens left for the Far East with definite instructions to find his way to China, Japan, and the Philippines. Nevertheless, he confined himself entirely to the Malay Archipelago.[28]

On February 2, 1606, the Board of Seventeen, which, as we saw, was in charge of the Dutch East India Company, made a resolution in which it was stated that the directors were to ask Prince Maurice for a letter written by him and addressed to the "king" of Japan. The directors added that a ship was to be dispatched to Japan carrying the message from Prince Maurice, and the captain of the vessel was to present the Japanese ruler with a gift. Paulus van Caerden, who, on April 20, 1606, departed for India, carried with him the letter addressed by Prince Maurice to the "emperor" of Japan. But the letter did not reach its destination, because Van Caerden was detained by the Spaniards in the Moluccas.[29]

More successful was the fleet which left the Netherlands on December 22, 1607, under the command of Admiral Verhoeff. Two vessels belonging to this fleet reached Nagasaki in July, 1609. The ships were called *Roode Leeuw met Pijlen* and the *Griffioen*. The crew of the *Griffioen* immediately got in touch with the surviving members of the crew of the ship that had arrived in 1600. The shogun received a fine present, and upon the advice of William Adams, the Dutch also gave a present to the governor of Nagasaki.[30]

There are also valuable Dutch sources which throw welcome light on the reception granted by the Japanese rulers to the two crews that had sailed respectively on the two first Dutch vessels that went directly to Japan. One of these sources is the report made by the merchant of the *Griffioen*, Jacques Specx, who, on July 25, wrote these words: "We were received with great friendship and we were invited to send commissioners to the court of the emperor, in order to obtain from him a contract for peace and trade with the Netherlands."[31] Encouraged by this report, some of the council decided immediately to take advantage of the invitation and dispatched two chief merchants, together with two assistants to the imperial court, while Melchior van Santvoort, one of the survivors of the first Dutch ship to appear in Japan, was to go along to act as the interpreter. On September 20, these two chief merchants presented a report of their experiences to the council. From this report and from a letter which the "emperor" sent to Prince Maurice in the Netherlands it appears clearly how well the Hollanders were received. They were granted free trade in all the harbors and places of Japan, as was shown in a special pass prepared for them and in a letter, to erect a factory for the East India Company which was to be built at the town of Hirado (or Firando, which was the Portuguese spelling for the town of Hirado). Jacques Specx was appointed the chief official of the Dutch settlement in Japan. On October 2, 1609, the two Dutch vessels left the harbor of Hirado and about one month later arrived at Patani, which was the headquarters for the trade of the Dutch between the East Indies and China and Japan.[32]

According to William Adams, a small vessel arrived, from the Netherlands, in Japan during the course of the year 1611. This was undoubtedly the ship used by the enterprising Dutch Captain Specx, who, during 1610, had looked in vain for the arrival of any Dutch ships. In November, 1610, Specx had sent two of his assistants to the chief Dutch merchant Heijn, in Siam, and on November 8, 1610, he wrote a letter to this merchant. Moreover, on November 3 he wrote another to the board of directors of the Dutch East India Company in Amsterdam. He urged the College of Seventeen to send a number of articles which were produced in the Dutch Republic. These were mirrors, textiles, cloths, carpets, glassware, leather, iron, and lead. He added that prices of Chinese goods in Japan were higher than before, which must have partly resulted from the fact that a richly laden Portuguese vessel had recently been wrecked in a storm.[33]

After Specx had written these letters, he seems to have gone to Patani, in order to fetch from there some goods that he needed for his business in Japan. It was with these goods that he went to the court of the Japanese ruler, to inform him of the reasons why the Dutch ships had not yet made their appearance. Besides, he wanted to pave the way for a favorable reception when the proper time came.

On June 16, 1611, Specx left the port and about the middle of August he arrived at the imperial court. He was promised an audience with the shogun on the very next day. In the meantime, Specx and his companion learned that a short time ago a Portuguese mission had arrived at the court, and although received by the shogun, they were given no reply to their questions. The Dutch also learned on the same occasion that a Spanish mission had met a like fate. The Spanish had insisted upon the privilege of building ships in Japan wherever they pleased, and upon the expulsion of the Dutch traders.

During the audience at the court of the shogun, William Adams was the interpreter and the official friend of the Hollanders. They asked for two commercial passes, giving them privileges to trade in all ports of Japan. They also requested the right to unload their ships without being subject to the strict supervision of the Japanese officials. He explained why their ships had not yet appeared. The shogun asked the Hollanders how many soldiers they had in the Moluccas, whether they traded with Borneo, whether the best camphor grew there, where the best aloe wood was to be found, whether fragrant wood grew in the Netherlands, and which fetched the highest price.

Also at the court in Yedo the Hollanders were very cordially received. Here they also left sumptuous presents. On August 29, the commissioners returned to the city of Suruga, and two days later they received the commercial pass that they had requested. It stated: "The Dutch ships that have sailed to Japan, in whatever port they shall anchor, may not be molested anywhere in Japanese waters, but on the contrary all favorable assistance shall be rendered them."[34]

In August, 1612, the Hollanders in Hirado were greatly relieved to see at last the Dutch vessel from the Netherlands that had been expected for such a long time. It was the *Roode Leeuw met Pijlen,* which has been mentioned above; now it arrived for the second time in this Japanese port. After it had returned to the Netherlands, Abraham van den Broeck, the commander, told the board of directors of the Dutch East India Company about the privileges which he and his companions had received in Japan. This occurred on August 2, 1610, and four weeks later the College of Seventeen decided to prepare a suitable memorial for the Japanese rulers in the form of a cargo. Two ships were dispatched to carry the merchandise to the Malay Archipelago, where the Governor-General would determine which ships and which persons would be sent to Japan. The merchants were instructed especially to take care that they would obtain a good quality of silver. Perhaps the officials in Amsterdam dod not know that in Japan very few false coins were permitted to circulate.

The cargo on this vessel was so large (being made up of spices) that it became necessary to load Chinese goods, such as silks and porcelain, in another vessel called the *Hasewint,* which was to arrive from Patani. In addition, the chief merchant at Patani should send over a third vessel whose home port was Bantam, and which was intended for coastal service in Japan for the use of the traders.[35]

Whereas the Portuguese were greatly hampered in their operations, owing to the extensive organization of foreign trade that they had built up in Japan, which naturally required strict supervision on the part of the Japanese officials; the Hollanders, like the Spaniards and the Chinese, were permitted to carry on their trade almost unrestricted.[36] The Dutch leaders now took advantage of this remarkable opportunity, and provided their men with suitable quarters for trading purposes. They opened up a lucrative import trade for goods coming not only from the Netherlands, but also from various Asiatic countries, including cotton from the mainland of India, as well as the silks from China. At first the Hollanders had contented themselves by renting a building for their factory, but by the year 1613 they had acquired two excellent buildings of their own, which had cost them a large sum, but they were fireproof and durable. This was one of the reasons why Brouwer had recommended that the Dutch settlements should not be moved away from Hirado. These warehouses the Dutch filled with a variety of fragrant and precious woods, deerskins, nutmegs, cinnamon, pepper and other spices.

In 1617, the first large Dutch fleet arrived in Japan. Four of the vessels had a capacity of between six hundred and nine hundred tons, and one measured four hundred tons. The appearance of this fleet caused the Portuguese no small envy, and they hastened to seek the ear of the important Japanese officials, in order to stem the tide of Dutch competition before it might be too late for the Portuguese. As a result of these activities, the Japanese government ordered all foreigners in Japan to cease quarreling, and to refrain from seizing ships which belonged to other nations.[37]

It was a sad blow for all the Europeans when they were told that hereafter all trade was to be restricted to two

ports, namely, Nagasaki and Hirado.[38] Nevertheless, the
pass which the Japanese government granted to the Dutch
in the year 1617, notwithstanding the interpretation given
to it by a number of modern interpreters, shows that the
Hollanders suffered no greater trading restrictions than
before.[39] It is true that nothing is said in this pass about
complete freedom of trade, but none of the passes had said
anything that could be so construed. The Dutch always
were obliged to submit to close supervision on the part
of the Japanese officials. Only in the letter from Ieyasu to
Prince Maurice, which was dated approximately August,
1609, and the remarks made by the shogun in 1611 at the
time of the trip to the court by Specx, is there any indication of real commercial liberties to be enjoyed by the Hollanders.

However, after 1623 the Dutch merchants in Japan
began to thrive more and more. The profits which they
derived from their trade with Japan were indeed extraordinary, and compared favorably with those obtained in the
Malay Archipelago. A wealth of figures were put together
by a distinguished historiographer in the Dutch East India
Company, to whom we owe a great deal of important information.[40]

At the same time the relations between the officials of
the Japanese government and the Dutch representatives
were quite cordial. For example, in 1626, the commis-
sioner of the Dutch East India Company was well received
by the shogun, who refused to talk with the embassies of
Portugal and Siam. Furthermore, in 1624, the Spanish
embassy, which had been sent to notify the Japanese ruler
of the succession of the throne of Spain to Philip IV, did
not even dare to go to Yedo. Their costly presents were
also refused, and their large and handsome vessel manned
by three hundred soldiers was closely watched, and all the
men on board were prevented from contact with the Japa-

nese. Thus the Spaniards had to return to Manila without having accomplished anything worth while.[41]

On December 20, 1623, the Dutch commander of the factory at Hirado wrote a letter to the Governor-General in Batavia, saying that all the results which the Portuguese had obtained from their complaints about the Dutch, were, in short, their own persecution. The Portuguese men had been compelled to leave Japan, while their wives and children remained there.[42] In a letter of April 28, 1624, he reported that the same fate had befallen the Spaniards.[43]

As a result of these developments, the Dutch finally obtained control of the trade of Chinese silk and silk goods in Japan. From 1624 to 1661, when Formosa was a Dutch colony, the Hollanders used their advantageous position in increasing the flow of trade between China and Japan. However, this remarkable success of the Dutch did not result in improved relations with the Japanese officials. The latter had hoped to extend their sway over Formosa, and naturally they resented the success obtained by Europeans in the waters of the Far East. Moreover, a number of Dutch officials were lacking in tact and caused a strained relation between themselves and the Japanese. Formosa was not wisely governed, and its commercial contacts, which had been very promising, were subject to neglect and abuse. Furthermore, the government of the Dutch colonies in the Indian Ocean ordered that the Japanese would have to pay for their trading privileges with Formosa, in order to help the Dutch pay for their fortifications on the island. The toll which they had to pay amounted to about 10 per cent of the value of the goods bought and sold.[44] This caused the Japanese to take serious reprisals between 1627 and 1630, but relations became more cordial when the Japanese rulers prohibited their subjects from going to Formosa.

From 1632 to 1641, the Dutch enjoyed a fair amount of prosperity in Japan. Japanese competition in Formosa had ceased, because the Japanese officials refused to give any more passports to their citizens who were bent upon going to Formosa for trading purposes. Portuguese competition was greatly reduced, and at the end of the period it completely disappeared because of the hostile action taken toward them by the Japanese officials. The hatred of the Japanese for the Catholic religion was of such a nature that it became absolutely repulsive to them. In addition to these factors it must be noted that Japan, during this period, was rather prosperous and enjoyed an increase in its foreign trade. The Dutch in these years did indeed carry on a very favorable trade in Japan.[45] On the other hand, it was no longer possible for the Hollanders to regain the extensive trading privileges which they had enjoyed before 1624. They had to endure many humiliations, but, being intent upon an extension of commerce, they willingly suffered them, and cautiously refrained from making too many complaints against the Japanese officials. In former years, the Hollanders were permitted to participate in the interior trade of Japan, but now this was forbidden. When their ships arrived at the factory in Hirado, trading could not yet be started until the governors at Nagasaki had told the Hollanders at Hirado what a fair price for the goods would be. The Portuguese were favored by the governors at Nagasaki, who deliberately increased the duration of the period in which they made up their minds. But the Dutch persevered in spite of all this.[46]

In the second half of 1637 and the opening months of 1638, a rebellion known as the Shimabara revolt broke out in Japan, which was partly supported by the Roman Catholics. About the middle of December, 1637, many thousands of Japanese subjects were in open rebellion. In one district, which contained about 28,000 inhabitants, about

85 per cent of the population joined the forces of rebellion.[47] In February, 1638, the Hollanders also became involved. When a Japanese general on his way to Nagasaki was informed that the Hollanders would gladly support his government with cannon and ammunition from their ships, he commanded that they loan him the use of five cannon and ten barrels of powder. The Dutch commander of the settlement dared not refuse the request, although he merely sent six barrels of powder instead of ten. About the middle of February the Dutch commander (Couckebacker) received the order to remove his ships to the scene of battle. On February 24, Couckebacker obeyed this order and had the one sea-worthy vessel, from which five cannon had already been taken, and one on which there were still fifteen left, dispatched to the besieged city of the rebels. For sixteen days the Hollanders took part in the siege of the fortification. Great was their relief when, on March 12, they received an order from the prince at Hirado to return to his port. But a large number of writers subsequently maintained that the Hollanders deliberately participated in the attack on the rebels, because the latter had among them a considerable number of Roman Catholics. But this interpretation does not seem justified in the light of the latest researches.[48]

The Shimabara Revolt was the final blow to the Portuguese in Japan. After the edict of 1637 the Portuguese had tried to maintain themselves on the island of Deshima in Nagasaki harbor, but in 1639 they were ordered from Japan upon pain of death. With the withdrawal of the Portuguese in 1639, the last European rival of the Hollanders was removed, and the Dutch alone now were to control the European trade to Japan until the second half of the nineteenth century.[49]

It must not be imagined that the Dutch in Japan continued to be treated very kindly by the local officials. In

1641, the Dutch company sent commissioners to have an audience with the emperor, who told them that the Japanese government did not want any more foreigners in the country, but that the Dutch might stay, provided that they leave Hirado and remove to the artificial island of Deshima in the mouth of the river at Nagasaki.[50] Just before that order was given them, they had been compelled to destroy their fine stone buildings in Hirado, because they had inscribed upon the roofs these words respectively: "1637 Anno Domini" and "1639 Anno Domini." The Dutch immediately had obeyed this command, tearing them down in five days with the help of two hundred of the crew of a ship lying in the harbor.[51]

Despite these hardships it was comforting for the Dutch to know that, by 1641, all the Portuguese had been driven out of Japan, and that the English were no longer there. The reasons why the Dutch alone among all European nations could continue to operate in Japan have been ably analyzed by a Japanese scholar, who recognized these three cardinal policies followed by the officials of the Dutch East India Company: (1) the removal of European rivals, (2) the desirability of maintaining the favor of the Japanese government, and (3) the need of keeping up with the demands and tastes of the Japanese population and of controlling the markets in Japan. Moreover, the Dutch would go out of their way to hunt for Portuguese priests and deliver them to the Japanese officials. Such actions greatly pleased the Japanese. For example, in 1620 they brought two priests to the Japanese, who executed them and richly rewarded the Hollanders. This action of the Dutch was called "loyalty" (goschusetsu) or "service" (gohokosuji). Incidentally, it was the only means by which Japan could learn about the outside world. In addition, each year the Dutch commander of the factory paid a visit to Yedo, later called Tokyo, bearing enormous gifts, and in later years he was accompanied by capable physicians who offered medical services and instruction.[52]

The Dutch imported to Japan such wares as raw silk and silk cloths, sugar, deer skins, shark skins, lead, tin, spices, ivory, woolen cloths from Europe, and various small objects for children and housewives.[53] They exported gold and gold objects, silver coins and silverware, copper and copper goods, camphor, grains, lacquerware, and porcelain. Eventually the export of precious metals was forbidden by the Japanese government. The annual profit of the Japanese trade was about 500,000 guilders, which greatly surpassed that derived by the Dutch from their commercial contacts with any other country in Asia. For example, the Dutch, in 1649, obtained a profit of 709,603 guilders from the trade with Japan, as compared with 467,538 from that with Formosa, at that time a Dutch colony, 326,842 from the Persian trade, 92,592 from Surat, 93,280 from western Sumatra, 42,964 from the Malabar coast of India, 43,523 from Macassar, and 20,526 from Jambi. In that same year, a loss was shown in the trade with the Coromandel Coast, Amboina, Banda, Malacca, Siam, Batavia, Mauritius, and Solor. The Dutch could very well afford to present the Japanese court with an annual gift of about 25,000 guilders, and they did not complain too much about certain inconveniences caused them by brazen officials who searched their vessels for crucifixes or Bibles. The Dutch were there to make money, not Christians.[54]

After the Dutch removed their factory to Deshima in the harbor of Nagasaki, they quickly readjusted themselves to their new location, and were able to increase their trade because of the favorable position occupied by the great port of Nagasaki in the island empire of Japan. Here the Portuguese formerly had been very well situated. The Hollanders were told by the Japanese officials that, although Japan was not benefited much by the trade of the foreigners, the Hollanders, because of passports granted by the former ruler, would be permitted to reside in Japan and trade there, on condition that their ships call only at the harbor of Nagasaki, where the island of Deshima was located.[55] However, now, the Dutch had to contend with the Chinese. After the Portuguese were forced out of Japan, in 1639, the Chinese took their place, buying the silk goods which the Portuguese used to do, directly from China and other places, especially from Tonquin, and then bringing them to Japan.

The Dutch did not always realize the advantages from their trade in Japan. Sometimes the trade was so bad that there was talk of closing the factory. But it was not considered advisable to do this, and the government of the Indies recommended to those in Japan that they conduct themselves with all modesty and humility, so as not to give the least offense to the Japanese, but humor their whims. The Dutch were to carry out the commands of the Japanese to the best of their ability, so that the latter would not find an excuse to deprive them of their commerce. This attitude, adopted by the Dutch officials in Batavia, explains in part, at least, why the Hollanders, after 1639 and up to 1859, were the only Europeans permitted to trade with Japan at all. It was their extraordinary tact that enabled them to keep their monopoly between Europe and Japan for a period of 218 years. Since the Dutch were Christians, they were also suspected, just as the Portuguese had been. They were ordered each year to send a new chief and to inquire what the rulers' orders were.[56]

What pleased the Dutch particularly about the location of their new factory, was the fact that the harbor at Nagasaki gave protection to the ships in times of bad weather, especially when the typhoons were blowing. Even when the vessels would break away and get stuck in the soft

mud, they would always get loose again when the high
tide appeared, but, at Hirado, typhoons would do considerable damage to the Dutch ships.

On the other hand, as soon as the Dutch were established in Deshima, they were immediately watched and
forbidden to talk to anyone. This was enforced much more
severely than it had been with the Portuguese, so that it
seemed as if the Dutch were looked upon as criminals and
dangerous to Japan. The Portuguese were at least partly
responsible for this treatment, because they gave the Japanese to understand that the Dutch were of the same faith
as the Portuguese. However, in the early months of the
new establishment at Deshima, the local officials treated
the Hollanders with a fair amount of cordiality. Le Maire,
the new commander of the factory, was forced in August,
1641, to draw up ordinances in order to maintain har-
mony. In other words, he established strict rules of conduct for his subordinates. Since the maintenance of the
Christian religion was forbidden on land and on ships in
the harbor, the observance of Sunday was prohibited, and
the Dutch were ordered to work on that day. The dead
had to be buried at sea, as the Dutch were not thought
worthy of Japanese soil.[57]

Each year the Dutch had to pay the Japanese 5,500
taels as rent for Deshima, which amounted to 19,530 guilders. The Dutch ships were inspected very carefully, and
light cannon, powder, and other ammunition were taken
from the ships and stored in the shogun's magazines. The
sails were tied up and the rudders were removed until the
day the ships were to depart. The inspectors treated the
sailors and the officers very rudely and impolitely, often
even beating them with sticks. Furthermore, no one could
go ashore without special permission from the inspectors.
It is true that at Deshima "the position of the Dutch in
their new abode was rather that of captives; however, as

they were tolerated in any case, whereas other Europeans were entirely excluded, they contented themselves with things as they were."

Van Dam, the historiographer of the Dutch East India Company during the seventeenth century, said that it might well have been the actions of the Hollanders themselves which brought upon them their unpleasant experiences. They had been engaged in debaucheries and misdemeanors with women and others, and they had also been noted for their extraordinary pride in their comportment with Orientals. The Japanese, who were a brave people, could not tolerate this characteristic, but desired a humble and modest demeanor, since they considered the Dutch as merchants and only interested in commerce. One Japanese authority has correctly maintained that, after 1640, the Dutch, who professed a different brand of Christianity from that of the Portuguese, and who were, from the beginning, dissociated from religious propaganda, were, for that very reason, tolerated by the Japanese. The only other foreigners who could trade at Nagasaki were the Chinese, who obviously would not be suspected of spreading the principles of the Christian religion.[58]

It can be easily understood why a large number of Japanese living in Nagasaki and its vicinity, hearing that the Dutch were Christians like the Portuguese, reasoned that the Dutch East India Company was doomed in the end, and that it soon would have to withdraw its factory, as the English had done before them. Consequently, many of them sold their investments and discontinued trading with the Hollanders, but it would appear to the present writer that their fear was unnecessary, since the Dutch, from the beginning, had shown little inclination for missionary work in Japan.[59]

Although the Japanese officials insisted on loading the ships for the Hollanders, and putting their goods into the warehouses, as well as sealing both, the Dutch sent six or seven ships a year to Nagasaki. In 1641, they sold goods to the value of eight million guilders, and in the same year they petitioned to be allowed to export copper, which had been forbidden in 1637. When this was allowed, silver exportation was prohibited. After three or four years of peaceful negotiations, the Japanese officials at Yedo became very much satisfied with the recent developments at Deshima. In the journal kept at Batavia a statement was written down to the effect that the Japanese liked the "new order" and that his majesty, the ruler, had declared that the Hollanders could peacefully continue their negotiations in Japan, partly because of the passes which his forefathers had granted them in earlier times.[60]

Not satisfied with the local trade in Japan, the Hollanders thought from time to time of exploring regions to the north, as well as to the south of Japan. In 1643, two yachts sailed from Batavia, having orders to discover the north coast of Tartary. The commander of the expedition was De Vries, who, coming to the northern coast of Japan near the city of Nambre, or Nambu, had the cannon on the Dutch ships fired, and anchored the ships there. But the vessels were promptly seized by the Japanese and the men taken to the imperial court at Yedo. Although, according to Japanese law, they were subject to the death penalty for their offense, they were set free by the ruler.[61] As a return for this kindness, the Dutch later sent an embassy to the imperial court with special honors and presents for the "emperor." The Hollanders also realized presently that there was not much to be gained by extending trading operations to the north of Japan. Consequently, they continued to concentrate upon the importation of Chinese silks, and the exportation of silver from Japan. After the Portuguese expulsion from Japan, the Portuguese got into closer contact with the Chinese and controlled the most important part of the silk trade, so that the Dutch could derive very little from the same. A proposition was then made by the government in the Indies to cut the Chinese off from the trade in Japan and annex it for themselves. It was alleged that if nothing were done, the Chinese would kill the Dutch trade; consequently, it would be more advisable for the Dutch to force them out of Japan.

However, the board of directors of the Dutch East India Company in Amsterdam did not agree with the Council of the Indies in Batavia. The directors in Amsterdam believed that profits should not be sought through the exclusion of all other merchants; that the Dutch should be satisfied with a reasonable profit and should not try to get more by unjust means. Furthermore, aggressive actions to gain all profits from the Japanese trade would also strengthen the false belief, held by many Japanese, that the Dutch were pirates and not merchants. The Hollanders in Japan wanted to use a capitalization of two million guilders in gold, which should be sent from the Netherlands to Japan and upon which a profit of 1,400,000 guilders was expected.[62]

Since the Dutch were very scrupulous in maintaining proper relations with the Japanese and in adjusting themselves as far as it was humanly possible, the Japanese rewarded them in turn by reducing the restrictions on their trade. But notwithstanding the flourishing conditions of the Dutch trade in Japan, and in spite of the more lenient attitude shown by the imperial officers, many of the old restrictions remained in force. For example, we read in one of the old Dutch accounts that on the gates of the island of Deshima an announcement was fixed of the closing of the island, the forbidding of natives to go to the island on pain of death, or to communicate to the Dutch what went on in the city. The Dutch also were prohibited from entering the city, and had to pay high prices for all the food that was brought to them.[63]

Relations between the Dutch and Japanese continued in much the same manner for several years. It is worth noting, however, that, in 1664, the Japanese expressed fears that the Dutch trade was declining. They had observed how the Hollanders had cut down the amount of the presents which they gave to the imperial court each year; so the Japanese wanted to know if the Dutch trade had decreased, and whether they were becoming poorer, because the presents were no longer as sumptuous and abundant as they had been in earlier years. One of the reasons why the presents had diminished, was, no doubt, due to the fact that two ships were lost in 1663, and they had had on board many rare gifts for both the shogun and his council.[64] Moreover, when the accounts of the Dutch factory in Deshima are examined, it will be seen that there was no appreciable drop in their trade between the years 1649 and 1664.[65] It is true that after 1664 there was a slight falling off, but the same may be said of the trade in the Malay Archipelago, or with Ceylon. The Dutch had to face increasing competition with the British in the Indian Ocean, on the mainland of India, and in America. It is no wonder that they could not continue to derive such huge profits as they had had in the year 1649. Nevertheless, their trade with Japan was always more lucrative on the average than was that with certain other colonies, such as some of the islands in the Malay Archipelago which they prized much more highly than Japan.[66]

The financial success which they experienced here would make the Dutch persevere amidst conditions that would have seemed intolerable to many other peoples. They would also combine consummate tact and diplomacy with their patience, in order to wrest from their European competitors the trade with Japan for a period of 218 years.

Even when the Dutch Republic would cease to exist, its flag would continue to wave over the factory in Japan until, in the place of the defunct state, a kingdom should arise which would resume the threads of diplomacy and commercial relations. Only after the Americans had opened the door of Japan's house to all other western powers, in 1853, did the tenacious Dutch merchants yield a share of the Japanese foreign commerce to the other powers.

CHAPTER VII

DECLINE, RECOVERY AND FURTHER EXPANSION

THE Dutch Republic was in its day of glory a very wealthy and a very powerful state. But many of its most distinguished citizens, like the plutocrats who controlled the government of ancient Carthage, were more intent upon securing for themselves increased profit than in promoting the security of the nation as a whole. Perhaps it was a bit premature when some leading English statesmen during the course of the third Anglo-Dutch War (1672–1674) contemptuously compared the United Netherlands with Carthage and said, *"Carthago est delenda"* ("Carthage must be destroyed"). Nevertheless, at that very time certain forces were in operation which undermined the political and economic power of the tiny republic. Sagacious burghers in Amsterdam likened England to a large mountain of iron and Holland to a small heap of gold. While speculators continued to make huge profits on the stock market in Amsterdam, both the army and the navy were being sorely neglected.

During the first half of the eighteenth century the British could easily have seized the whole of the Dutch colonial empire. One reason why they did not choose to adopt such a course was that they were allies of the Dutch against their common enemy—France. In the midst of the third Anglo-Dutch War a number of influential members of the Parliament came to the conclusion that the future rival of England was France, rather than the Dutch Republic. They despised King Charles II and his satellites for having made a secret agreement with the French monarch to wipe out the United Netherlands and to restore

Catholicism in England. In 1673 they succeeded in having the Test Act passed, which stated that henceforth no Roman Catholic could hold an important position in the English government. When peace was signed with Holland during the next year, a virtual alliance followed the war.

Anglo-Dutch ties of friendship were strengthened considerably when at the end of 1688 James II lost his throne and had to flee to France. His place was taken by the austere Dutch prince, William III, the son-in-law and nephew of James II. Now followed a bitter contest with France, in which the combined fleets of the British and the Dutch inflicted very serious damage upon the French. What most American historians have mistakenly called the War of the League of Augsburg, Professor G. N. Clark has more aptly termed the War of the Dutch Alliance (1688–1697).[1] After three years of peace with France, the allies prepared for a second war, which is generally known as the War of the Spanish Succession (1702–1713). Finally, in the War of the Austrian Succession (1740–1748), the British and the Dutch once more fought side by side against French aggression.

It was not the modern counterpart of the Roman Empire that ruined the Dutch Republic but rather the forces of interior decay to which a brief allusion has just been made. From 1672 to 1748 Holland was in mortal danger of being absorbed by the mighty kingdom of France. In 1688 the Hollanders gratefully accepted British aid against the Grand Monarch (Louis XIV). They were "irrevocably committed to the war before they sent their missions to London." Consequently, they were unable to "extort a price from England for their support." During the next seventy years Holland was a mere satellite of Great Britain. This period "contributed, above all else, to the greatness of England."[2] The writer remembers distinctly how one day his history teacher in the Netherlands told the class about the joint expedition to Gibraltar during the War of the Spanish Succession. We nearly wept tears when we were told how the British imperialists seized the town for themselves and kept it ever since. But the poor Hollanders got nothing for their hard work. What we overlooked that day was the bargain the Dutch had made with their allies. They wanted security against the French. This is what they received. Their dependence was placed upon the might of Great Britain. In the meantime the British succeeded in establishing themselves in North America and India, letting the Dutch retain the East Indies.

Although the British no longer molested the Hollanders in the East Indies and Japan, the latter began to slip badly. As early as 1662 they lost the valuable island of Formosa, owing very largely to inefficiency displayed by the local governor and also by the governor-general in Batavia.[3] A Chinese commander by the name of Coxinga overwhelmed the Dutch garrison, but permitted the defeated forces to withdraw to the island of Java. His sudden attack ended an enterprise undertaken by far-sighted merchants and navigators, whose work was nullified by weak-kneed officials. The same development might well have taken place in Japan if it had not been for the kind disposition shown by the Japanese rulers.

Even during the course of the fourth Anglo-Dutch War (1780–1784), in which the Dutch were decisively defeated, neither the British nor any other western nation could oust the Hollanders from their trading-post in Japan. This may have been partly due to the fact, however, that Dutch profits derived from the trade with Japan were dwindling. In 1688 the Shogunate had limited the number of Dutch vessels entering Nagasaki harbor to four or five a year. In 1743 the number was limited to only one.

During the period from 1715 to 1743 profits had declined from 500,000 to about 200,000 guilders annually. Much of this loss was ascribed by the Dutch to the debasement of the Japanese currency, and undoubtedly there was much truth in their calculations. Since the annual expenses amounted to about 175,000 guilders, sometimes running as high as 193,162 guilders (as in 1686), the Hollanders became ever more dissatisfied with their Japanese trade. For a time they actually contemplated starting war against the Japanese government, but the merchants and officials located on the island of Deshima in the port of Nagasaki advised against such a course of action.[4]

The period of greatest prosperity fell in the reign of Genruku, which began in 1688. One Japanese writer is of the opinion that this was chiefly the result of the favorable attitude displayed by the native ruler. He argues that in later years the loss of profits experienced by the Dutch merchants was caused very largely by the difficulties under which the Hollanders had to labor in Japan. He correctly repeats the complaints made by the Dutch themselves.[5] But we must take into account also events which transpired in Europe. As we have observed above, the Dutch reached the height of their commercial success between 1675 and 1725. What may be said about this trade in general can also be applied to the Japanese trade in particular. After 1725 the Dutch suffered reverses on nearly all fronts, and in 1795 the decrepit republic was overthrown, while three years later the Dutch East India Company ceased to exist. Is it any wonder that in 1800 the Hollanders in Japan were so hard pressed that they had to borrow money from the local Japanese rulers?[6]

Since Holland from 1795 to 1810 was to all intents and purposes a dependency of France, and from 1810 to 1813 a province of France, the British, then at war with the French, seized all of the Dutch colonies. At the peace settlement in 1815 (Congress of Vienna) the British retained one-half of Guiana on the mainland of South America, Cape Colony in South Africa, and the Island of Ceylon. But through all these dreadful years the humiliated Hollanders enjoyed the satisfaction of having their flag wave over the island of Deshima. Until 1859 they remained the only Europeans permitted to trade in Japan.

The leading statesmen of Europe assembled at Vienna in 1815 decreed that what was later the kingdom of Belgium be annexed to the former Dutch Republic. This union forced upon the proud Belgians did not prove a complete success, and in 1830 they revolted against their Dutch king. Nine years later the Kingdom of the Netherlands was formally reduced in size, retaining its name, but surrendering Belgium.

In the period from 1815 to 1918 the Hollanders took no part in any of the European wars. They realized fully their new position in international politics. No longer was their country a power of the first rank, nor even of a second rank. But slowly the Dutch people recovered from the terrible shock of the French Revolution and the Napoleonic era. Gratefully they turned their attention once more to the Far East, where their "Insulinde" began to assume a new rôle in the world of commerce and industry. With the discovery of immense tin and petroleum deposits, and with the increasing demand for rubber, tobacco, and certain valuable spices, the eastern portion of the Kingdom of the Netherlands acquired an importance exceeding by far that of the mother country itself.

But while the Dutch East Indies were growing in importance, Dutch contacts with two other areas in the Far East were suffering a relative decline. These were Australia and Japan. It has long been customary among teachers of history in American schools to assume that in the eighteenth century Australia was first discovered by the

English Captain Cook, and that in 1853 Japan was first opened to western civilization by the American Commodore Perry. Such interpretations are readily adopted because of the fact that the Hollanders who preceded the British and the Americans in these regions have since 1850 dropped far behind the latter. It is also assumed very naturally that the English helped to establish religious liberty and democratic principles in general at the very time when the Dutch were teaching the English these ideas. Recent events have crowded out in the minds of millions those things that came first chronologically.

Returning now briefly to the work of Dutch explorers along the coasts of Australia, we will recall why Australia was first called "New Holland," and why the island of Tasmania was named after the Hollander Tasman. We also recall why New Zealand was once regarded as a Dutch colony. Holland and Zeeland were the two most important Dutch provinces in matters of commerce and colonization. The earliest Dutch maps of the Far East show the west coast of New Zealand as being closely connected with the mainland of Australia.

As early as 1606 the Dutch explorers saw a large part of Australia, and in 1623 Cartensz. discovered the snow-capped mountains on the mainland which were not indicated upon reliable maps until in 1909, when this work was performed by Lorentz and Van Nouhys. In 1642, 1643, and 1644 Abel Tasman explored much of the coastline of Australia and Tasmania. He gave the name of Van Diemensland to the latter island, in honor of the Governor-General of the Dutch East Indies who had entrusted him with the task of exploration. (Only in recent times has this old name been changed at the request of the British inhabitants.) But he failed to find the strait that separates the northern portion of New Zealand from the southern part. This work was accomplished by Cook about

130 years later. In 1617, 1618, 1622, 1629, 1696, and 1705 various ships belonging to the Dutch East India Company reached a number of points on the Australian coast, where until this day many names commemorate the work of the intrepid Dutch explorers. But beginning with Governor Van Diemen, who died in 1645, the leading officials in the great commercial company were disappointed with the results obtained by these explorations. When in 1721 and 1722 the Dutch West India Company organized an expedition to Australia as a part of a trip around the world, little enthusiasm for colonization in Australia was aroused. Thus "New Holland" remained for the most part an empty name, and before long the British took possession of this region.[7]

The situation in Japan was somewhat different. Here the Dutch desperately clung to their position and frequently tried to improve it. They were virtually imprisoned upon the island of Decima (or Deshima), and many a year brought financial loss to them there. How they were restricted in their operations and their daily lives has been admirably described by an American scholar.[8] In order to reduce expenses, they greatly reduced the number of trips to the Japanese court in the capital of Yedo (or Edo), and they humbly acquiesced in their shameful rôle of playing the part of Christians who did not dare to practice their religion openly. John Calvin would have turned over in his grave had he known what these so-called Calvinists were doing there in the eighteenth century and in the first half of the nineteenth. But they derived immense satisfaction from the fact that they could maintain intact their monopoly of the European trade with Japan. To have possessed such a monopoly for a period of 218 years was at least a proof of extraordinary tact and diplomacy. Their patience must have been inexhaustible.

As we now approach the time of Commodore Perry,

we might well study the significance of a statement published recently by a reputable university press in this country regarding the opening of Japan's door to western civilization:

"Most Americans are thoroughly convinced that Japan was introduced to Western culture by Matthew Calbraith Perry's visit of 1853. They believe that the Mikado's secluded Empire was stunned by the Commodore's display of modern guns, machinery and scientific wonders. . . . Almost none of these beliefs—accepted even by many professional historians—is true. Europe and America were no mysteries to Japan."[9]

Four years after the publication of this statement many leading newspapers in the United States published another statement, which although erroneous indicates how little the average American knows about the way in which the Japanese were first made acquainted with the culture of the West. In the summer of 1941 the public was informed by these newspapers that the University of California had just issued a book on the Dutch East Indies in which the author proved that the Japanese were taught western civilization by the Dutch before Commodore Perry visited their country.[10] The papers said nothing about the work done by the Portuguese and the English, and, most astonishing of all, the book in question does not really discuss the subject that is supposed to have made it so important at the present time. The papers should have mentioned instead an excellent book which deals exclusively with the subject under discussion. Although this book was written in English, it is not easily accessible to American readers, for which reason a part of its contents is summarized below.[11]

Contrary to the opinion expressed recently by a number of American and British writers, the Dutch in Japan were in a position to learn a great deal about that country and its inhabitants. We gather from the writings of Charles Peter Thunberg, who from 1775 to 1777 was a Swedish doctor in the service of the Dutch East India Company, that the captains of the Dutch vessels in the port of Nagasaki were freely permitted to walk about the streets of that great city. Until shortly before Thunberg's arrival these captains had been in the habit of wearing loose, flowing silk robes, which enabled them to smuggle into the city a number of forbidden goods. Likewise, they could also carry away with them prohibited articles. Several Dutch scholars visited Japan, notably Izaac Titsingh, who did so on three successive occasions (1779, 1781, and 1784), and translated into the Dutch language the *History of Imperial Dynasties in Japan.* He added valuable commentaries and corrections.

The Japanese were particularly impressed by the skill displayed by the Dutch physicians, some of whom prepared treatises on medicine which were translated into Japanese. Very interesting also is the book by Engelbert Kaempfer entitled, *The History of Japan,* in which the western world was rather fully informed about the flora, fauna, and minerals of Japan. He was a doctor employed in Japan by the Dutch East India Company. He arrived there in 1690, when the Dutch had reached the height of their prosperity and influence in that country. After several years of diligent study he returned to his native country, Germany, and published there his remarkable history.

It is true that until 1745 the study of the Dutch language by the Japanese scholars and officials was not encouraged. Consequently, little was known among them about the great contributions which the Dutch had recently made to mathematics, cartography, the natural sciences, international law, art, and religion. But when in 1745 the Japanese interpreters were advised by the Shogunal Government to become better acquainted with the

Dutch language and thus read the most important books published in Holland, the way was opened for the sudden influx of western civilization into Japan on a fairly large scale. From 1775 onward Dutch books were freely printed and circulated in Japan.

A few instances of this new revival of learning in Japan will reveal the scope of the influence exerted by the Dutch in that country. Takahashi Yoshitoki, one of Japan's foremost astronomers in the latter half of the eighteenth century, procured the Dutch edition of Lalande's work on astronomy which in 1711 had been published in Paris. With the use of this book and information gathered from various Dutch sources, this Japanese scholar was enabled to write a highly important and accurate book on astronomy. He also was instrumental in rendering valuable assistance to the surveyor, Ino Tadataka, who near the end of the eighteenth century during a period of twenty-two years made a survey of Japan.

Particularly in the popular geographical literature of Japan the Dutch influence is clearly reflected, but unfortunately this influence has seldom been mentioned by western historians. The contents of these popular books "are not to be despised, and taken as a whole they serve to show that there was far more information about the outside world available to educated Japanese than most historians will allow." Most of these books were printed at Yedo and Kyoto, and some of them at Osaka, but none of them at Nagasaki. One of the earliest works of this kind appeared in 1695.[12] It was a geographical compendium, or encyclopedia, in two volumes, describing the products and inhabitants of all the countries known to the Japanese at that time. Each country was given one paragraph, with the exception of Holland, which received eight pages. No other Japanese book had ever discussed the geography of foreign countries except China and Korea. In 1708 a second edition was published, made up of five volumes. It contained a world map showing New Guinea and New Holland as one large land-mass.

Well-known to all scholars interested in Japanese history is the famous work, *Sankoku Tsuran Zusetsu,* by Hayashi Shihei, which first appeared in 1785 at Yedo, with five folding maps, and later was translated into French and published in 1832 at Paris. The French edition reproduced the maps in a separate Atlas. In this book the author mentions the fact that the chief of the Dutch factory at Deshima on his visit to Nagasaki had shown him a Dutch book on geography.

After 1800 a large number of Japanese books dealing with geography and cartography were printed. Particularly heavy was the production in the period from 1830 to 1843. They indicate that the Japanese scholars had become very familiar with the writings of British, American, German, and French geographers. Through their window at Nagasaki the Japanese could look out upon the western world, thanks very largely to the efforts of the Dutch, who, although they had come there primarily as traders, exerted a tremendously powerful influence upon Japanese culture, in so far as this was affected by the civilization of the West.

In the field of military science the Dutch were directly the teachers of the Japanese. But it should be noted that the Dutch were not eager to part with certain military secrets, believing that their security in the Far East depended largely on the relative weakness of the oriental nations. As we have seen, the Shogun Ieyasu in 1600 made excellent use of the guns and ammunition he had found on board the Dutch vessel, *De Liefde.* He also employed Dutch gunners in the celebrated Battle of Sekigahara, which he won in October, 1600. The presents which the Shogun appreciated the most were guns and ammunition.

In 1615 the Hollanders cast at Hirado a cannon weighing 600 pounds. Twenty-two years later, when the Japanese government had to contend with a serious uprising, and, the Hollanders had to be relied on to quash the rebels, it was made clear that the Japanese themselves had not yet acquired a sufficient knowledge of military science. According to the diary of the chief of the Dutch factory at Hirado, on February 26, 1639, "one mortar was cast in the presence of the Lord of Hirado who had come thither for the express purpose of seeing it." On March 24, 1639, the Dutch chief left Hirado for the capital, taking with him as a present from the Dutch East India Company two large bronze mortars and a large quantity of ammunition. Three hundred coolies were used in the service of the Shogun in order to transport this material to Yedo. On June 21st the Hollanders proceeded with the shooting, which amazed all the courtiers. Great indeed was the gratitude of the Shogun, who sent messages of thanks to the Dutch chief and the local ruler of Hirado. In the next year, as the reader will recall, the Portuguese and all other Europeans were forced to leave Japan with the sole exception of the Hollanders.

But the latter, now that they had been compelled to leave Hirado, chose to adopt a more cautious attitude in teaching military secrets to the Japanese. For one thing, all European competition had ceased, and now they need not fear any longer that if they themselves refused to instruct the Japanese, the Portuguese or the English would do so. Between 1639 and 1649 no mortar-gunner was sent by the Dutch to Japan. Perhaps no further efforts in this direction might have been necessary if it had not been for the fact that in 1643 a Dutch force landed at Nambu on the northeast coast of Japan, much to the anger of the rulers. Besides, in 1644 the Dutch concluded a truce with the Portuguese, which also angered the Japanese. It be-

came necessary, therefore, to placate them by sending four
gunners, who remained in Yedo for about six months.
Here they taught the Japanese "fire works." After 1650,
however, a long period of peace set in, and when the
rulers became ever more used to the new order, they began
to forget how badly they used to be in need of assistance
rendered by the Hollanders. Not until the last quarter of
the eighteenth century did they once more turn with eager
interest to the study of military science.

After the appearance of the British frigate *Phaeton* in
the port of Nagasaki in 1808, the Japanese rulers began to
think seriously about the possibility of invasion by one or
more of the great western powers. They became so alarmed
at this thought that henceforth a large number of Dutch
books dealing with the science of warfare were translated
and published in Japan.

The phenomenal power displayed by the British Empire in the first half of the nineteenth century was not lost
upon the Japanese. They often turned to their Dutch
friends for information and advice. During the course of
the Anglo-Chinese "Opium War" (1840–1842) they were
particularly concerned about the growing might of Britain. The first question they asked of the Dutch was, How
many English soldiers were dispatched to China? In reply
the Hollanders explained how many ships were sent and
how many guns and men were carried on each. The second
question dealt with the manner in which the English
soldiers were armed. In the next question the Japanese
inquired into the nature of the soil upon which the battles
were fought; they wondered whether the English were
able to level out the hilly soil, which according to the
Dutch was well-nigh impossible. But what the British
could easily accomplish was to conquer many millions of
Chinese with an armed force of only four thousand, because the natives in the Far East were no match for the

Europeans. There was also a question about steamships
used by the British, another one about the shape of steamships, and still another one about the damage inflicted on
steamships through hits on the machinery. The Japanese
also wanted to know about the results of heavy storms, and
the Dutch replied that the winds occurring near Japan
were as nothing compared with those near the Cape of
Good Hope. In the last question the ownership of Australia was brought up, which was somewhat embarrassing
to the Dutch. They replied that New Holland was for the
most part uninhabited by Europeans, but that the English
had occupied a number of small sections.

The general supremacy of the Europeans was also demonstrated in the study of the sciences, especially medicine. Several schools of medicine were established in
Japan, as a result of the excellent work done by the Dutch.
These schools were called *Oranda,* that is, Dutch, or
Komo, meaning "Red Hair," for the Dutch were usually
referred to as the red-haired people. Of considerable importance was the visit of Caspar Schambergen, the Dutch
physician, to the imperial court at Yedo. Here in the
course of the year 1650 he taught medicine, land survey-
ing, and gunnery. The school of science he established was
named after him, *Caspar-rvu.* From 1650 to 1700 a considerable number of Japanese physicians visited Nagasaki,
in order to become better acquainted with the Dutch
system of medicine, which even in Europe ranked very
high. In 1665 the Dutch in Deshima presented Arashi-
yama Hoan, a retainer of the local ruler of Hirado, with a
certificate attesting his skill acquired from his Dutch
teachers. It is not surprising that during the annual visit
of the Hollanders at Yedo the physician attracted more
attention than the chief of the factory in Deshima.

Much has been written about the first book published
in Japan that may truly be considered scientific. It was

called *Kaitai Shinsho,* and was published in 1774, as a result of the anatomical studies of the Dutch in Japan. The book caused a veritable sensation at the time of its appearance. The Shogun himself received a copy of the original edition, which was made up of five volumes. The chief editor was Maeno Ryotaku, the *Rangakusha,* or Dutch scholar. The book was based upon a Dutch translation of the great work of Johann Adam Kulmus.

Such was the influence of the Hollanders in the fields of botany, zoology, mineralogy, physics, and chemistry that for a long time Japanese scholars applied to these fields the Latin names taught to them by the Dutch, namely, *Botanica, Zoologica, Mineralogica, Physica,* and *Chemica.* It was not until about 1870 that Japanese titles were given to these subjects. By 1750 a remarkable work on the natural sciences in twelve volumes was compiled by the physicians at the court of the Shogun, who for this purpose utilized extensive Dutch sources.

In the realm of international diplomacy and foreign affairs the official language of the Japanese was Dutch until 1870, and not until 1872 were the Dutch language schools subsidized by the government closed, to make room for those in which English, German, and French were taught.

It has long been fashionable to think of the Hollanders at Deshima as prisoners in a land far from home, restricted to such a degree that one wonders how they ever chose to bear such an awful lot. That is why the author of *Aliens in the East* devoted the following titles to two of his chapters: "Curbing the Dutchmen," and "Only Deshima is Dutch." This writer explains that the Hollanders were in no position to become acquainted with more than a minute section of Japan. But we must not lose sight of the fact that after the year 1700 the relations between the Japanese and the Hollanders became increasingly friendly. In the days of Kaempfer, whose famous *History of Japan* does not go beyond 1700, conditions were indeed very unpleasant for the Dutch. Such chiefs of the factory as Titsingh and Doeff, on the other hand, were treated by the Japanese as fully their equals. Doeff must have been astonished by the extremely cordial treatment which he received at a time when Holland was no longer an independent state and no more Dutch ships could reach Japan. While living in Nagasaki, he was completely at the mercy of the local officials, who kindly supplied him and his subordinates with money, clothes, and food. During the first decades of the nineteenth century the Dutch chiefs on their annual visits to the court at Yedo were no longer required to play like clowns in a circus for the amusement of the officials and their concubines in the capital. They were accorded the same status and honor as the *Daimyos,* who alone could be received in a formal audience. Perhaps a few of the Hollanders may have been annoyed by the eager on-lookers who persuaded them to write some remarkable Dutch word upon their fans or on small pieces of paper. But such is the life of famous persons everywhere. In Yedo the Hollanders resided in an hospice or inn called *Nagasaki-ya,* where they enjoyed many privileges.

Much could have been done for the benefit of the Dutch people as a whole if their representatives in Japan had been inclined to take advantage of their unique opportunities. But only a few of them were willing to look beyond their own purses. They refused to treat the Orientals as worthy of their friendship. Even some of the directors of the Dutch factory were mediocrities who were more attached to their whiskey than to their duties as representatives of a great republic. All the more praise should be given, therefore, to a man like Isaac Titsingh, the *opperhoofd,* or director, of the factory at Deshima. He first reached Nagasaki in 1779, and immediately struck up a friendship with the local interpreters. Of them he said:

"They manifested an eagerness to procure for me every practicable information, to consult in various matters beyond their capacity the best informed individuals among the magistrates and clergy, and to furnish me with books which might serve as a guide to my labors."

In Yedo the tactful scholar met a number of influential persons with whom he corresponded for the next twenty years. During his second term as director at Deshima (1781–1783) he obtained valuable commercial privileges from the government, particularly that of exporting a larger quantity of copper from Japan each year. He was highly honored by the Shogun himself, and of the Prince of Satsuma, father-in-law of the Shogun, he wrote: "The Prince used our alphabet in his letters to express what he did not wish a third person to understand." Many prominent officials gladly learned the Dutch language at that time, and they read a large number of Dutch books. He was the most learned man ever employed by the Dutch in Japan. Partly for that reason it would be well if future historians would pay a little more attention to what he wrote and experienced, and a little less attention to Kaempfer, who lived at a time when the Dutch were suffering intense humiliation in Japan.

When the time came at last for the Dutch in Japan to yield part of their monopoly to other western powers, they were still in a position to exert great influence upon the Japanese rulers in their dealings with these foreign powers. The first Japanese warships were presented to the government by the Dutch, and the first negotiations with the United States, Great Britain, and other nations of Europe and America were carried on through the Dutch interpreters.[13] In the period from 1853 to 1859, when the Japanese rulers showed signs of unreasonable stubbornness, the Dutch officials at the court persuaded the former to make friendly overtures to the great western powers.[14]

But it is in the Malay Archipelago that the Dutch have achieved their greatest success as colonizers and empire-builders. From the very beginning they had set their heart upon the conquest of these rich islands. Nothing at first was known about the discovery of petroleum and tin, nor about the manufacture of rubber. It was the demand for spices that impelled the Dutch to concentrate nearly all their energies on the lucrative trade thus provided for them. The occupation of Ceylon and Formosa were only of secondary importance. The factory in Japan was but a small branch of the main office at Batavia. The explorations along the coasts of Australia and New Zealand caused little enthusiasm. But Java became and remained the center of activities in the Far East, and the Far East was the main attraction in the whole world.

After the fall of the East India Company, the Dutch government took over its assets. In 1824 it agreed with the British on some important transfers of territory in the East Indies, as embodied in the Treaty of London. Great Britain received from the Dutch the port of Singapore together with Malacca, that is, the southern portion of the Malay Peninsula. The Hollanders also surrendered to Great Britain their establishments on the mainland of India, but in return they obtained undisputed possession of northern Sumatra. Little did the Dutch know at that time how a century later the British would fortify Singapore and thus provide the Dutch with adequate protection against the Japanese. But at the time when the treaty was signed, there was much disappointment in the Netherlands. The loss of Singapore in particular was keenly felt.[15] Much consolation, however, was derived from the fact that the British had agreed not to establish factories in the Dutch East Indies. For the first time the Dutch had given up their possessions to the north of the archipelago, while the British had entirely withdrawn from the islands.

In the period after 1824 there occurred minor agreements and disputes. Upon the whole it may be said that the British and the Dutch gradually became more friendly toward each other. It had taken them almost exactly two centuries since the treaty of 1619 to arrive at a satisfactory arrangement. Since the Hollanders were so partial to Java and the other spice islands, they could devote themselves heart and soul to the exploitation of the same.

Many centuries ago a great teacher sagely remarked: "Where your treasure is, there shall be your heart also." This was true especially of the Hollanders, for they wept few tears when in 1667 they surrendered in a peace settlement with England the Hudson Valley in North America, thinking that they acquired in its place something that was far more valuable, namely, the western half of Guiana in South America. Again, in 1815, when they lost most of Guiana to the British, besides Ceylon and Cape Colony, they obtained sufficient satisfaction from the remnant of their vast colonial empire of the past. They wanted above all some tropical colonies in southern Asia. It was there that they had begun their colonial ventures, thinking of South Africa, Ceylon, Australia, and Japan as mere branches of their tropical realm. Their "India" was to them a dear treasure.

During the first three quarters of the nineteenth century the Dutch government permitted commercial companies to exploit the rich resources of the East Indies. In many instances the natives were not treated with proper consideration. The majority of the Hollanders in the Far East were still bent upon financial gains largely to the exclusion of other benefits. The administration of the Dutch East Indies in that period left much to be desired. But eventually a more liberal policy was adopted, with the result that since 1875 the Dutch have become famous for their enlightened form of colonial administration. Java and Bali have often been referred to as a veritable paradise upon earth.

Although in the early years of conquest the Hollanders were attracted very largely by the spices grown in the East Indies, during the nineteenth century they and the natives became ever more interested in the production of rice, coffee, sugar, tobacco, tea, and indigo. Gradually government enterprise was overtaken by exploitation begun by corporations, such as the famous *Nederlandsche Handelmaatschappij*, the *Handelsvereeniging Amsterdam*, and the *Nederlandsch Indische Handelsbank*. These corporations leased grants of land, furnished capital, and opened up large plantations, where natives were employed at extremely low wages.

The opening of the Suez Canal in 1869 gave a great impetus to big business in the Far East. Until this date the vast majority of Dutchmen had acquiesced in government control of the production of the staple products in the Indies. But after 1869 the spirit of private enterprise once more asserted itself. The East India Company was gone, never to return. But its place was taken by the Netherlands Trading Company, together with some of the lesser corporations. Much attention was given in the Netherlands to the possibility of gainful occupations for the younger generation of Hollanders. Perhaps the days of Coen might return. But at the same time both the Liberals and the Conservatives (Catholic and Anti-Revolutionary Parties) emphasized the need of humanitarian reforms.

As a result of these forces the Agrarian Law of 1870 was passed, stipulating that henceforth most of the land in the East Indies was to remain in the hands of the natives, who actually owned the property. But Dutch and other capitalists might lease land for a period of 75 years. In 1860 slavery in the Netherlands Indies was abolished, while in 1879 and 1880 enlightened labor legislation was introduced which offered more protection to labor and capital.

In the meantime native princes gradually lost much of their political power, and the administration of the whole area from the capital at Batavia became more effective and powerful. Under the benevolent rule of the Dutch government after 1870, agriculture and commerce expanded on a large scale. Between 1815 and 1845 the population of Java was doubled, and the same happened again during the next thirty years, while from 1880 to 1900 it increased from 19 to 28 million. Irrigation, improvement in transportation, and better instruction in the public schools added to the value of the natural resources.

Mining had been rather slow to develop, but now much was also done in this direction. As early as 1710 the Dutch discovered a valuable deposit of tin on the island of Banka, located not far from the great port of Singapore. The mines were worked for many decades, but little profit was derived from these operations until in 1850 a new company was founded for the mining of tin. In 1852 this company obtained a concession for forty years in the island of Billiton, which the Dutch in the Treaty of London of 1824 had secured in compensation for losing Singapore and the southern portion of the Malay Peninsula.

The mining of coal proved fairly profitable in Borneo, where from 1846 to 1859 considerable activity occurred. But a massacre of Europeans in 1859 frightened the investors, who now turned to the newly discovered coal fields in Sumatra, especially that near Padang. Since nothing could be done without railway transportation to Padang, the government in 1891 had to take over the mines in this area. Little was accomplished until after 1900, when a marked demand for fuel created a new exploitation. The following figures indicate the continued trend of expansion in the first three decades of the twentieth century: in 1890: 8,000 metric tons; in 1900: 203,000 tons; in 1913: 567,000 tons; in 1920: 1,095,000 tons; in 1925: 1,400,000 tons; in 1930: 1,870,000 tons. The reader will observe, however, that these figures are not impressive as compared with the production of coal even in the tiny mother country in Europe.

Quite different was the situation with regard to the production of gasoline. Although the existence of large deposits were known to the colonial government as early as 1863, prospectors could find no large ones until suddenly they made remarkable discoveries in Borneo, Sumatra, and Java. This happened shortly after 1880, and in 1883 the first concession was granted to a person named Zijlker, who was not able to attract sufficient capital, and had to turn to the government for support. But by 1890 he had made enough progress to found the famous Royal Dutch Company. Another important person in the oil industry was Munten, who discovered very large deposits in Borneo. But finding no adequate support in Holland he went to England, where he met Sir Marcus Samuel and with him founded a company named afterward the Shell Petroleum Company. A terrific struggle followed with a number of competing companies, which led the directors of the two large companies just mentioned to join forces. It was stipulated that 60 per cent of the capital was to be the property of the Royal Dutch Company and 40 per cent that of the Shell Company.

Ambitious American capitalists now entered upon the scene, with the result that the Standard Oil Co. in 1912 founded at Palembang in Sumatra the Dutch Colonial Petroleum Co. The Japanese, not to be outdone entirely, proceeded with the founding of a company of their own as well, namely, the Borneo Oil Co., established in 1930. Production figures for 1930 were as follows: total production in the Dutch East Indies: 5,531,000 metric tons, of which the Royal Dutch-Shell Co. owned 4,670,000, the Dutch Colonial Petroleum Co. 609,000, and the State Netherlands India Co. 240,000.

In recent years the production of oil in the Dutch East Indies has greatly enhanced the importance of this region. With Japan so near and so eager to obtain as much of the supply as possible; and with the British colonies in the Far East equally anxious to get a goodly share of the production, the Dutch have been placed in a position of a real world power. It was not for nothing that President F. D. Roosevelt in 1941 remarked: "If our government had not supplied the Japanese with some of their needs, they would have been impelled to invade the Dutch East Indies, and we would have had war." The president implied also that in 1939 the Dutch East Indies were not yet ready to defend themselves against the Japanese.

One reason why the United States has been so vitally interested in the Dutch East Indies is that much of the stock of the Royal-Dutch Shell Co. is owned by American citizens. Furthermore, large American investments in tobacco plantations in Sumatra account for some of our anxiety. Sumatra produces some of the finest tobacco ever known. But even more important for us is the rubber and tin which we buy each year in the Dutch East Indies. The greater we can make our share, the smaller will be that of our potential enemies.

Rubber production until 1942 was dependent on the agreement made at regular intervals by the British and the Dutch, who for some decades have controlled nearly the whole of the world's production. Since Great Britain is a much greater European power than is the Netherlands, it seemed fitting for the British to control more than one-half of the combined rubber production, just as in recent years the British government has insisted that in the Royal-

Dutch Shell Co. more than half of the stock shall be British-owned rather than Dutch. The Dutch East Indies could easily supply all of the world's needs of rubber, but the agreement just mentioned specified that some 60 per cent of the world production was to be in the hands of the British. In the year 1935 exports of rubber from the Dutch East Indies were valued at 70 million guilders (florins), and in 1937 the figure was 208 million, a guilder being worth about 55 cents. Sumatra and Java produced most of the Dutch share, while the British grew theirs in the Malay Peninsula.

Nearly all of the tin mined in the Dutch East Indies comes from the islands of Banka and Billiton. During the years of depression from 1930 to 1937 the colonial government had to subsidize the mining of tin, and even now the Billiton Co. is partly owned and operated by the government. Much of the tin from these two islands was smelted in Singapore, but some of that mined in Banka was smelted there. The British produced a little more than the Dutch did, while Bolivia has been also a heavy producer.

The Dutch did rather poorly in the field of shipping during the first three quarters of the nineteenth century. But when in 1888 the *Koninklijke Paketvaart Maatschappij* was founded, the situation suddenly took a turn for the better. It was high time that the Dutch regained their proper share in the sea power and shipping in the southern Pacific. During the first ten years after the opening of the Suez Canal, British ships dominated even the waters of *Insulinde,* for the Dutch were much too reluctant to replace their slowly moving sailing vessels with steamships. "The whole traffic was dominated by the Netherlands Indies Steamship Co., which by this time (1878) was linked up with the British-India Steamship Co. The headquarters were in London, no ships were built in Holland, nor even a boiler renewed."[16]

Since the Netherlands Indies Steamship Co. had enjoyed a practical monopoly of the shipping controlled by the government and often abused its privileges, the government in 1891 transferred this privilege to the newly founded company (often referred to by the Dutch as the K.P.M.). From 1872 to 1893 excellent port facilities were constructed at Batavia, which now has a population exceeding the half million mark. Moreover, from 1886 to 1893 the port called Emmahaven was constructed to enable the producers of coal at Padang in Sumatra to ship their product more cheaply. Numerous railway lines were also built at this time and during the next three decades.

By 1902 the K.P.M. operated 45 ships, and during the next ten years the number was increased to 80. The World War of 1914 placed the Dutch in a very favorable position to regain some of their lost shipping, at least in the three years of it. After the final peace settlement the Hollanders continued to take advantage of their newly found opportunities, so that by 1930 the number of ships employed by the Royal Packet Co. was 113 steamships and 32 motor ships. In addition to its numerous short runs within the archipelago, it began to operate lines to Burma and Australia. In 1902 the Java-China-Japan Line was founded, which did a thriving business during the following thirty-five years. In 1930 it used 19 passenger ships and carried valuable cargoes between Europe and the Far East. Such was the nature of commercial expansion in the Dutch East Indies that between 1900 and 1930 the number of ships calling at the harbor of Batavia (called Tandjong Priok) increased from 800 to 3134. As a result of this extraordinary development, new harbors were constructed at Sourabaya, the second port of Java; and Semarang, located on the central coast of northern Java. Furthermore, even at Macassar in southern Celebes it became necessary to improve port facilities.

During the first world war the officials in the colonial government at Batavia realized that the Dutch East Indies, cut off from the outside world in times of such a conflict, should become more self-sufficient. Consequently, many new industries were founded, which produced large quantities of cement, carbide, gas, beer, biscuits, vermicelli, etc. It appears very likely that in the near future the standard of living among the natives will rise considerably and will create a huge demand for plumbing supplies and household utensils.

In the period from 1870 to 1914 the Dutch were greatly worried about the increasing amount of British capital invested in their East Indies. By 1912, for example, the British owned 50 rubber companies in Java out of a total of 101. But the World War of 1914 checked the expansion of British investments in the Dutch East Indies, while at the same time the Dutch intensified their efforts to gain a larger share for themselves. Interesting are the following figures for the year 1929: Dutch capital invested: 1,536 million guilders; British: 278 million; French and Belgian: 112 million; American: 53 million; Japanese: 20 million; German: 18 million.[17]

CHAPTER VIII

THE UNITED STATES AND THE DUTCH EAST INDIES

THE three thousand islands that comprise the Dutch East Indies have been of inestimable value to the United States in the present war. If there had been nothing but water between Manila and Singapore, our valiant soldiers fighting under the superb command of General Douglas MacArthur would have had little incentive for their amazing stand on the Bataan Peninsula. They fought for time in which our government could bring up reinforcements to the Dutch East Indies, from where our men were to attack the Japanese. These Dutch islands have a combined area of some 750,000 square miles—that is, four times as much as the whole of Japan. They constitute a huge barrier between Japan and the Indian Ocean, and they form a multitude of bases suitable for future attacks upon the land of the rising and the setting sun.

Moreover, these fabulously rich islands support a population of seventy million who are now looking with eager anticipation to the day when the Yanks will come to free them from the threat of Japanese aggression and brutal exploitation. The natives are intensely loyal to Queen Wilhelmina, who, as they all know, is living in exile upon foreign soil—in the same British capital where her ancestor, Prince William V of the House of Orange, found refuge under very similar circumstances. In his day it was Napoleon who strutted upon the prostrate bodies of untold multitudes. Now it is another conqueror, but a man with the same unlimited ambition to rule the whole of Europe and to wreck the British Empire. Under Napoleon the French humbled the Germans, and under Hitler the Germans have humiliated the French. In each case the Dutch people lost their own country together with all or a large part of their colonial empire. But whereas in Napoleon's time it was the British who seized the Dutch colonies, now the Dutch are relying upon the British to save their East Indian empire. Now the British themselves are in mortal danger—such as they have not known since the eleventh century. For this reason the many millions of natives in the Dutch East Indies are hoping and praying that their queen will be restored to her throne with the aid of the Americans. In other words, our soldiers in the Far East will not only find admirable bases of operations against the Japanese but also seventy million persons who will receive them as allies and deliverers.

There is still another factor to be considered in the immense value of the Dutch East Indies to us. The men who were placed in charge of the armed forces in that region had behind them a tradition of extraordinary efficiency going back to the beginning of the seventeenth century, when the Dutch first arrived upon the scene as conquerors and empire builders. They were ready even before the treacherous enemy had time to dash upon them and stab them in the back. More than three hundred years of continued vigilance brought the Dutch huge rewards when their own forces of 120,000 men faced the fury of one hundred million Japanese. Well did the *London Times* at the end of January, 1942, testify: "They alone of all the Allies were fully armed in their own defense and ready for the attack which fell on them, and they have played their part from the first with exemplary skill, courage, and determination." Equally generous and appreciative was the verdict of A. V. Alexander, First Lord of the British Admiralty, who at that same time in a letter addressed to a Dutch official wrote: "The Dutch East Indian forces have shown, as they did against us many years ago, that they are brave, tough, and skillful fighters." What also pleased this particular British observer was the scorched earth policy employed by the Dutch, thus depriving the Japanese of the oil they needed so badly. In short, during the time that we ourselves were in no position to revenge the notorious attack upon Pearl Harbor, the Dutch East Indies provided for us a much needed breathing-space in which we could get ready for the grand knock-out blow to the Japanese and the Nazis. The land was there, the native population needed support, and the European leaders were doing all in their power to hold the aggressors at bay.

From a point far to the west of Singapore stretching eastward to the center of huge New Guinea, which lies east of the Philippines—the Dutch East Indies cover a vast area of both land and sea. If this empire of the Dutch in the Far East had been a large continent, the Japanese would have encountered little difficulty in conquering it. But immense numbers of ships were required to subdue the island of Java, where the Allied Nations established the headquarters for the defense of their stake in the Orient. This island, smaller than the state of Michigan, supports a population of over forty-five million, despite the fact that 90 per cent of the people depend upon agriculture for a living. These astounding figures will give some idea as to the natural resources of the Dutch East Indies and the difficulties that will be experienced by the Japanese in trying to subdue the native population. Even if they were not to be disturbed by the Americans, their task would require years of bloody conquest and bestial persecution. The Hollanders would continue indefinitely to pounce from their secret aerial bases upon the hundreds of ships which the Japanese would have to employ constantly. You can easily imagine what the end will be for the Japanese when once our own pilots appear with thousands of new airplanes to wrest from the enemy the places conquered by him thus far and then to pursue him into the bay upon whose shore stands Tokio.

All of these things are to a considerable extent familiar to the average American citizen. The newspapers and magazines which he or she had read during the past two months have sung the praises of the Dutch in the East Indies and have also told of the rubber, tin, gasoline, coal, tobacco, tea, and spices that are produced there in great abundance. Some day the island of Sumatra will have a population of one hundred and fifty million, while Borneo and New Guinea will also teem with agricultural and mining activity. Nowhere else could we find such a wealth of raw materials for our own industries and at the same time such a friendly reception for our manufactured products. If our leaders add consummate tact and good will to the armed forces which are sure to be sent there, we shall be able to reduce unemployment in this country to the vanishing point. Thus we face the possibility of warding off another economic depression as a result of the flow of merchandise and raw materials across the Pacific Ocean. Never before in the world's history has such a volume of trade been realized, and naturally the general public in this country follows with great interest the exploits of our fighters in the Far East. To add new wealth to a great military victory, would seem almost too good to be true. But if these things were accomplished this war would not have been fought in vain as far as the United States is concerned. Is it any wonder then that our newspapers delineate with great care what occurs from day to day in the Far East, while the campaign of the British in Libya, which used to attract so much attention in this country, seems to have lost nearly all of its importance?

While these speculations pass through the minds of a great many Americans, the historian pauses to reconstruct the events that have produced the present situation in the

Old World. He reads documents which show how the great nations of the past have come and gone, to make room for others. Thousands of little incidents can be put together in the same manner as we sometimes solve a crossword puzzle. Certain questions occur to the historian which are seldom discussed in our newspapers but which nevertheless turn out to be very interesting and instructive when we take the time to answer them. For example, let us consider this question, Why did the Japanese fail or refuse to attack the Dutch East Indies during the first two weeks after the incident at Pearl Harbor?

We all know very well that the Japanese are much closer to the Dutch East Indies than we are. Consequently, they must be more vitally concerned with the future of these islands than we happen to be. Why is it then that they seemed so reluctant to bomb Batavia rather than Manila? Our newspapers have pointed out the bravery of the Dutch fighters. We have been told repeatedly that the Dutch were fully prepared while the Americans and the British were by no means ready. As a result we have been led to believe that the Japanese did not dare to attack these strongly fortified Dutch places; they picked out the weaker ones first. All of this is very flattering to the Dutch, but our question remains for the most part unanswered until we look much farther below the surface of world events.

As we survey the long history of the Japanese people we are struck by age-long ties of friendship between Japan and one of the western powers, namely, the Dutch Republic, or Holland, which after 1815 has been known as the Netherlands. Beginning with the year 1600, this friendship lasted until the end of the nineteenth century. From 1641 to 1859, as we saw, the Hollanders were the only Europeans who were permitted to trade in Japan. Such was their tact and their tenacity that they suffered untold humiliations rather than give up their business relations with the Japanese.

The Japanese are well aware of these facts. Like the Chinese, they have great respect for their ancestors. They have been taught that at one time the Dutch were the benefactors of Japan. They have often told the Dutch in recent years that they would rather have them rule the Malay Archipelago than any other power. During the first half of the year 1941 they were still trying to maintain friendly relations with the Dutch and to wean them away from their allies, the British. What they wanted was peaceful penetration of the Dutch East Indies after having driven the Americans out of the Philippines and the British out of the Malay Peninsula and Singapore. Furthermore, the Nazis were the allies of the Japanese and Holland was to be united with Germany. At least some of the Dutch islands were to become German.

Why did the Dutch refuse to cooperate with the Japanese? The answer is not hard to find. The Dutch have been comparing Hitler with Napoleon. Their ruler is in exile again, once more in Great Britain. The people want to be delivered from German oppression. They are furious whenever they hear of further reverses suffered by their fellow-countrymen in the Far East. Unlike the British, their heart was always set upon colonial conquest in the Far East. They did not mind losing the Hudson Valley, but their beloved East Indies have seemed almost sacred to them. They have had to choose between the United States and Japan, and for obvious reasons they preferred us. Their sagacity in making this choice should convince the most pessimistic soul in this country that in the end Uncle Sam will emerge wholly victorious. Thus in a final sense the Dutch have become our invaluable ally.

The European mother country naturally can no longer hope to control the lion's share in the export and import trade of the East Indies. Some ten thousand miles separate these two parts of the Kingdom of the Netherlands. Only nine million inhabitants live in Europe, and nearly seventy million in the East Indies. Japan, with ten times as many inhabitants as the Netherlands in Europe, and being situated so much closer to the Asiatic dominion, draws to itself in normal times a very large share of the trade. The United States, as we have just observed, also does an immense amount of business with this region. It would seem to the writer that the United States must make an effort to forestall the Japanese in making very close connections with this fabulously rich dominion. Here is room for two hundred million people, who will want to sell to us their tin, rubber, tobacco, sugar, coffee, tea, quinine, indigo, peper, cinnamon, nutmeg, and rice. We could sell them an immense amount of machinery, plumbing supplies, radios, household utensils, building materials, automobiles, and sundry other articles. We could exchange cotton and some fruits for the raw materials of the East Indies. In this manner we would tide ourselves over periods of depression without suffering such terrific times of unemployment as we witnessed in the years 1931–1936.

Perhaps some gentle soul might argue that we would not want to deprive a small country such as the Netherlands of its legitimate share in the trade with its own dominion in Asia. The Hollanders shed their blood in the conquest of the archipelago. They spent an immense amount of energy in building roads, searching for minerals, establishing refineries, founding schools, and other fine institutions. Why should we turn imperialistic and rob them of their treasure? The plain figures of the years gone by, however, make such a process of reasoning superfluous. From 1830 to 1930 the share of the mother country in the export trade of the East Indies fell from

52.5 per cent to 15.3 per cent; and in the import trade from 41.9 to 16.8 per cent. This loss was not caused by imperialistic Americans. The latter have been a boon to both the native population and the European inhabitants. Trade relations between the United States and the South American republics could never produce such happy results as the commerce between our country and the Dutch East Indies. For that reason and others just given we must conclude that as soon as the fear of depression and unemployment haunts us again, we should think a little more often about the Dutch in the Far East. They need us there, and we need their products. In matters of religious and political liberty they gave us a splendid example to follow, but now they are looking to us for leadership in the future. The writer sincerely hopes that such leadership will soon be forthcoming.

How deeply interested the Hollanders themselves are in attracting commercial contacts with the United States may be gathered from the perusal of the periodical entitled *Knickerbocker Weekly,* which has appeared under the auspices of several important Dutch commercial establishments. In the issue of October 20, 1941, we read this illuminating statement: "That the Netherlands East Indies are second only to Great Britain and its dominions as a customer of the United States was made clear in an article by Eugene Hess which appeared in the *New York Herald-Tribune* recently." Moreover, Professor A. A. L. Rutgers, in an interesting article on the development of the Dutch East Indies in the reign of Queen Wilhelmina, published in *Neerlandia* for November, 1938, referred to the fact that from 1898 to 1937 the share of the mother country in the import trade declined from 36 to 18 per cent, and in the export trade from 36 to 13 per cent. He also indicated that in the year 1935 the figures for the import and export trades were respectively 12 and 7 per cent, but owing to more energetic measures adopted by the Dutch in Europe a very marked improvement was shown in 1937. He made this remark: "One may lament the steady decline in the share of the mother country, but this decline must be regarded as the inevitable result of the development of the East Indies as a part of Eastern Asia." On the one hand we note the enormous increase in the export to the great powers, and on the other hand the growing importance of the Japanese trade. Professor Rutgers emphasizes the effect of certain methods employed by Japanese merchants who cheapened their products and thus made heavy inroads upon the home market.

The years of crisis, so he continued, had come to an end so very recently that there was no need to say much about them to Hollanders. He was still worried about the Japanese competition, and reminded his readers of the strong steps that had to be taken by the colonial government in order to check the flood of Japanese imports. In comparing conditions prevailing in 1938 with those of 1898, when Queen Wilhelmina ascended the throne, he showed that the year 1898 ended the period of government control of trade and industry, but that 1938 came at the beginning of a new era of very extensive government supervision. During the forty years of free trade the imports of the Dutch East Indies increased from 168 to 490 million guilders, and the exports from 217 to 989 million guilders. Nowhere did Professor Rutgers express concern about the growing trade with the United States.

Of particular interest to Americans in the study of hygienic improvement in the Dutch East Indies. Whereas in 1898 millions of Europeans and Americans dreaded to think of the unpleasant climate in this tropical region, in and after 1938 infectious diseases have been drastically checked. At the end of the nineteenth century there was only one satisfactory supply of drinking water, while today there are more than 250. There are also more than 600 hospitals, with at least 50,000 beds. Equally striking are the figures which indicate the improvement in education. From 1898 to 1938 the number of pupils in the schools rose from 70,000 to 2,000,000. More than twenty thousand excellent schools provide instruction for both natives and Europeans, and many are the high schools and technical schools. Three universities have recently been founded.

The year 1941 has indeed been a landmark of importance in the history of the Dutch East Indies. More and more the Hollanders have begun to rely upon contacts with the United States. Particularly in Los Angeles and New York the leading commercial companies have opened branch offices. Here the colonies of Hollanders have for the first time since 1664 (when New Amsterdam became New York) felt bold and aggressive enough to be equal to all competitors. The appearance of the *Knickerbocker Weekly* in that year was definitely a sign that a new era had dawned upon the Dutch empire in the Far East. An alliance between American and Dutch interests was established, which bids fair to have very important repercussions in the Far East. Even after the conclusion of the present world conflict the ties that bind American economic interests to the growth of economic power in the Dutch East Indies will continue to increase in strength. For this reason it behooves us all to watch with keen appreciation the expansion of commerce and industry in the Dutch East Indies.

Of particular importance also is the establishment in New York City of the institution called The Netherlands Information Bureau. It has recently issued an attractive booklet entitled, *The Netherlands East Indies,* profusely illustrated and attractively written. It contains a chapter on the commerce with the United States, which is reproduced below.

The Netherlands East Indies is one of the richest parts of the world. It has the advantage of combining a great wealth of raw materials with the agricultural productivity of the tropics. Thus it can maintain a large population without much difficulty on a reasonable standard of living, without exporting those materials which are needed by other parts of the world.

Three of those materials, in particular, are always connected with the Indies—quinine, rubber and tin. Netherlands India is the world's leading source of cinchona, the raw material for quinine. It is grown mainly in the western section of Java and in several districts of Sumatra. Originally the trees grew only in South America and the bark is still commonly referred to as Peruvian bark. In the latter part of the nineteenth century unsatisfactory conditions of production and shipping in South America threatened the world supply of quinine, the only reliable treatment for malaria. This induced British and Dutch officials to begin cinchona cultivation in Southeast Asia.

The first plantations in British Malaya were not successful. In Netherlands India, however, constant research and experimentation was carried on and today more than 90 per cent of the world's supply of the bark comes from the Indies. The islands' production is regulated by the government through a system of licenses which are granted periodically to cinchona estate companies. This is to insure regular production, prevent an over-supply and stabilize the price level.

Before the invasion of the Low Countries, most of the cinchona bark was sent to the factories in Holland for the manufacture of quinine salts. There was, however, a small but growing factory in Bandung. Since May 1940, when all shipments to the Netherlands ceased, the Bandung factory has been expanded and today it takes up most of the cinchona production. Though cinchona and quinine are shipped to all parts of the world, the leading consumers are British India, Burma, China, the United States, Great Britain, the Balkan countries and Japan.

Southeast Asia produces more than 90 per cent of the world's supply of rubber, with the remainder coming chiefly from India and Ceylon. Netherlands India alone accounted for nearly 40 per cent of that supply in 1940, almost paralleling the production of British Malaya, for years the world's leader.

As was true of the cinchona tree, South America was the native habitat of rubber. The first plants were introduced into Southeast Asia in the latter part of the nineteenth century, or at about the same time as cinchona seeds. In Netherlands India rubber is grown by natives on small plots of land as well as by European and American companies. The chief producing regions are located on the island of Sumatra, in the western and southeastern parts of Borneo and in several districts of Java.

For the past seven years rubber production has been subject to international control. This was introduced as a means of coping with problems of over-production and cut-throat competition between the various rubber producing countries. An international committee consisting of representatives of the main producers determines, according to a basic production quota, the amount each country may export each year.

Another essential product from Southeast Asia—and more particularly from Netherlands India—is tin. This region produces around 65 per cent of the world's tin supply which is vital in the manufacture of many an industrial standby such as electrical equipment, tubing and piping, tin foil, soldering, galvanizing, cans, etc.

Like rubber, tin production is subject to international control to stabilize output and price. Each member country of the International Tin Committee is allotted a quota which it may export during each quarter year. Though Netherlands India accounts for only around 20 per cent of the world's supply, the Dutch are perhaps the world's most efficient producers. During the early part of the present war when the International Tin Committee constantly raised export quotas to meet rising wartime demand for the product, the Indies was the only member which could fill and even surpass its allotted share. The mines are located on the islands of Banka, Billiton and Singkep off the Sumatra coast and are for the most part owned and operated by the Dutch government. Outside Southeast Asia the only tin regions of any importance are Bolivia and the Belgian Congo. Yet, the supply from Bolivia and the Belgian Congo probably would not be sufficient to meet wartime demand if the supply from Southeast Asia were suddenly cut off.

An important factor in tin production are the tin smelters to work the ore into material fit for industrial use. Before the war, much of Netherlands India's tin was sent to Holland to be smelted despite the fact that there were large smelters at Singapore and Penang. Since September, 1939, however, increasing quantities have been worked at Singapore and the tin exported directly from that part of the world. With the closing of smelters in Europe and the consequent scarcity of such plants in the world, the United States government decided to begin the construction of a smelting plant in Texas which is to be completed and in operation in the near future.

Aside from quinine, rubber and tin the Netherlands Indies also ranks as a source of other important tropical products such as sugar, spices, copra, fibers, tapioca, tobacco, coffe and tea. Copra from the Indies, for instance, is considered one of the best qualities on the world market. It is cultivated mostly by natives in various sections of Sumatra, Celebes, the Moluccas and other scattered areas of the Archipelago. Nearly 30 per cent of the world's copra comes from these islands. Most of the copra and its derivatives, coconut oil and copra cakes—a cattle fodder— was shipped to Europe. These shipments have, of course, been stopped. The situation among the native population who depended upon coconut cultivation as a source of livelihood, at first was very serious. Since copra is an important source of fat, with a variety of uses, and since its consumption is expected to increase after the war, the Netherlands Indies government decided to aid coconut growers and thereby prevent the entire cessation of its cultivation. Large warehouses are now being constructed to store the copra which the government buys from producers, and which it plans to sell when there will once again be demand for this commodity.

For hundreds of years Netherlands India, and more particularly Java, has been famous for its coffee. Today the beverage is still commonly referred to as "Java." It is grown by natives on their own plots and by European estate companies in Java and Sumatra and also in various smaller islands. Before the war most of Netherlands Indie's coffee was shipped to Europe. When shipments to the European Continent ceased, however, the islands' product suffered a loss of markets. Dutch authorities therefore decided to buy up a major portion of the coffee production; what cannot be sold immediately is, as in the case of copra, stored away until more favorable times.

Long ago the East Indies was called the Spice Islands because it was the main pepper producing region in the world. Today, the islands account for 85 per cent of total world production; smaller quantities are produced in other areas of Southeast Asia. The two kinds, black and white pepper, come from the same plant and differ only in method of preparation. Black pepper is dried with the skin, pulp and all, and is piled in heaps and trampled upon so as to separate the stalks from the berries. White pepper, on the other hand, is prepared by removing the outer covering and pulp through fermentation. Cultivation is done mainly by natives, white pepper being grown on the island of Banka, in Bendulen and in the western and southeastern parts of Borneo, and black pepper being produced on Sumatra.

Of the other spices produced in Netherlands India, nutmeg is the most important, making up about three-quarters of the world's supply. It is cultivated mostly in the Molucca islands. Mace is the red leafy cover enclosing the nut. Nutmeg is also edible when made into jam or preserves. Other spices grown include cloves, vanilla, cinnamon and ginger.

The East Indies is the world's largest producer of sugar, being exceeded only by Cuba. Cane is grown only in Java, for the most part by Dutch companies. Owing to the well-developed organization of the industry and more particularly to scientific research and experimentation, Java has reached the highest production per space unit of all sugar countries in the world. A notable feature of the Java industry is the management staff's familiarity with all the various branches of factory and plantation work, for which men are trained in special schools. Domestic production is controlled by an Association for Sugar Sales, known as the N.I.V.A.S.; all sugar producers are members of this organization which stabilizes the price level and prevents cut-throat competition. Sugar exports are also subject to international control.

Netherlands India began tea cultivation early in the nineteenth century and today ranks among the foremost producers. This fact is seldom known to the consumer who generally associates tea with Japan, China and Ceylon. Yet Netherlands India's export is greater than that of China or Japan and is surpassed only by British India and

Ceylon. The increasing production and improvement in tea qualities during the past few years was made possible largely through the work of the experimental station at Buitenzorg (in Java.) In commercial circles, tea is now known under the various qualities such as "broken," "Leaf teas," "fannings," and "dust." As with the other chief products, tea exports are subject to international control. Ever since trade with the European Continent ceased, exports of tea have declined. This was offset, however, when in the summer of 1940 and again early in 1941 the British government signed an agreement with the Netherlands government for the purchase of a certain fixed amount of Netherlands Indies' tea to be delivered within a specified period.

An excellent example of the efficiency of Dutch enterprise in developing the potentialities of their island empire in the Pacific, is illustrated by the cultivation of the oil palm. This tree originally grew in equatorial Africa. According to one story, an interested traveler took a small tree back to the Indies to plant it for ornamental purposes. The commercial value of its cultivation was soon discovered. At the present time Netherlands India is the largest exporter of palm oil. The manufacturing of the palm fruit into oil is an interesting process. The bunches of fruit are put into large drums for sterilization; this frees them of their stems, thus facilitating the threshing process which is done by machine without bruising the individual fruits. The fleshy mass around the kernel is then loosened under steam heat and is later pressed to obtain the oil. The waste material given off in the process has as yet little commercial value and is used only as fuel. The palm oil itself is used principally in the manufacture of soap, candles and margarine.

Netherlands India produces more than two thirds of the world's supply of kapok. This fiber is generally known as a filling for mattresses and pillows; yet it has a variety of other important uses. Because of its buoyancy it is an essential material in life belts. In 1939 the British Ministry of Shipping called for the best quality of Java kapok to be used in the new type of life belts. Aside from this, it is used as insulating material in aircraft and in refrigerators; because of its lightness, resiliency and imperviousness to vermin and bacteria it proved invaluable during the last World War as a surgical dressing and padding. The kapok fiber grows within a pod on trees in almost every part of the islands. It is most frequently found and commercially grown in Java and South Celebes where climatic and soil conditions are particularly suitable. The islands also produce large quantities of sisal fiber and are producing small but increasing quantities of cotton.

In tapioca production, Netherlands India ranks first. Tapioca, which in America is sometimes referred to as "fish-eye pudding" is obtained from the root of the cassava plant. Although generally known as a food, comparatively small quantities are actually consumed for that purpose. Vast amounts are taken up by the paste and glue factories, and by the textile industry as a sizing for cotton and rayon goods. Cassava also is cultivated mainly by natives.

Aside from being a storehouse of tropical agricultural products, Netherlands India is also vastly rich in mineral resources. It is the fourth largest oil producer. Petroleum is found in Sumatra and Borneo with smaller amounts in Java and on the island of Ceram. At the present time New Guinea is extensively explored and may in the future become important. The main refineries are in Palembang and Balikpapan. The oil industry is controlled for the most part by British and Dutch interests; Americans also have a share through a subsidiary of the Standard Oil Company of New Jersey.

Manganese and phosphates are found in Java; gold and silver in Sumatra, Borneo and the Celebes. Bauxite, the source of aluminum so indispensable in the manufacture of aircraft and munitions, is found in the Riouw Archipelago off the coast of Sumatra. Diamonds are mined in Borneo; sulphur in Java, Sumatra and the Celebes; and coal in Borneo and Sumatra. Besides this there are vast unexplored and unworked regions throughout the Netherlands Indies which contain valuable deposits of iron ore, nickel, lead, zinc, sulphur and copper.

Economic well-being in Netherlands India depends largely upon its trade in raw materials. One of the most important consumers is the United States. Since the outbreak of the European war in September, 1939, the latter's share in the islands' trade has assumed increasing importance. This is the result of a larger volume of exports going directly to the American continent instead of by way of Europe as formerly. This can be seen from the figures. In 1939 Netherlands India exported 146.9 million guilders worth of goods in the United States; in 1940 this figure was practically doubled and amounted to 290.9 million guilders. This rise also meant that the United States increased its share of 20% of total exports from Netherlands India in 1939 to 33% of total exports in 1940.

In examining the exports of specific products, this percentage appears even greater. During 1940, for instance, rubber shipments to the United States represented 61% of the islands' entire rubber exports, while tin shipped to the United States amounted to 64% of total tin exports, and manganese ore to the United States to 67% of total exports of the product. Netherlands India, moreover, sent 60% of its total palm oil exports in 1940 to the United States, 59% of its tapioca, 72% of its sisal, 40% of its kapok, 38% of its pepper and 32% of its cinchona bark. Coffee exports to the United States in 1940 almost tripled those of 1939. In the latter part of 1940 a tobacco exchange was set up for the first time in New York to replace the one in Amsterdam which was closed when Germany invaded the mother country. This new exchange takes care of all Netherlands India's tobacco sales in the Western Hemisphere and those parts of Europe which can still be reached.

Though the proportion of rubber exports from the Indies to the United States is smaller than that of British Malaya, it is significant that the islands have gradually increased their share. Before 1929 the United States took 15–20% of its rubber from Netherlands India; by 1939 this had climbed to 29% and in 1940 the islands supplied as much as 35% of total U. S. requirements. The Netherlands Indies government recently announced that all available cargo space in ships plying to the American Continent would be primarily devoted to U. S. orders of rubber and tin. American rubber investments in the Indies in 1936 were reported to be in the neighborhood of $40,000,000. The first rubber-tire factory in the islands was established six years ago by the Goodyear Tire and Rubber Company, Inc., and was protected by import contingents on tires imposed by the Dutch government. Other American rubber companies operating in the Indies are the United States Rubber Company and the Firestone Tire and Rubber Company.

Practically all of the pepper consumed by the American public comes from the Netherlands Indies; the United States imports up to 75 million pounds annually. The Indies also supplies more than half of the United States requirements of nutmeg and mace. Though there is only a small quantity of Netherlands Indies tobacco shipped to the American Continent, it is of a variety produced in Sumatra and which cannot be obtained anywhere else in the world. Because of its distinct flavor, it is used as cigar wrapper and is highly in demand. Palm oil, tapioca and kapok are also obtained by the United States chiefly in the Netherlands Indies.

Just as the United States is an important market for the Netherlands Indies, the Indies itself is finding America an increasing source of goods formerly obtained in Europe. The United States is now the islands' main supplier of machinery and tools, metal goods, chemicals and—most important of all—aircraft, arms and munitions. The increasing industrialization of the islands heightens rather than diminishes the dependence upon American goods. Recently the government of Netherlands India appropriated ten million guilders in the 1941 budget for the establishment of a number of industries important to the economy of the islands, such as chemical, textile, paper and glass factories, and a plant for the smelting of scrap iron. The major portion of the machinery and tools for these industries will be imported from the United States. At the same time the United States government issued unlimited licenses authorizing exportation to the Netherlands Indies of a broad range of iron and steel products, brass, bronze and nickel and certain tools to aid the military and economic defense preparations of the islands.

The industrialization of Netherlands India, furthermore, is one indication of the islands' economic progress. This was possible only through the far-sighted administrative policies of a stable colonial government. For a number of years the Netherlands Indies government has focused a great deal of attention on improving the standard of living of the native population, giving it opportunities for education and technical training and encouraging its initiative in developing its small industries. The government sends thousands of natives each year from the densely populated sections of Java to the sparsely settled regions of the Outer Provinces, both to relieve the population pressure in Java and for the development of these fertile islands.

For the United States, economic progress in Netherlands India has meant an increase in its trade relations with the islands and Americans have also begun to realize the benefits of mutual economic dependence. It is significant, for instance, that while during the depression years total American investments in foreign countries declined, Americans increased their investments in the Netherlands Indies.

Long ago a famous Dutch administrator introduced the phrase *"rust en orde"*—peace and order—as one of the aims of colonial government. The realization of this aim in Netherlands India has been responsible for its economic growth.

CHAPTER IX

THE JAPANESE INVASION OF THE DUTCH EAST INDIES

ONE of the most perplexing episodes in the history of the Far East has been the manner in which the Japanese sought to occupy the Dutch East Indies long before the outbreak of World War II. Seemingly oblivious of the debt which they owed the Dutch, the masters in Tokyo from 1919 to 1941 bent much of their energies on the task of arousing the natives in the great achipelago against European rulers. They used tactics that today remind us forcefully of those employed by the Politbureau in the Kremlin, while previously some of the Nazi leaders proved adept in the same maneuvering.

The American public knows little as yet about the measures adopted by Hitler and his Japanese allies in the Orient in their endeavor to oust the Dutch as well as the British and the French from the Far East. The Japanese had much in their favor, for the time had come to announce a new regime in East India. "Asia for the Asiatics" was as suitable a phrase in Indonesia as it had been in the Philippines. Thanks to the well-intentioned sentiments and labors of the Americans who set the Philippines free from colonial dominion, the Indonesian leaders naturally hope to achieve total independence from Dutch control, not only political but also economic and cultural. Their aspirations were thoroughly sound and wholesome in so far as they sought to employ evolutionary tactics rather than revolution, bloodshed and theft. Some of them realized perfectly that peaceful and orderly conduct would gain more for their people than subversive activities.

The occupation by the Japanese of the Liuchiu Islands
(1873), Formosa (1896), Korea (1910), Manchuria
(1931), and a large part of China (1937-1940) preceded
other conquests to the south, much to the amazement of
certain European and American statesmen. When in September 1940 the Japanese warlords received permission
from the abject Vichy Government to annex the northern
section of French Indo-China, Capitol Hill in Washington was considerably disturbed. There was much reason
for this, since anybody with some knowledge of modern
history could easily foresee what would come next. It did
not take long for the next step to materialize. Today we
rub our eyes in wonder as we reminisce a bit, still confused
and perplexed as we review the catastrophies suffered by
our Allies in World War II. The Japanese were riding
high as they encouraged the Siamese government to occupy a large part of Indo-China that had not yet been
occupied by the Japanese. The conflict between Thailand
(Siam) and Indo-China was obviously engineered by
Japan, but it was made to appear as if the rulers of Indo-
China had precipitated hostilities. Consequently, the
"grateful" government of Thailand soon became all too
subservient to the men from Nippon. The latter quickly
seized the southern section of Indo-China (July 1941),
proclaiming to the world that the sovereignty of France
was fully recognized in all of Indo-China, but actually
carrying on the old program of "Asia for the Asiatics."
How Thailand itself fell into their hands is well known
by now, while the conquest of Malaya which followed
early in 1942 was of such agonizing a nature for all American patriots that further mention here would be superfluous.

Beyond Singapore lay the Dutch East Indies, storehouse of oil, rice, sugar, spices, tobacco, nickel, tin and

coal, with tantalizing prospects of fabulous wealth for the Nipponese. Here was also the large area of western New Guinea, with room for ten million Japanese settlers. What an empire in itself! Moreover, the gentle and peaceful natives of Java and Sumatra would offer little resistance to the wily plotters from Tokyo. They would gladly obey the orders to help build the co-prosperity sphere of action and show the colonial powers how foolish they had been in trying to throttle the reasonable demands for independence.

Long before Pearl Harbor a large number of Japanese fishermen, photographers, journalists and diplomats had been very active in preparing for the military invasion that was bound to follow in due course of time. Particularly noticeable were the operations of the Japanese businessmen when in 1931 and 1932 the great economic depression with the subsequent devaluation of the Japanese currency precipitated a veritable inundation of products from Japan all over the Dutch East Indies. Japanese shops sprang into existence like mushrooms, according to a report by the Dutch government at that time. The economic invasion was naturally accompanied by political measures. The scholars in Tokyo kept telling the military bosses that inexhaustible riches were waiting for exploitation, in contrast with the meager results obtained in Manchuria, China, Formosa and Indo-China. What the military machine would appreciate particularly was the oil in Sumatra and the tin near Singapore. In the meantime the farmers were constantly complaining about the lack of land for suitable cultivation. Why not get permission to migrate to Sumatra and New Guinea? Yes, why not? A mere handful of Hollanders could not stop mighty Nippon!

In 1940 Japan announced that the "Communal prosperity sphere" was finally taking shape. The attractive phrase, "Cooperation to achieve mutual prosperity" appealed readily to millions of young Asiatics. What the Japanese had in mind was not exactly the same as that which they officially proclaimed, for they wanted simply more space for the teeming population of their own country, and also more markets for their factories at home. Such a scheme was in keeping with precedents established by their own teachers of the period between 1641 and 1853, when the Dutch guided their foreign policy and revealed the secrets of their own success in the seventeenth century. The merchants in Amsterdam had in their day of glory and power played a few tricks not to the liking of their competitors. Now the Japanese decided to imitate their masters. This is not the way recent Dutch accounts delineate events in the Far East, for it is rather difficult for the Hollanders to view things in the light of their own past performances. Even the magnanimous Americans occasionally exhibit similar tendencies.

The Dutch government in exile announced in London that it was not willing to join the lovely scheme proposed by its former pupils. And in November 1940 the Governor-General of the Dutch East Indies proclaimed a similar message . That seemed to surprise the statesmen in Tokyo, who kept up their old line of approach by reminding the Dutch of the old ties of friendship, going back to the first decade of the seventeenth century. No doubt the insidious poison of British and American propaganda had obscured the minds of the Dutch rulers. Henceforth other measures must be taken, and these were indeed forthcoming.

Financial support given to Indonesian traders who were buying Japanese products was freely offered, but only a few natives in the Dutch East Indies responded, largely because the numerous Chinese storekeepers had matters well in hand for their own benefit. These Chinese businessmen, numbering altogether about two million, including their families, exercised enormous power and influence which was much stronger than their Nipponese friends realized at the time. Other factors, such as swift counter-moves by Dutch merchants, helped to frustrate the attempts made on the economic front.

In the second place must be mentioned the opportunities offered to Indonesian students who were willing to study in Japanese universities. The objective was laudable in many respects, because the Indonesians could obviously learn much from their northern neighbors, who were willing to accord them financial assistance and various privileges. A few students took advantage of this offer, and some of them attended various meetings of the Pan-Asiatic groups. Here they were addressed as Indonesians, rather than as subjects of a European power. It is true that in some instances they were urged to rise against the Dutch rulers, but in general the idea of emphasizing the dignity of a great race was certainly not subversive. Eventually the Indonesians had to break away from the tutelage of a colonial power. On the other hand, it was not necessary on such an occasion to submit to the guidance of the Japanese. Perhaps an honorable connection with the Kingdom of the Netherlands would prove very advantageous.

The Japanese also attempted to impress upon the Indonesians their great respect for Mohammedanism and their profound interest in the Koran. In October 1939 a Mohammedanism exposition was held in Tokyo, where some Indonesian leaders examined various displays. Upon their return to their native land they reported that the Japanese knew very little about Mohammedanism and had done almost nothing for its propagation.

Similarly the propaganda campaign through the use of newspapers produced comparatively little in return for all the effort and expense involved . Unfortunately for Japan, its officials who ruled Formosa and Manchuria did not carry out the benign policies that the slogan of "Asia for the Asiatics" seemed to imply. Many well-educated Indonesians traveled widely in Asia, some on their way to Mecca, others on mere business or as tourists. As a matter of fact, vast sums of money were spent on the pilgrimages to Mecca, for the religious aspirations of the Indonesian Mohammedans were productive of pious acts. Other Mohammedans in India, Iran, Iraq and Arabia would converse with their brethren from the southeast. The great majority of them had long been aware of the religious toleration practiced by the Hollanders in Asia. They also appreciated the benevolent attitude of the Dutch in matters of politics and social customs.

It was Pearl Harbor that changed everything. Hitherto the Japanese merely plotted and worked at a great disadvantage. They could not offer the natives any real benefits from their proposed assistance. The Chinese were as truly Asiatic as were their eastern neighbors, and in an official document issued by the newspaper editor T. Yishizuma to the agent attached to the Japanese Consulate at Batavia called Mr. Toyoshima published recently by the Dutch government, he indicated clearly the difficulties experienced by him: "Naturally, the anti-Japanese action of the Chinese contains many sentimental elements but peace between China and Japan is not important for their existence."[1]

The Japanese attack on Pearl Harbor on December 7, 1941, was followed almost immediately by a declaration of war by the Dutch. The latter had long been aware of American support in case their possessions in the southwest Pacific should be attacked by Japan. On November 7, 1941, President F. D. Roosevelt had polled his Cabinet on the question of whether he would receive popular support "if it became necessary to strike at Japan in case she should attack England in Malaya or the Dutch in the East Indies. The Cabinet was unanimous in the feeling that the country would support such a move." Such was the statement penned by Henry L. Stimson in his *Diary*.[2] However, Hull believed that before the people were to render such support there would first have to be held many meetings in which the citizens would be informed about the danger of taking no decisive action. Admiral Stark wrote to Admiral Hart on the same day: "The Navy is already in the war of the Atlantic, but the country doesn't seem to realize it. Apathy, to the point of opposition is evident in a considerable section of the press. . . . Whether the country knows it or not, *we are* at war."[3]

This was true for the United States had been actively engaged in providing the British with naval supplies. The British and the French and the Dutch hoped that they could count on American aid in case their possessions in the Far East would be attacked by the Japanese, and they were also well aware of assistance rendered even before December 7, 1941. For this reason the Dutch government did not hesitate a moment in siding with the Americans, and during the night which followed the attack on Pearl Harbor the Dutch issued their declaration of war, informing the Allies of their momentous step.

On Sunday, February 15, 1942, Singapore fell. After this the loss of Java seemed certain. On Friday and Saturday, February 27 and 28, 1942, Admiral C. E. L. Helfrich, Commander of the Allied Naval Forces in the southwest Pacific, offered battle to the Japanese fleet which was protecting sixty transports on the way to the north coast of Java. Twelve days of heroic action followed by the Allied vessels under Helfrich. The latter informed the present writer at the end of May 1953 how the Japanese official records, just released, indicated that he had followed a course of action which at the time did not please Americans but now (May 1953) appeared in a new and better light, thanks to the Japanese revelations. Helfrich in 1950 published the first two volumes of his memoirs,[4] and the third volume was being prepared in the autumn of 1953. A popular work in one volume, made up of two parts, one devoted to the war and the other to the subsequent peace, is now in the process of publication. It will prove illuminating to those who wish to understand the exact reasons why Admiral Helfrich replaced Admiral Hart in the midst of apparently futile operations.

Much has also been written about the Japanese occupation, of which perhaps the best account is that issued by the Dutch government on May 1, 1946. It is impartial and packed with astonishing facts. The Japanese, so we are told on high authority, did their best to end once and for all Dutch prestige and influence. They were naturally displeased by the firmness displayed by the Dutch in stopping one attempt after another to inundate the East Indies with goods and propaganda.

As a result of Admiral Helfrich's offensive actions and the work of Dutch and other planes the Japanese suffered far greater setbacks than was realized before the summer of 1953. Many heroic deeds on the part of American and British forces also require further attention, for they help explain why General MacArthur was able to win back important areas very soon after the fall of the Philippines. General Charles A. Willoughby, who for eleven years was the intelligence chief under MacArthur and a close friend of Admiral Helfrich, happens to know a great deal about the terrific fights in the Java Sea and other areas of great strategic importance. The Allied forces did far better than most of us knew at the time. Although the Japanese on March 27, 1942, announced that they had occupied the whole of Sumatra, fighting went on there for months. Even in Java the situation was such that during the second week in April several units of the Java Army made their escape to Australia. Other Dutch forces in Java continued the struggle until June, according to the Japanese reports. On the small island of Timor the Japanese never were able to gain the upper hand, until a year later the Dutch forces were removed to Australia, while in the southern half of Dutch New Guinea large areas remained in the hands of the Dutch until the end of the war. At the port of Merauke, the Capital of southwestern New Guinea, the Dutch flag always remained in the air, protected by Dutch soldiers and the airplanes commanded by General Douglas MacArthur.

To the south of the Philippines the native population proved so troublesome that large groups of Amboinese, Timorese and Menadonese were hauled away to concentration camps, where they suffered untold privations with their old friends the Dutch. Moreover, thousands of Chinese were treated in the same manner. It will serve little to allege erroneously, as has been done by John Coast in his Chauvinistic book, *Recruit to Revolution* (London 1952, p. 9), that the "arrival of the Japanese in 1942 had been greeted hopefully by most Indonesians." Moreover, the slogan of "Asia for the Asiatics," as observed above, meant much less for the Indonesians in 1942 than Mr. Coast would want us to believe.[5]

Propaganda was extensively used by the Japanese in order to undermine the respect among the natives for the Dutch. A decadent European country had been utterly defeated by the triumphant men from Nippon. It was clear that Western civilization had seen its best days, and now it must yield the scepter of dominion to Oriental peoples, under the leadership of Japan. All visible memorials of great Hollanders and their work were swiftly removed. For example, the statue of Jan Pieterszoon Coen, the founder of Batavia (now named Djakarta, as it used to be called before 1619), disappeared from the scene. Those who remained friendly to the Dutch were interned. The use of the Dutch language was prohibited, even in the churches. Nothing should be left that might remind the Indonesians of the days when they enjoyed peace and prosperity under Dutch rule.

In order to win the favor of the masses of people, the Japanese made clever use of certain nationalistic leaders who had been sent away to remote spots where the Dutch would not be disturbed by their artivities. The most promising of these was Sukarno, who hated the Dutch for having refused to let him organize a movement for the establishment of independence. Uprisings had occurred in the past, and it would seem that the Dutch officials did not take the right sort of action at the time. Refreshing and also surprising are the comments by a Dutch scholar published in a book bearing the imprint of a well-known firm: *De Indonesische quaestie* by Dr. C. Smit, Leiden: E. J. Brill, 1952. The author claims that the European businessmen in Indonesia did not want the natives to earn adequate wages in order to reap greater profits for themselves: "The source of all the misery was the colonial system, but at the beginning of the twentieth century the natives did not yet realize this." He also remarks that the strikes and other disturbances in the period from 1919 to 1926 were not caused primarily by Communists but by the low standard of living.[6]

Sukarno and his associates were active long before the Japanese invaded Indonesia. He himself was imprisoned for "subversive, Communist-inspired activities," but on December 31, 1931, he was set free. Shortly after that date he founded the party known as the *Partindo,* a screen for the Communists. In August 1933 he was arrested again and interned, first on Endeh, later at Benkulen, and during the Japanese encroachment in the city of Padang. On March 17, 1942, he offered his services to the Japanese as collaborator, and during the next four months he worked for them in the former Dutch bastion named Fort de Kock. In July 1942 he left Sumatra for Java, where he became the chief collaborator among the population.

Another nationalist leader was Sutan Sjahrir, who was a native of Sumatra. He studied extensively in the Netherlands, where he acted as the Secretary of the Indonesian labor union called *Perhimpunan Indonesia.* In 1933 he arrived in the East Indies, gaining favor with the native workmen. Before long he was President of the *Pendidikan National Indonesia,* which was a Communist front organization. In 1934 Mohammed Hatta became the President of this same party, while Sjahrir served as President of a labor union. In the same year he was arrested for "subversive, Communistic activity." It appears that at the time he was in close contact with the Japanese Marine. But during World War II he, unlike Sukarno, did not act as collaborator for the benefit of the invaders. The latter did not retaliate but let him do as he pleased. After having been in exile for seven years (1934-1941), he was set free by the Japanese at the place called Banda-Neira. His adverse criticism of the Dutch colonial system was such that he could safely be trusted by the Japanese. His diaries for the years 1934 to 1938 reveal lofty sentiments from the standpoint of a nationalist leader. He was justified in bemoaning the unwillingness on the part of the Dutch officials to meet the nationalists part of the way.

Hatta in 1925 was President of the Perhimpunan Indonesia in the Netherlands. In 1927 he was delegate at the convention of the Communist League of Oppressed Peoples, an organ of the Comintern. He became an active member of the executive council . In 1932 he arrived in the Dutch East Indies, and on March 25, 1934, he was arrested. He was sent to the same places where Sjahrir was, and he assisted Sukarno in founding the new republic under Japanese guidance.

Sjarifudin before World War II belonged to the Communist front party called *Gerindo*. He was extremely pro-Russian and Communist, for which reason he refused to collaborate with the Japanese, who imprisoned him in 1943. In the first period after World War II he exerted considerable influence for the benefit of the Communists. In 1947 he acted as Prime Minister of the Indonesian Republic.

Japanese propaganda was very effective in Java, but less so elsewhere. It seemed as if the white races had lost their former prestige and power, while Japan should emerge as the leading nation in the whole world. Sukarno presided over the *Djawa Hookoo Kai,* an association of Java civil servants. It was also called officially the Central Organization of the People's Will. On March 9, 1943, various other groups and parties were all integrated in this central body. The four presiding officers were Sukarno, Hatta, K. H. Dewentra (well known for his extremely anti-Dutch sentiments), and K. H. M. Mansur. They were collectively known as the Four-leaved Clover. Each day the members had to swear an oath that they would strive for the destruction of the power of "our enemies, America, England and the Netherlands, to the very roots."

On the Emperor's birthday that year Sukarno as Chairman of the whole organization loudly proclaimed that "we will smash the English with the crow-bar and flatten out the Americans."

It is interesting to note that when on August 17, 1945, Sukarno and Hatta announced the founding of the new republic, they placed the following date on their proclamation: Djakarta, *hari* 17 *bulan* 8—2605 or Djakarta, the 17th day of 8th month, Year 2605. That was the Japanese reckoning in line with their national calendar. Nevertheless it has often been argued by Sukarno's friends that he was not a real collaborator but used the Japanese in order to get independence for his own people.

On November 8, 1944, the campaign against the white races reached its greatest fury. A procession moved along the streets of the capital and portraits of three distinguished men were borne along and then burned. These men were the Dutch statesman Van der Plas, President F. D. Roosevelt and Prime Minister Winston Churchill. Sukarno gleefully presided over the bonfire and made a thrilling speech, denouncing the very government that would soon raise him to the highest pinnacle of power and prestige in Indonesia.

The unspeakable crimes committed by the nationalist leaders and their followers must seem strange when we consider the gentle nature of the Indonesian natives before the Japanese invasion. It goes to show what propaganda can accomplish among people deprived of news from the outside world. Disorderly bands of youths were whipped together for the purpose of punishing the Dutch for their alleged crimes. Sukarno was ever present to give vent to his old hatred and his desire for revenge. If only the Dutch officials of the prewar days could have seen this tragedy we may surmise that they would have tried some reconciliation.

CHAPTER X

LIBERATION

I N THE process of liberation from Japanese control many errors were made in all directions, by the British, by the Americans and by the Dutch. Needless to say, the Indonesian nationalists contributed a large share of their own. In the midst of almost incredible confusion and swift events befalling the greatest experts to their utmost surprise it was obviously difficult to do the right thing at the right place. For this reason it might be well to suggest that all the accusations and counter-accusations cease, and that all parties concerned in the rebuilding of Indonesia pull together in a common task of decent and honest effort.

In the period from September 9, 1952, to June 5, 1953, the present writer had interviews with Dr. J. W. Meijer Ranneft, the former President of the People's Council in the Dutch East Indies, and with numerous other officials who happen to know a great deal about Indonesia that outsiders should also know. Dr. Ranneft has been very frank in admitting three faults on the part of the most important Dutch officials in the most critical years, namely, from 1929 to 1945. Other qualified persons in the Netherlands have also admitted quite readily that serious mistakes were made. Let us therefore begin our present survey with the errors of the most responsible Dutch officials.

Dr. Ranneft in December 1945 published a highly illuminating booklet entitled, *Rechtvaardigheid voor Indië: Indië in den maalstroom,* Maastricht: Leiter-Nypels. He said that these were the three great mistakes made by the Dutch: (1) During the Great Depression

from 1929 to 1934 the Dutch government followed the
wrong course in maintaining the gold standard and trying
to save every penny for the distant future rather than
freely spend to sustain a healthy economy, which was very
detrimental to the people in the East Indies. (2) In the
disastrous years of the Second World War the Dutch government in exile was too vacillating to help the Indonesians enough in their preparations for the Japanese attack.
(3) During the process of liberation the Dutch leaders in
the Parliament and elsewhere did not rise to the occasion
and show the other Allied powers the justice of their cause.
Nearly all foreigners condemned the Dutch at the very
moment they should have remembered what had actually
happened in Indonesia. When a person is accused he
should not run into a corner and hide his face in shame.
On the contrary, he must defend himself with all the facul-
ties at his disposal.

In Indonesia there was no more pro-Japanese sentiment than in the Philippines or in any of the British possessions. In 1942 the Indonesians rallied bravely in their
efforts to save the Dutch control over the archipelago.
Even in 1942 the general economic and social situation was
good, particularly when compared with other areas over-
run by the Japanese. The chaos that befell Indonesians
was probably less extensive than that which would have
occurred under similar conditions in any other Asiatic
country.

Now let us examine the errors committed by the
British and the Americans. They showed so little concern
over the situation in the Dutch East Indies that the Japanese were permitted to turn their arms over to the Indonesian nationalists. If this sort of thing had happened
in the colony of another Allied power the outside world
would immediately have been informed about the injus-

tice done to this particular country. But the Dutch officials in The Hague were too feeble and too confused to take proper steps; they let their former friends ruin their stake in the Far East. While the British retained their own colony in Borneo and the Portuguese were permitted to stay in their half of Timor, the Dutch had to surrender the whole of Indonesia. (Dutch New Guinea does not belong to Indonesia.)

Throughout the year 1941 and the first half of 1942 the loyalty of the Indonesian population remained about the same as before. On December 12, 1941, the newly founded Federation of Nationalist groups, which included members of the labor unions and the Moslem organizations, declared officially that it was the people's duty to resist all attacks by foreigners and to support the government of the Dutch East Indies. The nationalists naturally expressed the hope that in the near future the native population would receive a greater share in the government than had been the case hitherto. But this desire was a continuation of earlier requests; each time the Dutch officials carefully considered how much could be granted, although it must be admitted that the measures adopted were not always just the right kind of liberalism. In 1941 and the opening months of 1942 the sultans, together with the political leaders on a lower level and the Indonesian corps of civil servants, joined the Dutch side in the hour of national peril. With the increasing danger of a Japanese invasion on a large scale the natives could easily have reasoned that now the time had come to dispose of the colonial regime. Such a thought, however, did not enter their minds until after the Japanese had indoctrinated them over a fairly long period of time. There was practically no passive resistance, nor insurrection, nor inflammatory propaganda against the Dutch. Strikes and demonstrations of an unfriendly nature were extremely rare, particularly as compared with the general situation after 1945. The great majority of Indonesian nationalists were men of integrity. They knew that national independence was certain to come, for in each decade some progress had been made in the right direction.

One of the most amazing things in modern history is the manner in which the British and the Americans have discussed the occupation of various Asiatic countries by the European powers, notably Russia. It is almost always assumed that Russia has the right to do what no other European nation may do, that is, to occupy and annex vast areas, up to six million square miles, twice as large an empire as the whole of the United States . There she may remove political institutions, destroy native customs, obliterate the former language and religions, and settle the country with Russian citizens. But little Holland may do none of these things. In her case this would be called colonialism. She let the Indonesians retain their languages, their religion, their real estate property, etc. When the natives were too lazy for their own good and had no money left for elementary education the Dutch were blamed for illiteracy, although the rate was just as high in many other countries similarly situated. Now we discover that the Indonesians are even more indolent than ever before, thanks to their beloved *merdeka,* the liberty to loaf and destroy the property of others, particularly of European businessmen. *Merdeka* has a wonderful sound, for this time there are no severe laws and punishments with which to curtail robbery, murder and destruction of libraries, archives and utilities.

Ever since 1918 the Russian Communists have made it their business to undermine the authority of all other European powers in Asia. While the Russians consolidated their own holdings and even enlarged them, the natives of India, Burma, Ceylon, Indo-China and Indonesia were told how terrible was their lot under the domination of colonial masters. What Russia was doing in Siberia and Outer Mongolia was not colonialism. No, that was philanthropy. And when in 1936 and 1937 the Communists in the Kremlin fanned the sit-down strikes in Michigan the present writer was the only person of some importance locally who dared to warn against their methods. In his book, *Christianity, Capitalism and Communism* (Ann Arbor, Michigan, 1937), he pointed out that Walter Lippman and other friends of the Russians were mistaken in ignoring the dangers of Communist infiltration in this country. They naively believed that the sit-down strikes originated in the U.S.A. The only reward the writer received was an attempt to remove him from the Campus at Ann Arbor. His warnings were premature at the time.

Now we are living in another era, but the Americans have been accustomed so long to view the Russian foreign policy in a light very harmful to themselves that it will take considerable indoctrination before any great American statesman will have the courage to tell the Russians how to behave in Asia. Little Holland can easily be silenced, but mighty Russia can go on some more without interference from the British or the Americans.

When the Indonesian Republic was officially proclaimed by Sukarno and Hatta, the latter were not consulting the proper representatives of their own people. On the contrary, they were then in Indo-China. On August 7, 1945, they were summoned by the Japanese Supreme Army Command to go to Saigon, which city they reached on August 9th. They were given suitable instructions by Terauchi, the nature of which, however, has not yet been revealed. They apparently were allowed to select their own date for the consummation of their plans. Japan was to announce the great news on August 19, but on the 15th she capitulated. For a moment the two Indonesian nationalists hesitated, not knowing how to proceed without instructions from their Japanese masters. They returned to Java, where they suddenly were kidnapped by the Communist Students Committee.

The moment Japan was out of the war her star began to decline swiftly. The Communists in Indonesia saw their chance to make Russia replace Japan in the race to conquer Indonesia. They carried with them instructions from Moscow, which have been identified in the so-called last will of Sukarno and Hatta. Four other leaders were designated as their successors, namely, the comrades Tan Malakka, Iwa Kusuma Sumantrie, Sukarni and the well-known Sutan Sjahrir, who, as we saw, refused to collaborate with the Japanese, largely because he preferred to serve Russia rather than Japan. It was feared by the Communists that Sukarno and Hatta might be unwilling to assist their aims. The Indonesian Republic was not actually proclaimed by Sukarno and Hatta but by the Communist Students Committee. The latter was very careful, however, not to annoy the Japanese army commanders in Indonesia, for the Communists wanted to make use of their war material. Outwardly Japan was the foster mother of the new republic, but the master minds of the Kremlin were in real charge of local operations, just as they were in the sitdown strikes in Michigan. Finesse works better than crude and premature publicity.

It took four years to carry out the instructions from Moscow. First came the agreements with the Dutch known as the Linggadjati (Cheribon) Agreement of March 25, 1947, and the Renville Agreement of January

17, 1948, on board the American ship *Renville*. In the latter it was stated that "sovereignty throughout the Netherlands Indies is and shall remain vested in the Kingdom of the Netherlands until, after a stated interval, the Kingdom of the Netherlands transfers its sovereignty to the United States of Indonesia. . . . The status of the Republic of Indonesia will be that of a state in the United States of Indonesia." On January 20, 1948, the State Department welcomed the agreement as "a healthy basis for the political and economic development of Indonesia."

It was indeed an excellent agreement. But the officials in the State Department did not know at the time that Sukarno, who had been made President of the new republic, and Hatta, the new Vice-President, did not have the slighest intention of keeping their part of the bargain. They wanted something entirely different, but they could only obtain it through forceful measures later on.

A certain Indonesian expert in The Hague on June 3, 1953, placed at the disposal of the present writer an accurate copy of a highly illuminating document dated October 22, 1948. At the top we read: "Secret Indonesian Republic." It was No. 378 SEK, Cabinet of the Indonesian republic, removed by a very bold Dutch captain in person or one of his accomplices. (The writer spent an hour at the captain's home in May 1953.) The document, according to the Postscript, was issued by the Secretary of the Cabinet in the name of the President of the Indonesian Republic, that is, Sukarno. At the bottom appears the name of Asaat. The ministers of the republic are informed that neither the Linggadjati nor the Renville Agreement was binding on the new republic, since some of the political parties in Indonesia had not been consulted. Curiously enough the document quotes Article 1 of the Pact in the German language. More than that, it was "not the government of the Indonesian Republic which was bound by the agreement but only those who signed it, and they acted without authority; consequently the Pact is not valid." Such is always the reasoning of Communists and fellow travelers. The same thing may be said about the truce signed by the government of the U.S.A. with "Chinese volunteers," in order to end hostilities in Korea. Such a pact has absolutely no value.

The next section in the document under discussion is devoted entirely to the fortune inherited by President F. D. Roosevelt. His grandfather, Warren Delano, was an opium smuggler, "whose ill-gotten wealth is now a part of the vast fortune controlled by the White House incumbent." The whole section is in English except the last line, which says that it is high time this information be made known.

Section 4, which is the last one, says that certain persons must be thanked for having sent newspapers and periodicals. The first mentioned is *The New Times,* published in Russian, English, French and German. The publishers are Koran Trud, Moscow. The second is called *Soviet Weekly,* a magazine in the English language, published in London at 630 Grand Building, Trafalgar Square. The third is the *Second Anniversary Republic of Indonesia,* an English paper issued by the Central Committee of Indonesian Independence, 246 Boundary Street, Brisbane, Australia. The fourth is *Merdeka,* a periodical in English, issued by the Indonesian Information Service, Constitution House, Curzon Road, New Delhi, India. The last is a paper in the Malay language published in Singapore, Utusan Malaya Press Ltd.

It should be noted here that these Communist papers and periodicals emanated directly from Russia or from British possessions in which certain persons tried to unseat the Dutch in Indonesia. This is in line with certain developments in Java immediately after the Japanese capitulation. General Mountbatten could have and should have demanded the unconditional surrender of the Japanese in Java before the arrival of the British troops. Such was indeed his original plan. On or about September 3, 1945, he ordered the Japanese in Java to dissolve the newly proclaimed republic unconditionally. Later in that month he gave an order to the Japanese to refrain from giving over the administration of Java to any political party. Unfortuntely these admirable orders were never executed.

This development does not exonerate General Mountbatten entirely, but it shows that on the highest level in British military circles the American position was well understood. The State Department in Washington naturally favored the idea that the Allied powers should first of all regain their territorial possessions liberated from the Japanese before they were to be given over to any other party. But General Christison, who commanded the British forces in Java under Mountbatten, made concessions to the nationalists. Near the end of September the British Broadcasting Corp. announced that Christison was proposing a round table discussion with the Indonesian nationalists.

Admiral Helfrich, Commander of the Netherlands forces in the Far East, on September 30, 1945, sent a telegram to Lord Mountbatten in which he uttered a strong protest against the proposed action of General Christison. Mountbatten now changed his mind on the matter and insisted that the Dutch must first negotiate with the Indonesian nationalists. He did not know just who the latter were or where they had gotten their authority and titles. But he refused to let British troops be used until the Dutch come to terms with Sukarno and Hatta. It has been fash-

ionable in certain quarters to argue the whole matter in an
entirely different manner. Admiral Helfrich's protest is
not mentioned, and it is made to appear that the British
were in no position to cope with the situation, having only
a few thousand troops on hand for operations.

In the *Saturday Evening Post* for May 16, 1953, we
read that "On the other side of the curtain in this fateful
year of 1942 the Indonesians greeted their fellow Asiatics
with great rejoicing." The reader gets the impression that
Sukarno was now hailed by the whole population as the
founder of the republic. When liberation came at last
the British were so busy with their own possessions that
they could do very little in Java: "Mountbatten had already given up most of his amphibious equipment to the
European theater and, besides, he had Britain's own Malaya and Thailand and Indo-China to think of." Very
true, but even in this fair article no mention is made of
the fact that when the British troops did arrive General
Christison refused to recognize Dutch authority. The
article just mentioned does have this illuminating and
correct statement: "The independence movement got unexpected *de facto* recognition from the British general,
Sir Philip Christison, who announced as he set off for
Java that his handful of troops expected the co-operation
of 'the Indonesian authorities,' " That is indeed a revela-
tion, though it merely says that the "Dutch were furious—
but helpless." The article certainly is not pro-British or
anti-Dutch. The fault lies in the lack of information about
the actions by Helfrich and the early careers of Sukarno
and Hatta. Nothing is said about the Communist Students Committee which kidnapped the two leaders and
produced the action which is generally thought to have
come from the masses of people. But we are told that the
Dutch had not created the paradise which travelers in

pre-war days described with enthusiasm. Those travelers must have been partly blind or biased in favor of the Dutch. Perhaps they had been hypnotized by the European masters in the Dutch East Indies. In 1945 Sukarno and Hatta were the duly appointed representatives of the Indonesian people. Christison understood this well, although his action was unexpected. However, since the Netherlands was still the recognized source of authority, the *Saturday Evening Post* should have stated the facts as they actually were. For example, Mr. Noel Baker on October 17, 1945, said in the House of Commons that "Great Britain recognizes only the Netherlands Government." What else could any British statesman say? Why then do American commentators still beat about the bush and refuse to tell the truth?

Helfrich asked for permission to land Dutch troops, since the British did not want to take any positive action. He mentioned the obvious fact that Sukarno and his friends did not represent the Indonesian people and for that reason were not the proper persons with whom to deal in the great crisis. The Japanese should lay down their arms and not hand them over to their puppets, which Sukarno and Hatta plainly were at that time. Law and order had to be restored. If the British would not do it the Dutch should have the chance to rule in their own house. But on November 19, 1945, General Christison issued the order that no Dutch troops were to land in Java, though this island was as much a Dutch possession as Malaya was a British one. The differences between the two situations are as follows: In Malaya the rebels are called terrorists, for they are fighting against a major power. In Java they are nationalists, for Holland is too small and too weak to receive justice.

In September and October the Dutch authorities in

The Hague refused to let any of their representatives deal with Sukarno. But Christison treated him with great deference and his superiors in Great Britain began to listen more and more to his arguments with outright approbation. Consequently the British suggested to their Dutch friends in The Hague that the latter relent and pay no more attention to Admiral Helfrich. Gradually this happened; Helfrich was completely repudiated by his own government. On November 1, Dr. van Mook had a conference with Sukarno in apparent defiance of his instructions. Admiral Helfrich protested but was informed by Van Mook in the presence of Van der Plas that Professor Logemann, the Minister of Overseas Territories, had personally given him permission to talk with Sukarno. This statement was false, but the harm done could no longer be remedied. It seemed as if evil forces too strong for Helfrich and his friends combined against those who fought for law and order.

It should be noted here that Admiral Conrad E. L. Helfrich was a naval officer of very considerable skill and long experience. When the war with Japan broke out in December 1941, he had already served in the Dutch Navy for thirty-five years and now was appointed Commander-in-Chief of the Netherlands naval forces. Previously he had taught at the Naval War College in The Hague. On February 14, 1942, he took over as Allied Fleet Commander the direct command of Admiral Thomas C. Hart, U.S.N. On February 25, 1942, the supreme command of the Allied naval forces, instituted under the supreme command of the British General Sir Archibald Wavell, was terminated, and Helfrich now assumed charge of all Allied naval operations in the East Indies. At that time the joint forces of the U.S.A. (American), Great Britain, the Netherlands and Australia were collectively referred to as the ABDA, the D standing for Dutch. After the Battle of the Java Sea, Helfrich was commanded to evacuate all remaining forces to Ceylon and Australia, and to establish new Dutch headquarters in Colombo, the capital of Ceylon. From now on he was merely the commander of the Dutch forces, and he operated under the command of Admiral Lord Louis Mountbatten's Southeast Asia Command and General MacArthur's Southwest Pacific area Command. After the Japanese surrender he returned to Java, remaining there until February 1946. He witnessed many scenes of bloodshed, destruction of property by terrorists, torture of numerous Dutch women and children, besides inflammatory speeches. He retained his position until October 1, 1948, when he resigned it because he could not support the negotiations with irresponsible terrorists. In 1946 and 1947 the British permitted some Dutch troops to land in Indonesia, but these were not commanded by Helfrich.

On August 1, 1953, Major General Charles A. Willoughby wrote the following statement in a letter addressed to the present writer: "I have known and worked with the Admiral, at MacArthur's Headquarters, during the Pacific war, in Brisbane and Port Moresby. I consider him an outstanding naval officer and our war-time association was of the most pleasant character. . . . It is my opinion that the story of the Netherlands East Indies and its betrayal through international appeasement of Russia and Communism should be written."

General Willoughby is not the only American commander who remembers with regret the pro-Russian machinations of certain statesmen in the U.N. and outside of it. It was not untli 1952 that the U.S. Government finally published the official reports about the war in the Southwest Pacific, for which reason the book by Professor

Morison, *The Rising Sun in the Pacific,* issued in 1947, is hopelessly misleading. Helfrich writes on July 27, 1953, that with a little more material help from the U.S.A. he would have checked Japan in the Southwest Pacific. He wonders why the Dutch government has refused to publish the highly compromising documents captured by the Dutch forces at Jogjakarata in 1948, and suggests that pro-Communist authors may have had something to do with the reluctance on the part of the Dutch government to open up the archives of the Dutch Intelligence Service. But he admits that the operations of the British in 1945 and 1946 must not be too hastily criticised in an adverse manner. According to him the most recent reports indicate that some of the earlier condemnations of Dutch experts were premature and not grounded upon actual facts: "We still do not understand just what did happen."

It would be well for some American commentators if they read p. 104 in a book entitled, *Indonesia* and written by P. S. Gerbandy, Wartime Prime Minister of the Netherlands. It was published in 1950 and again in 1951 by a fine British firm with offices in London, New York, Melbourne, Sydney and Capetown, that is, Hutchison and Co. After having enjoyed the hospitality of the British when the Dutch government in exile resided in London, he was shocked to learn about the events just narrated above. To think that a person who was obviously a tool of the Japanese and the Russians should be deemed worthy of sharnig full authority with a government that had been in operation for more than three hundred years was absurd. Gerbrandy said: "The outcome is serious. The Kingdom of the Netherlands has been badly shaken, the labours of generations have been lost and the dangers of which Governor-General Tjarda van Starkenborgh Stachouwer gave warning unhappily have been and are being experienced to this very day. . . . Negotiations were to be guided in such wise that British interests in Asia would not be harmed, or, put more positively, that British interests would be served." It was all the more agonizing for Gerbrandy to note that at the very same time the British possession called Sarawak in northern Boreno was now proclaimed a Crown Colony, while the Dutch portion of Borneo was being given over to Japanese puppets. At the same time British forces were withdrawn from Java to help reinforce the British colony of Malaya,. just a few miles from Sumatra. Gerbrandy goes on by saying on p. 106 that Helfrich "was doomed to powerlessness in the face of (1) a weak-kneed policy such as that of the Netherlands Cabinet, (2) a Lieutenant-Governor the extent of whose power was too wide (3) a British High Command which appeared to show too little concern for the interests of the Netherlands. Despite all Helfrich's protests and advice, the nation was rent in twain while he had to stand by powerless."

These matters are indeed serious. It is not surprising that others followed in their train. In accordance with instructions from Moscow, Sukarno and Hatta violated one of the most important terms in the Union Statute of 1949. They did not like the fact that besides their Indonesian Republic there were other states, such as East Java, Madura and East Indonesia. These had been joined with the Indonesian Republic into a great nation called the United States of Indonesia. They were soon liquidated by force of arms. The Republic of the South Moluccas put up a fierce resistance, but the natives were helpless in the face of superior forces with the latest equipment. Thousands of the latter finally fled to the Netherlands, where the housing shortage was terrible, but something had to be done for these displaced persons. They make little noise in the outside world, but those who have been willing to talk with them have learned a few things about Communist tactics.

On September 15, 1951, Sukarno, for the first time since the end of the war, said in a speech at Bandung in Java that he supported the principles of "marheinisme," which is Indonesian for Communist multi-nationalism. It is not surprising that soon after that speech Russian submarines were sighted near the oil port of Sorong in Dutch New Guinea. Sukarno since that time has been spending a great deal of energy in reminding his people of the fact that Dutch New Guinea is an integral part of Indonesia, and must henceforth be called Irian. But this has not been to the liking of the U.S.A., nor of Australia. The latter country has since 1950 turned more and more toward the Netherlands and with some feeling of appreciation for what the Dutch accomplished for it in 1942. No doubt the Americans will also live to see a day in which they will welcome law and order in Indonesia.

To return to the founding of the Indonesian Republic on August 17, 1945. Here was the supposedly Glorious Revolution lauded frequently by misinformed spectators from afar who never took the trouble to investigate just what happened. Two outspoken enemies of the U.S.A. and Great Britain, who hated the Dutch with poisonous feelings of revenge, were made the supreme commanders of the infant republic. When on August 11, 1945, Sukarno once more went to Saigon at the request of Terauchi he expressed allegiance to the Japanese Emperor. He used to march up and down the roads of Java and through the streets of cities and villages with hundreds of youths, shouting the Japanese Salute and with outstretched arm crying *"Merdeka,"* which were the external symbols of the Five Fundamentals of Indonesia's part in the Asiatic co-prosperity sphere. The first of these five fundamentals read as follows: "Together with the other East Asiatic Nations we shall live or die with *Dai Nippon* and we will make our sacrifice willingly, knowing that the present war is waged to vindicate peace and justice." The other four were very similar.

After the capitulation the Japanese, in violation of their own pledges and the terms of the official armistice, continued to assist the new republic with arms. They deferred the announcement of the end of the War until the founding of the Indonesian Republic had been proclaimed. The Japanese army commander in Java said: "We swear never to forget our oath to live and die together with Indonésia." What is still more remarkable, Japanese officers continued to serve as instructors and leaders in the Indonesian army for at least six years after the cessation of hostilities.

Even more sinister were the ties with Russia. In December 1926 the Perhimpoenan Indonesia, in which Hatta was an influential member as we saw, made an agreement with the Partai Kommunis Indonesia, according to which the former was to direct the policies of the latter. This agreement was canceled by the masters in the Kremlin, for they were opposed to the subordination of a Communist organization to a nationalistic one. Nevertheless, the Communists continued to cooperate very actively with the nationalists in Indonesia. Very important was the work performed by Hatta at the conference of the LIGA held in Brussels during the month of February 1927. This was the League Against Colonial Oppression fostered by the Communists. The Russians, who were the chief colonial power in Asia, made it appear as if they originally had been an Oriental nation and thus fully justified in wrecking the work of the other colonial powers. Hatta gleefully assisted the Communists in this task. The Americans were sleeping peacefully while these sinister events took place.

Long ago the present writer had an occasion to test the ethics of the Communists. In the summer of 1920 he took a trip from Cologne to Munich. First he received from the German consul a visa on his Dutch passport, giving him permission to visit Bavaria and all other parts of the German Republic. When the writer said that according to many German citizens in Cologne it was not permitted to travel in Bavaria without authority of the Bavarian government, the consul replied by saying that Germany was still a sovereign state, which Bavaria obviously was not . But the conductor on the train warned the writer against proceeding any farther than the Bavarian border. He went on to Munich just the same, but was pulled out of bed that night by two Bavarian officials who told him he had violated the laws of the great state of Bavaria, which was no longer a part of the German Republic. The next morning the writer and some other foreigners were haled before a court and forced to pay a fine to the Communist state of Bavaria.

It would seem that Communism breeds lack of integrity. Hatta should have known that before he let himself be used by the enemies of Great Britain and the United States. The League Against Colonial Oppression was not what it seemed on the surface, for it actually was an organization which intended to ruin Great Britain, France and the Netherlands in Asia for the benefit of Russia, which was not considered a colonial power. Furthermore, the officials who controlled the foreign policy of the Dutch nation in 1945 and 1946 should have known what it meant to bargain with men lacking in good faith. To sign a treaty with Communists or fellow travelers is to put confidence in a worthless piece of paper.

In April 1947 the present writer had a long discussion with His Eminence Johannes Cardinal de Jong in his home in Utrecht. The writer complained about the fact that the Roman Catholic Party had forsaken its ancient ally, the Anti-Revolutionary Party, and joined with the Socialists in a common front. This, so reasoned the writer, would lead to a weak foreign policy. The Cardinal replied as follows: "It is an *alliance de raison;* my heart is not in it." It was easy to see that this prince of the Roman Catholic Church was not happy in his present situation. During the Second World War he had boldly defied the Nazis and had refused to collaborate with the Liberals and the Socialists, let alone the Communists. But now he was allied with his former opponents, which made him rather uneasy.

The events of 1945 and 1946 had very serious consequences for the Indonesians as well as for the Americans. If the Dutch officials had realized their errors of the past and seen that the leaders of the Indonesian nationalists had been driven into the arms of the Japanese and the Communists partly because of a policy by the Dutch that had been too stern in the past, they would have taken measures quite different from those that they did adopt in an evil hour. Unfortunately for the Dutch nation it so happened that Lord Mountbatten, who assumed responsibility for the liberation of the Dutch East Indies, chose to deal with men who were not reliable nor representatives of the Indonesian people as a whole. Dr. van Mook, the Lieutenant-General, also decided to bargain with the Japanese puppets Sukarno and Hatta.

The mess left behind by the Japanese in Indonesia was certainly no worse than that which the Germans had bequeathed to the Dutch people in 1945. Just the same, the Dutch got busy at once and cleaned up their mess at home, while the Indonesian leaders let things go from bad to worse. Racial hatred went on unabated because there was no desire on the part of the leaders to use common sense. The enemies of the U.S.A. and Great Britain were treated with the utmost deference and cordiality by the very persons whom the Indonesian nationalists had burned in effigy a short time before. Dr. van Mook should have noted that his instructions were as laid down in Art. 45 of the Indies State Regulation, which was the Constitution of the Dutch East Indies. He was to protect the people against oppression from any quarter. But this law meant nothing any more to those who chose to cater to the desires of their own enemies. Many thousands of Chinese and Eurasians were murdered under the most criminal circumstances and in the most inhumane manner.

One Governor of East Java has estimated that in the republican disorders of the years 1945 to 1949 some two million natives and other inhabitants lost their lives due to lack of protection from the proper authorities in Indonesia. For months and months the civilian internees and prisoners of war were left behind barbed wire while the constituted authorities bargained with men who had usurped their powers without consulting their own people. The Dutch officials should certainly have insisted upon the release of the internees and prisoners of war before the talks with the unelected representatives of the so-called republic were begun!

In the year 1949 an amiable young Indonesian official named Almassawa came to Ann Arbor and gave a talk before a student body in the basement of Lane Hall on State Street. The present writer presided over the meeting and the next day he took Mr. and Mrs. Almassawa to Detroit. The latter styled themselves Federalists. They explained their position as follows: He had an important

office in Batavia, or Djakarta, where he helped the cause
of the Indonesian nationalism by working for the establishment of a federal republic in imitation of the U.S.A.
During World War II he had assisted the Dutch with all
the means at his disposal, and there were many thousands
of intelligent young men in Java who were going to work
the same way. There should be a well-ordered government with all the earmarks of true parliamentary practices. In Mr. Almassawa's opinion the Indonesians could
very well afford to use the Dutch scholars and businessmen
in exploiting the great natural recources of their country.
He bemoaned the ruthless manner in which the associates
of Sukarno and Hatta had stifled free elections. There
should be close friendship with the countries of the West,
rather than the senseless racial hostility and persecution
recommended by Sukarno and Hatta . Since Queen Wilhelmina in December 1942 had officially promised that
Indonesia would soon become an independent nation, the
Federalists and the Dutch did not quarrel over the question of a future colonial status . The old colonial days were
gone, as the Queen had admitted in 1942. Why then all
this fuss about the unwillingness of the Dutch to grant full
independence to the Indonesian people? The Federalists,
who were very numerous, and the Dutch in 1949 were
ready to set up a system of government that would strongly
resemble that in the U.S.A. They did not want to turn
all authority and power over to a few men who wished to
rule without proper elections and proper representation.

Public opinion in the U.S.A. was upon the whole
poorly informed. The average citizen believed that the
Revolution in Indonesia was very similar to that of 1776
in America, when Great Britain had to give up her political hold on the American colonies to the south of Canada.
The thought seldom occurred to the leading journalists

and radio commentators that perhaps there was a difference between the two revolutions. The Dutch started out
by promising full independence, and they meant exactly
what they said. Queen Wilhelmina was a very religious
person, and she never intended to deceive her former subjects. But the British in 1776 did not offer full independence nor did they intend to give it without a struggle.

In the year 1949 the celebrated Round Table Conference under supervision of the United Nations Organization (U.N.O.) was held. The Dutch negotiated directly
with the men who had set up the new republic, thereby
checking the aspirations of the Federalists. The first meeting was opened in The Hague on August 23, and the last
one closed on November 2, 1949. It was agreed that the
transfer of sovereignty would take place before 1950. The
title of the new republic would be The United States of
Indonesia, but the Indonesian leaders took instant care
that in the future no such state should exist, notwithstanding their own written agreement. When the natives of
Amboina and other territories wanted to assume their
right they had just received their masters in Java quickly
put down their "rebellion." Their desire was to have a
state of their own, somewhat analogous to a state in the
U.S.A. They discovered to their sorrow that the men who
set up the federal state had no intention of keeping it that
way. They almost immediately broke their agreement
with the peoples of the islands to the east of Java.

It was hoped by all parties concerned that in the future
the pre-war trade and industry would be fully restored. In
1948 the situation had looked very favorable for the Dutch.
Exports to Indonesia were 7.5 percent of all the exports,
and imports from Indonesia had risen to the figure of 6.8
percent. In 1938 the figures were respectively 9.7 and 7.2
percent. In pre-war days the total of Dutch investments

in the East Indies was about 2,800,000,000 guilders, while that of all other nations combined was only 1,800,000,000 guilders. The Indonesians themselves also profited from the Dutch investments and labors. In 1938 the local government received 200,000,000 guilders in the form of taxes, and the workmen 400,000,000. These figures are revealing, for they refute the arguments of those who sought to show that the Dutch fleeced the natives in a scandalous manner.

The Round Table Conference produced good results in the matter of trade and industry. The Indonesian delegates realized that they were in no position to insist upon the right to make separate commercial agreements with all the nations in the world. They were willing to let the Dutch help to sell their products in various countries, largely by transporting them to Dutch markets, where they would fetch just as high prices as would be the case if they were sold somewhere else and in many smaller quantities. Consequently, during the period from 1949 to 1953 a large amount of Indonesian tobacco and tea has been sold at good prices by the Dutch. Oil and tin have also been disposed of in an amicable manner, allowing the Dutch a fair amount of profit and leaving the Idonesians a handsome residue. It should be noted, however, that American oil companies have recently taken over a large share of the business, but that was in line with previous developments.

In the night of December 8 and 9 the Second Chamber in The Hague finally took a vote on the treaty with the Indonesians. All of the 100 members were present, a unique situation. Of these 71 voted in favor and 29 opposed. The Roman Catholics (32 members) were unanimous in their support, and the Anti-Revolutionary Party solidly opposed. The Socialists, now called Labor Party, were also in favor. In the First Chamber 49 votes were cast, the total membership being 50; 34 were in favor and 15 opposed. On December 27, 1949, Queen Juliana in the large *burgerzaal* of the former City Hall, now called the Royal Palace in Amsterdam signed the treaty. Wilhelmina's daughter executed the promise made by the Queen nine years earlier. The old order of things had passed away.

Although the Roman Catholic and the Labor Parties had not opposed the transfer of sovereignty, many members of the two parties regretted the fact that they could not have witnessed a period of transition. Everybody knew well that the Indonesians required at least ten years of careful guidance, but outside interference by misinformed American and British idealists had wrecked the program envisioned by both Catholics and Calvinists. The baneful results of this intereference are now visible on every hand, and they are exactly what many well-intentioned Hollanders had predicted to the present writer in 1947, when he talked with them. Those who fought so bravely, notably Admiral Helfrich, are now asking what sort of reward the Dutch got for their fighting. Helfrich, in a letter dated July 15, 1953, wonders why he ever had expected recognition from the Allied governments for the work done by his subordinates. Why did Sukarno and Hatta seem more important than hard-working men like Almassawa? And why were those men cast aside who were real friends?

The *Saturday Evening Post* of May 16, 1953, and the *Reader's Digest* of August 1953 allege that the Dutch were unable to put down the rebellion of the nationalists. This is entirely misleading. On July 30, 1947, the U.N.O. began its campaign against the Netherlands, which had completed its first active offense against the nationalists. The

Dutch government called it a police action, but the name is of litle significance. Australia and India invoked Articles 35 and 39 of the Statute, and although neither power considered the question as to whether or not the U.N.O. was competent in this matter, it was immediately placed on the agenda of the Security Council. The draft resolution made by Australia read as follows: "The Security Council, noting with concern the hostilities in progress between the armed forces of the Netherlands and the Republic of Indonesia, calls upon parties (a) to cease hostilities forthwith, and (b) to settle the disputes by arbitration or by other peaceful means and keep the Security Council informed about the progress of the settlement."

The Dutch government complied with this order, believing, however, that the Security Council of the U.N. did not have the proper authority with which to issue such an order. Since according to the terms of the agreements made so far between the Dutch government and the nationalists there was not yet an actual Indonesian Republic within the framework of the Dutch East Indies, it was not proper nor ethical for the Security Council to intervene in the domestic affairs of the Dutch government in the East Indies.

The second action by the Dutch government, called the second police action, was swift, orderly and extremely successful. Contrary to many foreigners the natives had very little desire to support Sukarno and Hatta. The latter with all their apparatus at Jogjakarta were captured by the Dutch forces. In a few more weeks almost complete order and stability would have been restored in all parts of the Dutch East Indies. It was now January 1949, and the Renville Agreement was supposedly still in force, that is, the Dutch had abided by its terms while the Indonesian nationalists had for the most part refused to comply with them. The document was dated January 17, 1948. It stated that there must be a cease fire order immediately, and that after six months "free elections will be held for self-determination by the people of their political relationship to the United States of Indonesia." Those elections were never held for the simple reason that they would have meant the end of the power exercised by the chief leaders of the nationalists.

The success of the second forceful action by the Dutch government was so spectacular and so satisfactory to the great majority of Indonesians that many foreigners were thoroughly displeased. Particularly those small powers which never had had any colonies themselves did not want the Dutch to enjoy further rule of any sort in the East Indies. The Committees of Good Offices of the U.N.O. had stated on January 17, 1948, in an appendix to the Renville Agreement, that "Sovereignty throughout the Netherlands Indies is and shall remain with the Kindom of the Netherlands until, after a stated interval, the Kingdom of the Netherlands transfers its sovereignty to the United States of Indonesia." That is the reason why Sukarno and his associates did not want to accept the terms of the Renville Agreement.

As soon as the Dutch officials saw that they were dealing with irresponsible persons they decided to check their subversive activities. The reader may have asked why in 1948 the Dutch government acted in such a different way from that adopted in 1945 and 1946. The reason is easy to understand. As long as the Dutch experts thought that they could make some progress in negotiating with honest representatives of the masses of the people, they were quite willing to carry out Wilhelmina's promise of total independence even under Sukarno and Hatta. But how could they trust the latter after they had captured secret documents in Jogjakarta, the capital of the so-called Indonesian Republic? Moreover, how could there be a sovereign state within a larger sovereign state? The great error made by well-meaning men in the Security Council of the U.N.O. was that they could somehow envision one sovereign state as a part of another sovereign state. Such a thing had never existed before, as it was completely at variance with the fundamental concepts of international law and human reason. But a wave of mob phychology swept over the most learned statesmen in 1949. They never thought of consulting some dependable Indonesians who really loved their own people, nor did they listen to the voice of their own consciences. It would seem incredible to the British or the French or the Belgians now if they were to make the same concessions the Dutch were called upon to offer in the opening months of 1949. A sovereign power was forced to recognize within its dominions another sovereign power, although the latter was not called by that title. It received the real essence of recognition, while the experts still used the proper terminology. Granted that the Kingdom of the Netherlands exercised sovereignty in the Dutch East Indies, how could anybody in the Security Council argue for the desstruction of the same before an orderly development had removed it?

On December 17, 1948, the Dutch government started the second "police action" because it was then apparent that the followers of Sukarno and Hatta were terrorists rather than nationalists. The government issued an illuminating booklet at that time entitled *Why Political Negotiations between the Netherlands and the Indonesian Republic Failed.* Although published in the English language, it is very seldom quoted in any country outside of the Netherlands. That is not a bit strange, for a booklet drawn up by men who had originally tried to assist Sukarno and Hatta in their attempt to lead the people into independence and showing that there was justice in the Dutch cause as opposed to that adopted by jealous powers in Europe, Asia and America, was obviously not to the liking of the latter.

In this illuminating booklet we read: "Although the Renville Agreement was signed, after long and painstaking negotiations, by plenipotentiary representatives of the Republic and so undeniably constituted a lawful obligation of the Republican Government and all its services including the armed forces, it was straightaway made clear by the Commander-in-chief of the Republican National Army that the *forces at least* would never stop the fight, truce or no truce." In other words, the order for a cease fighting was binding only upon the Dutch, not upon the Indonesian forces.

On January 25, 1948, General Sudirman said in a formal Broadcast: "The forces of the Republic of Indonesia have throughout never given up the struggle and they will not do so until their ideals of complete liberty have been realized. Moreover, the decision to accept the truce was made by the Cabinet. *Both orally and in writing all the commanders of units in the forces have made known their determination to continue the fight in defense of the sovereignty and liberty of the Republic of Indonesia.*" The italics were supplied by the Dutch government in December 1948.

The military dictators on August 4, 1948, came out with the following remarks: "Those who took part in the Bandung Conference are nothing but traitors who deserve to be shot." This conference was held peacefully by non-Republican, Federalist Indonesians, who believed in parliamentary procedure and free elections. They also thought that self-respecting citizens should abide by the terms of an agreement made by their government with another government. According to General Sudirman the men who negotiated with the officials representing the U.N.O. on the American ship *Renville* were not properly qualified to act for the armed forces, and so the latter felt free to carry on the armed fight, regardless of the truce order issued by the U.N.O. When the Dutch saw that their men were being attacked by the soldiers of General Sudirman, they finally took up arms again. This is not the way the story reads in numerous accounts published thus far by those who preferred to listen to lawless terrorists rather than to peaceful citizens of Indonesia.

One example may suffice here: In the book by James A. Michener entitled, *The Voice of Asia,* one of the "Bantam Giants" and sold by the thousands at 35 cents a copy, we read this: "Few Americans visit Indonesia today without instinctively wishing that the Dutch were back in control. . . . Comparing 1935 with today's anarchy one begins to rationalize that perhaps the Indonesian himself was better off under Dutch rule. . . . The evil fact about colonialism in Asia is that the laudable reforms were always just about to take place. . . . I am even for the bewildered people who think that if they can only wrest Irian from Holland somehow everything will magically be better." Mr. Michener reports some conversations he had with a few persons who did certainly not represent the masses of the people. He also talked with a Dutch citizen whose words he quoted at great length. What he should have done is to do a little research in the libraries and archives, rather than rely on the comments of those who gave him only what he wanted to hear. He thinks that Indonesia will get Dutch New Guinea. In that position he is greatly mistaken, as he is in some others. The Dutch in the Far East put through many notable reforms in the past, as any

historian will readily admit, and henceforth they will continue, in spite of errors, to make further progress in the
right direction.

There are some facts that may nullify the efforts of the
extreme nationalists to become entirely independent of
the Dutch. Article 5 of the Union Statute says that "at
the head of the Union shall be Her Majesty Queen Juliana, Princess of Orange-Nassau, and in case of succession
Her lawful successors in the Crown of the Netherlands."
Article 6 adds these significant words: "The Head of the
Union effectuates the spirit of voluntary and lasting co-
operation between the partners." In the Preamble of the
Union Statute appears this sentence: "The Kingdom of
the Netherlands and the Republic of the United States
of Indonesia, having resolved on a basis of free will, equal-
ity and complete independence to bring about friendly
co-operation with each other and to create the Netherlands Indonesian Union with a view to effectuate this
future co-operation, have agreed to lay down in this
Statute of Union the basis of their mutual relationship as
independent and sovereign States." Furthermore, it was
provided that three ministers of each of the two partners
were to hold conferences twice a year "and further as often
as the partners shall deem necessary." The Union is to be
served by a Secretariat; each of the two partners has a
secretary-general. Joint regulations are to be submitted
for ratification to the parliaments of the two partners. A
Union Court of Arbitration has also been provided for,
consisting of six members, three for each partner. Common defense measures, financial and commercial agreements, and cultural stipulations have been drawn up in
great detail, as stated in Articles 21-23. These details are
to be found in separate documents of a supplementary
nature.

The Round Table Conference could not come to an agreement regarding the status of western New Guinea. After many conferences on the subject the Dutch government suddenly announced in 1953 that it would henceforth consider this area as Dutch territory pure and simple. The Dutch flag now waves at Hollandia, the capital, and Merauke, which was mentioned above, as well as in other places. They Royal Dutch Oil Co. has agreed to share with American companies the exploitation of the very substantial oil deposits in Dutch New Guinea. Near Hollandia rich nickel deposits have been located, while coal supplies are known to be adequate for future use in the area. Vast acreages of rich clay soil are to be found in the southern region, while in most sections valuable forests are awaiting exploitation. In the center are mountains covered with glaciers, being more than 15,000 feet in altitude. Waterfalls can be harnessed to provide electricity, and immense fisheries are a distinct possibility. The rainfall is heavy in the lowlands along the southern coast, where no doubt some day enormous rice fields will provide a living for several million persons. After the work of more than three centuries in Indonesia the Dutch cannot be expected to fold their hands in lassitude and regret over the disasters that befell them in the period from 1940 to 1945. Their own country has done so well that half of the American investments in Europe happen to have been concentrated in the Netherlands.

The native population in Dutch New Guinea is not of the Malay race, as is the case in Indonesia. The Papuans are a simple people, different in many respects from the inhabitants of Java or Sumtra. Although they have lived in New Guinea for many centuries, they are not nearly so numerous as their northern neighbors. According to the latest statistics they number about 700,000. Since the western half of New Guinea has greater oil deposits than Sumatra and Bornea combined, and since the higher plateaus offer pleasant living conditions for the Dutch, it may be expected that in the near future many Hollanders will emigrate to this area. Their crops will not be subject to drouths and the heat of the tropics will generate luxuriant plant growth. Lumber will be plentiful for generations to come. It is likely that Dutch New Guinea, which is close to Australia, will resemble this sub-continent in becoming a distinctly white man's country. In Java and the outer territories the natives were too numerous to permit such a development, but New Guinea is entirely different.

The Dutch were the first to chart the coasts of Australia, which during the eighteenth century was generally called New Holland, while New Zealand was named after the Dutch province of Zeeland. They still have a large stake in Indonesia. Under the guidance of the new governor, Van Baal, formerly a fiery Anti-Revolutionary member of the Second Chamber of the Dutch Parliament, the Dutch settlers may look for orderly progress and suitable exploitation of the natural resources. They will find swamps and forests, as did their cousins when in 1847 they founded the city of Holland, Mich. under the indomitable Albertus C. Van Raalte. Much hard work will have to be done, but that should not cause them to grow impatient. Whereas in the first half of the nineteenth century the Dutch settlers in western Michigan did not have at their disposal such advantages as air-conditioning and heavy machinery for breaking up the soil, the founders of new cities in the Far East will enjoy the conveniences provided by our scientists. The Dutch in the Far East will perform wonders such as Java never saw before 1949.

BIBLIOGRAPHICAL ANNOTATIONS

NOTE FOR THE PREFACE

[1] S. Takdir Alisjahbana, "Tensions in Indonesian Life and Culture," in *Confluence: An International Forum*, March 1953, pp. 13–22. Mr. Alisjahbana is a Lecturer in Indonesian culture and literature in the Akademi Nasional, Djakarta; also editor of *PudJangga Baru* (culture and literature) and *Pembina Bahasa Indonesia* (modernization of the Indonesian language). Being a participant in the Harvard International Seminar of 1952, he was asked to write his highly illuminating article. *Confluence* is published by Harvard University.

This Indonesian scholar naturally represents those interests which hope to make their country entirely independent of the Dutch in matters of commerce as well as of industry, utilities, transportation and cultural life. He admits that "many of the present difficulties are undoubtedly due to the lack of experienced and trained personnel, both in the business world and in government, and this has resulted in much uneven and indecisive action." Among eighty million inhabitants there are only some one thousand physicians, three hundred attorneys, eighty fully qualified engineers and ten economists to lead the way of the morass he has mentioned. The liberation and the revolution, so he continues, did not actually solve but render more acute the problems of Indonesian culture.

There is much "controversy, chaos and doubt," but Indonesia also is producing real reconstruction. For example, the school system shows some signs of improvement. "The Dutch left us with a heritage of eight million children between the ages of 7 and 12 who had not had the opportunity to attend any kind of school." Very true, but the author does not tell us what was done by the native population to force more children to enter school. The Dutch also left the people with their own religion, unlike the Spaniards in the Philippines, who took care that their subjects become Roman Catholics. Moreover, the Indonesians were left with their two hundred languages and their political and social ways of life. Such was their own desire, hence they received what they wanted: as little interference from the Dutch as possible under the circumstances.

Owing to the influence of Japanese and other diplomats and businessmen the Indonesians adopted a frame of mind that tended to overlook certain good features of the old order. For example, the Mohammedan laws had been carefully preserved and studied. Theft and murder were properly and promptly punished, Plantations owned by foreigners were protected from sabotage, while the natives still continued to own the soil.

NOTES FOR CHAPTER I

[1] G. N. Clark, *The Seventeenth Century* (Oxford, 1929), pp. 14–15.

[2] G. M. Trevelyan, *England under the Stuarts*, 12th ed. (New York, London, 1925), p. 50.

[3] See especially the influential work of J. E. Barker, *The Rise and Decline of the Netherlands: A Political and Economic History and a Study in Practical Statesmanship* (London, 1906), pp. 279–291.

[4] See J. B. Manger, *Recherches sur les relations écnomiques entre la France et la Hollande pendant la Révolution Française (1785–1795)* (Amsterdam, 1923), p. 23.

[5] This article was written by C. H. Wilson; it appeared in the issue of May, 1939. The writer refers to the wrong pages of Manger's book, and he exaggerates when he says that, according to Mr. Sagnac, "the carrying trade between France and northern Europe from 1697 to 1713 was entirely in the hands of the Dutch."

[6] See C. H. Wilson, *op. cit.*, p. 113.

[7] See J. G. van Dillen, "Amsterdam, marché mondial des métaux précieux au XVIIe et XVIIIe siècle," in: *Revue Historique*, Vol. CLII (1926), pp. 194–201.

[8] Max Weber's thesis is indeed approved of in the doctoral dissertation submitted by W. F. van Gunsteren, in The Free University and published in Amsterdam in 1934. The title is *Kalvinismus und Kapitalismus: Ein Beitrag zur Erkenntnis der Beziehungen zwischen Kalvinistischer Sozial-ethik und kapitalistischem Wirtschaftsgeist.*

[9] See p. 3 of this issue of the *Standaard* of April 13, 1939.

[10] Even Mr. J. B. Manger (who has been mentioned above), when he presented his thesis of the economic relations between France and Holland just before the French Revolution, which he did as a student of the University of Amsterdam, and not of the Free University in Amsterdam, felt called upon to devote the second of his propositions connected with the presentation of his doctoral dissertation to the relation between capitalism and Calvinism. He stated in this second proposition, which was publicly defended by him on May 23, 1923, that Professor H. Pirenne was mistaken when he saw a connection between capitalism and Calvinism. See his famous work, *Histoire de Belgique*, Vol. III, 2nd ed., p. 433.

[11] The place of publication is Cambridge, England.

[12] See pp. 171–172 of his book.

[13] He wrote the admirable work, *Cattolicesimo e Protestantesimo nella formazione storica del capitalismo* (Milan, 1934). An English translation appeared in New York in 1936, entitled, *Catholicism, Protestantism and Capitalism.*

[14] A. Fanfani, *Catholicism, Protestantism and Capitalism*, p. 168.

[15] The figures about the Baltic trade given above are drawn from a very useful work: N. E. Bang, *Tabeller over skibsfart og varetransport*

gennem Oresund 1497–1660 (Copenhagen and Leipzig, 1906); and the same for 1661–1789, published in 1930. They show that, until the war of the American Revolution, the ships of the Dutch Republic kept abreast of the English merchant marine in the Baltic Sea. They explain why Oliver Cromwell said such bitter things about the Dutch in the Sound, as may be seen especially in Speech XVII, in the edition of Thomas Carlyle. It is indeed remarkable that in 1653, when Cromwell's sailors were said to be successful in fighting the Dutch, not a single ship from England sailed through the Sound. It is also remarkable that the province of Zeeland did no better in the years 1673, 1676–1678, 1691, and 1695; when Holland sent respectively, 500, 723, 961, 627, and 701 ships. The highest number attained by Friesland and Groningen (the two northern Dutch provinces) was 1,498 in 1740, when Holland sent 1,106, and England 718. In 1775, England boasted of 2,038, Holland of 982, and Friesland and Groningen of 1,422.

[16] M. Weber, *The Protestant Ethic and the Spirit of Capitalism* (London, 1930), pp. 103–104.

[17] See A. Hyma, "Calvinism and Capitalism in the Netherlands, 1555–1700," in: *The Journal of Modern History*, Vol. X (Sept., 1938), p. 324.

[18] Sir Walter Raleigh, "Observations Touching Trade and Commerce with the Hollander, and other Nations," in: *The Works of Sir Walter Raleigh, now first collected to which are prefixed the lives of the author, by Oldys and Birch*, Vol. VIII (Oxford, 1829), p. 370. See also the same treatise in the book entitled *Remains of Sir Walter Raleigh* (London, 1702), pp. 149–150.

[19] See P. J. Blok, *Geschiedenis van het Nederlandsche volk*, Vol. II, (Leyden, 1913), p. 370.

[20] See W. Raleigh, *op. cit.*, pp. 357–358.

[21] See W. Raleigh, *op. cit.*, p. 356.

[22] The complete title runs thus: *"Memoirs of the Dutch Trade in all the States, Empires, and Kingdoms in the World. Shewing its first rise and amazing Progress: After what Manner the Dutch manage and carry on their Commerce; their vast Dominions and Government in the Indies, and by what Means they have made themselves Masters of all the Trade of Europe as also What Goods and Merchandize are proper for Maritime Traffick, whence they are to be had, and what Gain and Profit they produce. A Treatise very necessary for every Englishman.* The treatise in the original language is entitled, *Memoires sur le commerce des Hollandois dans tous les etats et empires du monde.* The author's full name is Pierre Daniel Huet. The French edition consulted by the present writer is that published at Amsterdam in 1717.

[23] On the last subject see the admirable work by Dr. J. H. Kernkamp, *De handel op den vijand*, Vol. II, 1588–1609 (Utrecht, 1935). The author shows that from 1588 to 1609 trade between Spain and the Dutch Republic continued regardless of the proclamations and

placards of both governments. He concludes that the large number of prohibitions issued is an indication of the violations (see p. 348 of his work).

[24] Pierre D. Huet, *op. cit.*, pp. XII–XVIII of the French edition, and pp. V–XI of the second English edition.

[25] P. D. Huet, *op. cit.*, p. 33 of the French edition, and p. 28 of the English edition.

[26] Huet, *op. cit.*, p. 32 of the second English edition.

[27] P. D. Huet, *l.c.*, p. 58 of the second English edition. The commercial relations between the Dutch Republic and Sweden have been ably discussed in W. J. Kolkert, *Nederland en het Zweedsche imperialisme* (Deventer, 1908), especially pp. 4–11. The writer makes this significant observation on p. 4: "Het is licht te begrijpen, dat in een handelsstaat als de Republiek bij uitnemendheid was, welks 'geheel leven ende welvaren, mitsgaders reputatie' van den stand der 'commercie ende navigatie' afhing, de belangen van dien handel van den versten invloed moesten zijn op al zijn staatkundige betrekkingen." Dutch trade with Muscovy is treated in S. Muller Fzn., *Geschiedenis der Noordsche Compagnie* (Utrecht, 1874). See also S. van Brakel, *De Hollandsche handelscompagnieën der zeventiende eeuw* (The Hague, 1908), pp. 28–29, 55. The reasons why Dutch commerce grew so rapidly during the seventeenth century are analyzed in the Introduction, pp. XI–XV. A more recent work is F. Breedvelt-Van Veen, *Louis de Geer 1587–1652* (Amsterdam, 1935), in which De Geer is described as a typical "big businessman" in Amsterdam and later in Sweden. Note the excellent bibliography on pp. 233–235. King Gustavus Adolphus was heavily indebted to this Dutch merchant and industrialist, for he enabled the Swedes to exploit their huge deposits of iron ore.

[28] This subject has been more fully discussed in K. Heeringa, *Bronnen tot de geschiedenis van den Levantschen handel*, Vol. II (The Hague, 1917), pp. 1–52.

[29] See his *Oeuvres complètes* (Paris, 1823–1825), XVIII, p. 339.

[30] Montesquieu, *Voyages* (Paris, 1894–1896), Vol. II, p. 230.

[31] Descartes, *Oeuvres* (Paris, 1897–1913), Vol. I, p. 203.

[32] See R. Murris, *La Hollande et les Hollandais au XVIIe et XVIIIe siècles vus par les Français* (Paris, 1925), pp. 42–44.

[33] *La Richesse de la Hollande.*

[34] See Vol. I of this work, pp. 78–80.

[35] See A. Hyma, article on John de Witt in the *Encyclopedia of the Social Sciences.*

[36] See Ernst Baasch, *Hollaendische Wirtschaftsgeschichte* (Jena, 1927), p. 241–245. See also G. N. Clark, *The Seventeenth Century*, pp. 14–15.

[37] A. Eekhof, *De Hervormde Kerk in Noord-Amerika*, Vol. II (The Hague, 1913), p. 1.

[38] *Acta van de Nederlandsche synoden der zestiende eeuw,* ed. F. L. Rutgers, in *Werken der Marnix-Vereeniging,* Series II, Vol. II (Utrecht, 1889), pp. 13, 22, 25, 134, 140, 144, 154–156, 158, 163, 168–169, 220, 231, 235, 264, 283, 285, 318, 323, 325–326, 321–330, 365, 402–403, 418, 420, 426–427, 433–434, 439, 442–443, 446, 449, 452, 488, 495, 498, 500–501, 513, 542, 557, 595–598, 602–603, 612, 618, 624–625, 627–628. See also A. Hyma, *Christianity and Politics* (Philadelphia, Pa., 1938), pp. 234–250.

[39] *Verclaringhe van twee vraghen door D. Franciscus Iunius. In sijn leven Doctor ende Professor der Heylighe Theologie in de vermaerde Hooghe-Schole tot Leyden. De Eerste, Van de overeencominghe en het onderscheyt der Politijcke ende Kerchelijcke bedieninghe. De Tweede, Van het Recht des Magistraets in de sichtbare Kercke.* This work was published in Amsterdam in 1610 (Knuttel, 1770).

[40] The book has been reproduced in 1935 by the Baptist Historical Society in England and is entitled *The Mistery of Iniquity.*

[41] Herbert I. Bloom, *The Economic Activities of the Jews of Amsterdam in the Seventeenth and Eighteenth Centuries* (Williamsport, Pa., 1937).

[42] See H. I. Bloom, *op. cit.,* p. 15.

[43] Pieter de la Court, *Interest van Holland ofte Gronden van Hollands-Welvaren* (Amsterdam, 1662), p. 38.

[44] One of my students, Dr. Frank Dykema, has recently completed a doctoral dissertation in which he discusses in considerable detail the commercial relations between France and the Dutch Republic between 1648 and 1672. He mentions numerous cases where both French and Dutch pirates operated and had to be restricted by their respective governments.

[45] H. Dunlop, *Hollandsche zeerovers in de zeventiende eeuw* (Zutphen, 1938).

[46] A. C. Kruseman, "Aanteekeningen betreffende den Boekhandel van Noord-Nederland in de 17 de en 18de eeuw," in *Bijdragen tot de Geschiedenis van den Nederlandschen Boekhandel,* VI, 1893, p. 497. See also M. M. Kleerkooper and W. P. van Stockum, *De Boekhandel te Amsterdam, voornamelijk in de 17e eeuw* (The Hague, 1914–1916), pp. 361–362.

[47] H. I. Bloom, *op. cit.,* p. 49. Mr. Bloom says that it is not clear to him what were the purposes of these musical notations, but he has done an important service in presenting a mass of details concerning the economic activities of the Jews of Amsterdam.

[48] M. James, *Social Problems and Policy during the Puritan Revolution 1640–1660* (London, 1930), pp. 188–191.

[49] A. S. P. Woodhouse, *Puritanism and Liberty being the Army Debates (1647–9) from the Clarke Manuscripts with Supplementary Documents* (London, 1938), p. 138.

[50] Published at Cambridge in the year 1922. See Ch. VII, pp. 110–118.

[51] G. Edmundson, *op. cit.*, p. 110.

[52] J. E. Barker, *The Rise and Decline of the Netherlands* (London, 1906), p. 165.

[53] R. Fruin, *Geschiedenis der staatsinstellingen in Nederland tot den val der republiek*, ed. by H. T. Colenbrander (The Hague, 1901), p. 184.

[54] P. Geyl, *The Netherlands Divided (1609–1648)*, translated by S. T. Bindoff, M.A., in collaboration with the author (London, 1935), p. 248.

[55] R. Fruin, *op. cit.*, pp. 264–346.

[56] C. H. Wilson, "The Economic Decline of the Netherlands," in: *The Economic History*, Vol. IX (May, 1939), pp. 115–127.

[57] E. Baasch, *Hollaendische Wirtschaftsgeschichte* (Jena, 1927).

[58] C. H. Wilson, *op. cit.*, p. 111.

[59] E. Baasch, *op. cit.*, pp. 316–317.

[60] See D. Campbell, *The Puritan in Holland, England and America*, Vol. II (New York, 1892), pp. 325–327.

[61] J. E. Barker, *op. cit.*, pp. 190, 195, 248–251, 264.

[62] See S. A. Kahn, *The East India Trade in the XVIIth Century in Its Political and Economic Aspects* (London, 1923), pp. 22, 25, 26, 27, 29, 36, 41, 42, 44, 48, 49, 51, 53, 55, 56. Moreover on pp. 42 and 43 there are references also to Davenant and Sir Dudley North.

[63] See Charles M. Andrews, *op. cit.*, Vol. IV, pp. 48–49.

[64] See H. E. Becht, *Statistische gegevens betreffende den handelsomzet van de republiek der vereenigde Nederlanden gedurende de 17e eeuw (1579–1715)* (The Hague, 1908), pp. 186–189; R. Fruin, *op. cit.*, pp. 306–309. Mr. Becht shows that the great wars from the period from 1600 to 1750 had relatively little effect on the extent of Dutch commerce, as the revenues of the government plainly reveal.

[65] W. Sombart, *Der moderne Kapitalismus*, Vol. II (Leipzig, 1917), p. 957.

[66] M. James, *Social Problems and Policies during the Puritan Revolution*, pp. 69–70.

[67] R. Coke, *A Detection of the Court and State of England* (London, 1697), pp. 350, 356.

[68] M. James, *op. cit.*, pp. 72–73.

[69] M. James, *op. cit.*, pp. 73–74.

[70] C. M. Andrews, *The Colonial Period of American History*, Vol. IV (1938), p. 46.

[71] C. M. Andrews, *op. cit.*, p. 47.

A similar opinion has been expressed by L. A. Harper in his excellent work, *The English Navigation Laws* (New York, 1939), pp. 51–52. He shows that the English colonies in North America objected to legislation enacted in Great Britain unless they had been consulted first.

On the other hand, he claims that the Acts broke the Dutch hold on England's carrying trade and kept Holland from sharing in the profits of the English colonies. (See p. 306 of his book). Unfortunately, he seems to err on this point by overlooking other factors. His documentation here is inadequate.

72 See J. D. Elias, *Het voorspel van den eersten Engelschen oorlog* (The Hague, 1920), p. 127.

73 S. Elzinga, *Het voorspel van den oorlog van 1672. De economisch-politieke betrekkingen tusschen Frankrijk en Nederland in de jaren 1660–1672* (Haarlem, 1926), pp. 197–219.

74 S. Elzinga, *op. cit.*, pp. 275–293.

75 H. de Vries. *The Anglo-Dutch War, 1672–1674* (not yet published). This is a doctoral dissertation submitted in the department of history in the University of Michigan in the spring of 1939. The writer has shown in this work that an influential Hollander, called Du Moulin, persuaded a number of important officials in England during the course of the year 1673–74 to become friends rather than enemies of the Dutch.

76 The title of the first work is *A Justification of the Present War against the United Netherlands. Wherein the Declaration of His Majesty is Vindicated, and the War Proved to be Just, Honourable, and Necessary; The Dominion of the Sea Explained, and His Majesties Rights Thereunto Asserted* (London, 1672). The title of the second work is *A Further Justification of the Present War against the United Netherlands* (London, 1673).

77 H. Stubbe, *A Justification of the Present War*, pp. 2–3.

78 H. Stubbe, *A Further Justification of the Present War*, p. 16 (C 3).

79 G. van Alphen, *De stemming van de Engelschen tegen de Hollanders in Engeland tijdens de regeering von den koning-stadhouder William III, 1688–1702.* Leiden Dissertation, 1938.

80 C. H. Wilson, "The Economic Decline of the Netherlands," p. 126.

81 H. T. Colenbrander, *De Patriottentijd.* 3 vols. (The Hague, 1987–99). For the fourth Anglo-Dutch war see Vol. I, pp. 208–233.

82 Published in The Hague in 1925. For the subject mentioned above see pp. 147–151.

83 For many details on this subject see the doctoral dissertation submitted in the University of Amsterdam by H. E. Becht, entitled, *Statistische gegevens betreffende den handelsomzet van de republiek der vereenigde Nederlanden gedurende de 17e eeuw (1579–1715)*, pp. 78–106. The tables in the Appendix indicate that the volume of Dutch commerce remained very high throughout the seventeenth century and that the city of Amsterdam reached the highest volume during the year 1699.

84 See N. W. Posthumus, *De nationale organisatie der lakenkoopers tijdens de republiek* (Utrecht, 1927), pp. 238–241.

85 K. Heeringa, *Bronnen tot de geschiedenis van den levantschen handel*, Vol. I, 1590–1660 (The Hague, 1910), pp. 570–571.

86 N. W. Posthumus, *op. cit.*, pp. 172–174.

87 This is also done by one of the latest European authorities; see T. P. van der Kooy, *Hollands stapelmarkt en haar verval* (Amsterdam, 1931), pp. 1–2. The writer mentions several earlier experts.

88 An excellent discussion of this second factor, called the organization of Dutch commerce, has been presented in T. P. van der Kooy, *op. cit.*, pp. 16–34. Here we observe how the merchants employed salesmen abroad, how they made use of skilled labor wherever they could, how they divided the whole field of commerce and industry into special categories so that specialists could facilitate export and import trade, how they provided cash for the immediate sale of anything that the foreigners wanted to sell in Holland, and how they refined and improved raw products or unfinished goods which had been purchased abroad at a very low cost.

89 An excellent brief summary of the latest research on this subject may be found in the article by Dr. H. J. Smit in *Bijdragen en mededeelingen voor vaderlandsche geschiedenis en oudheidkunde* VIIIe Reeks, Vol. I (1939), pp. 140–143. See also the forthcoming article by the present writer entitled, "Protestantism and Capitalism in Colonial America and the United States before 1860," to be published in *The International Review for the Social Sciences* (Amsterdam).

90 John L. Motley, the author of *The Rise of the Dutch Republic*, which is a brilliant piece of work, but pays almost no attention to economic factors.

91 Preserved Smith, *The Age of the Reformation* (New York, 1920), pp. 275–276.

NOTES FOR CHAPTER II

1 This is the admirable work by Mr. J. K. J. de Jonge, which fills ten volumes. Of especial value to us is his fourth volume, which was published in 1869. But every one of the ten volumes is a scholarly piece of work and based almost entirely upon original sources. The many documents that are published in this book for the first time throw much light upon this important subject. The title of this work is *De opkomst van het Nederlandsch gezag in Oost-Indie. Verzameling van onuitgegeven stukken uit het oud-koloniaal archief.*

Of great value also is the second edition of the original sources that deal with the first trip made by the Dutch navigators to the Malay Archipelago in the years 1595 to 1597. It was prepared by J. C. Mollema and published in 1935, and again in 1936. Mr. Mollema has added a valuable introduction, in which he discusses first of all the reasons why the Dutch began to trade in the Malay Archipelago. This discussion is of considerable value, because it throws much light on the prelude to the rise of

Dutch sea power in the Far East. Mr. Mollema refers here to the excellent work done by the Dutch society called the Lineschoten-Vereeniging. which published the accounts dealing with the first trip of the Hollanders to the Malay Archipelago in three volumes, dates respectively 1915, 1925, and 1929. He also points out the admirable work done in this field by Dr. J. W. IJzerman, who made an extensive survey of the commercial operations of the English, the Portuguese, and the Spaniards during the whole of the sixteenth century. Dr. IJzerman made a valuable collection of notes which he left to the Linschoten-Vereeniging.

Mr. Mollema's work is entitled *De eerste schipvaart der Hollanders naar Oost-Indië 1595-1597 naar de oude journalen.* Another work of importance is the famous essay published in 1868 by Professor R. Fruin, of the University of Leiden. It appeared in the periodical entitled *De Gids,* and an English translation has also been published, but it is far from satisfactory. For that reason the present writer, in 1931, prepared a new translation. It deals with the masterpiece of Hugo Grotius, *De Jure Praedae,* and it explains more accurately than any writer has done between 1868 and 1938 the motives which guided Grotius in preparing his work on the law of Prize in 1604 and 1605, and the arguments he presented to the English in the year 1613. We shall see that there is an apparent difference between the two sets of arguments.

Although it is to be regretted that the Dutch historians have devoted so little time in recent years to the study of Dutch navigation in the Far East, we are very fortunate in possessing the momentous work of De Jonge. Curiously enough, Mr. Clark, in discussing the origins of the Dutch sea power in the Far East, on page 46 of his article, completely ignores this comprehensive account, and refers the reader to the book by J. E. Elias, *Het voorspel van den eersten Engelschen oorlog.* He says that the general account by G. Edmundson, *Anglo-Dutch rivalry* (1911), is much less satisfactory than the book by Elias. As a matter of fact, the brief treatment by Elias is practically worthless when compared with the only comprehensive discussion, namely, that by De Jonge. A new history of the subject was published in 1939. It consists of four large volumes, without documentation, and was edited by F. W. Stapel. Numerous references to it will be made below. In addition to these valuable works, we now possess the monumental biography of Jan Pietersz. Coen, the greatest of the Governor-Generals of the Dutch East Indies, written by Dr. H. T. Colenbrander. In the sixth and last volume in this series, Dr. Colenbrander presents a brilliant discussion of the factors that led to the commercial contacts established in the Far East by various European powers. He is right in observing that not only the Portuguese and the Spaniards, but also the Dutch were impelled to go around Africa in search of spices, owing largely to the obstacles placed in their way through the Near East by the Ottoman Turks. Large numbers of European scholars during the past four hundred years have consistently supported this viewpoint, and although in recent times a group of American historians have come to the conclusion that the Ottoman Turks were not nearly so opposed to commercial contacts with the western powers as was once generally believed, the present writer feels that the concrete facts in the case will vindicate the old opinion.

See H. T. Colenbrander, *Jan Pietersz. Coen*, Vol. VI (The Hague,, 1934), pp. 10–17. He argues that "the Ottoman Turks, imbued with a deep-seated hatred for the Byzantine Empire and all Christendom, conquered Constantinople in 1453 and Egypt in 1517. Now the trade with India was disrupted; how was it to be restored? The Italians sought the solution in dislodging the Turks from the Near East." Even the remarkable revival of trade in the Mediterranean during the second half of the sixteenth century did not fundamentally alter the course pursued first by the Portuguese, then by the Dutch, and finally by the British. They knew why they were avoiding the old trade routes which had ended in Constantinople, Antioch, and Alexandria.

It might be argued that it was twenty-five years after Columbus sailed west in 1492, before Egypt was taken by the Ottoman Turks. It is also well known that the Portuguese sailed around Africa before 1500, and that, in 1502 the Venetians found virtually no spices in Alexandria because the Portuguese had collected them at the original source of supply in India. It is absolutely necessary to remember, nevertheless, that the Christian nations of Europe, ever since 1350, feared the occurrence of a great calamity in the Near East, a fear that was tremendously stimulated in 1453, when the Ottoman Turks seized Constantinople. We may well raise these questions: How did they know where the Turks would encourage trading? All they certainly knew before 1500 was that the Turks did little more than fight, invade, destroy, and levy tribute.

Curiously, the religious factors involved in the commercial revolution that occurred between 1400 and 1600 have thus far been almost completely overlooked, largely because the world today is so different from that which witnessed the dawn of modern civilization. We are too likely to regard Prince Henry the Navigator as a mere navigator, whereas his earliest biographers thought that religious zeal was the principal factor in his repeated endeavors to explore as much of the west coast of Africa as possible. Nor was it for nothing that shortly after the occupation of Constantinople by the Turks, in 1453, two popes in succession issued bulls urging the Christians to wrest some of the lost lands from the Turkish infidels, who were styled "infamous dogs." The literature of the time is filled with thousands of references to the "unspeakable Turks," and until the end of the sixteenth century the leading writers, preachers, and educators of central and western Europe continued to speak of the Turks as the most contemptible people on the face of the earth. Among the Dutch Protestants of the seventeenth century, it became a popular proverb to say that one would rather be a Turk than a Catholic, meaning that only Catholics were worse than Turks. And when reformers preached against usury and graft, they would say that a usurer was even more detestable than a Turk.

Especially significant is the verdict of Erasmus of Rotterdam, the prince of the humanists, who was personally acquainted with a large number of distinguished statesmen, prelates, and scholars. He reflected the popular sentiment current in western Europe during the first three decades of the sixteenth century. Although he was strongly opposed to warfare, he did not hesitate to condemn the barbarous Turks. See his treatise on the Turkish War (*De Bello Turcico*) of the year 1530 (in his *Opera Omnia*, Vol. V (Leyden, 1704), vols. 349, 350, 352, and 353).

Martin Luther was even more prolific in his condemnations of the Turks. One example selected from a large number of similar utterances must suffice here. It has been taken from his celebrated treatise, *Address to the German Nobility*, dated 1520: "Italy is almost a desert now: the convents are destroyed, the sees consumed, the revenues of the prelacies and the churches drawn to Rome; towns are decayed; the country and people ruined . . . Why? Because the cardinals must have all the wealth. No Turk could thus have desolated Italy and overthrown the worship of God."

See also *Die Türkenbulle Pabst Calixtus III*, being a photostatic reproduction edited by P. Schwenke (Berlin, 1911), p. 11: Cum his superioribus annis impius nominis Christiani persecutor Turcorum tyrannus post oppressam Constantinopolim civitatem, in qua omne genus crudelitatis exercuit . . ."

And see *Aeneae Silvii Piccolomini Senensis qui postea fuit Pius II Pont. Max. Opera inedita descripsit . . . J. Cugnoni*, published in *Atti della R. Accademia dei Lincei anno CCLXXX* (Rome, 1883), p. 416: "Hostilis gladius in viscera nostra properat, Rasciam populatur, Hungariam invadit, Germaniae atque Italiae minatur. Sunt inimici nostri potentes ac numerosi . . . Exterminandum est Turchorum impurum genus. Nunquam tuti erimus, nisi hanc pestiferam gentem funditus deleverimus." These words appear in a letter dated January, 1454.

² In this connection Mr. Mollema answers a question that had been raised by Mr. G. N. Clark, but which he had not fully answered himself. On page 49 of Mr. Clark's article the writer discusses the circumstances and the motives which led the earliest Dutch navigators into the Far East. In his opinion they were partly intended as a means of increasing Dutch commerce in the Far East, and partly as an opportunity of inflicting damage upon Spain, which is true in general. The original sources plainly reveal what was in the minds of the founders of the Company of the Far Regions. While treating Portugal as a neutral power, and while avoiding piratical operations, the aim of the

Dutch merchants who sent out the earliest expeditions was not merely to inflict damage upon the Spaniards (which does not appear to have been considered of great importance), but first of all to capture the bulk of the spice trade regardless of who their opponents might be. As one clerk in the employ of the Dutch merchants so succinctly stated, "It is to be hoped that Holland will take precedence over Portugal in building a strong fortification at the port of Bantam." This would give the Dutch control of the important Strait of Malacca. See J. C. Mollema, *op. cit.*, pp. 14–32.

³ See R. Fruin, *Verspreide geschriften*, Vol. III (The Hague, 1901), pp. 372–375.

⁴ This work was published in the original Dutch version as Vol. II of the *Werken der Linschoten-Vereeniging* (The Hague, 1910), and continued in Vol. XXXIX (1934).

⁵ J. C. Mollema, *op. cit.*, pp. 82–357.

⁶ *Geschiedenis van Nederlandsch Indië*, Vol. II (The Hague, 1939), pp. 321–378.

⁷ *Geschiedenis van Nederlandsch Indië*, Vol. II, pp. 379–419; J. K. J. de Jonge, *De opkomst van het Nederlandsch gezag in Oost-Indië*, Vol. I, pp. 99–103, 120–129, 153–228; Vol. II, pp. 210–225.

⁸ Of particular interest is the scholarly account of what happened to the fleet of eight ships which under the command of Admiral Van Neck and Admiral Warwijck sailed directly to the East Indies by way of the Cape of Good Hope: *De tweede schipvaart der Nederlanders naar Oost-Indië*, ed. J. Keuning and published by the Linschoten-Vereeniging, Vol. XLII (1938). This volume contains much valuable information about the separate companies which later were amalgamated to form the Dutch East India Company (see pp. XXI-LV). Very interesting is the journal by Van Neck (pp. 1–111), and helpful are the copies of the original documents and extracts from important secondary works, such as the *Jaarboeken* by Hugo Grotius. Equally illuminating are the two volumes by J. W. IJzerman entitled, *De reis om de wereld door Olivier van Noort, 1598–1601*, in the works of the Linschoten-Vereeniging, Vols. XVII and XVIII. See especially Vol. I, pp. 1–265 and Vol. II, pp. 45–92.

⁹ W. van Ravesteyn, *Onderzoekingen over de economische en sociale ontwikkeling van Amsterdam* (Amsterdam, 1906), pp. 272–362. See also J. K. J. de Jonge, *op. cit.*, Vol. I, pp. 101–103, 217–218; Vol. II, pp. 225–239, 375–459.

¹⁰ Articles 34, 7, and 35 of the Charter.

¹¹ Articles 1, and 2 of the Charter.

¹² Nearly all writers have stated that the number was 73, but the correct figure was discovered by F. W. Stapel. See his article "Het aantal Bewindhebbers der Oostindische Compagnie in 1602," in *Bijdragen voor vaderlandsche geschiedenis en oudheidkunde*, Sixth Series, Vol. VI (1927), pp. 146–148.

13 Articles 18–26.

14 Article 10.

15 H. I. Bloom, *The Economic Activities of the Jews of Amsterdam in the Seventeenth and Eighteenth Centuries* (Williamsport, Pa., 1937), p. 118.

16 *Gesch. van Ned. Indië*, Vol. III, pp. 28–29. Lemaire not only owned stock from the very beginning, but he also was one of the founders of the Brabant Company, and for years he actively bought and sold stock in the East India Company. See the interesting work by J. G. van Dillen, "Isaac le Maire en de handel in actiën der Oost-Indische Compagnie," in *Economisch-Historisch jaarboek*, Vol. XVI (1930), pp. 1–165.

17 A list of the different editions of the charter of 1602, together with valuable information about the same, is to be found in P. van Dam, *Beschryvinge van de Oostindische Compagnie*, edited by Dr. F. W. Stapel, Book I, Vol. I (The Hague, 1927), p. 43.

18 See Pieter Van Dam, *Beschryvinge van de Oostindische Compagnie*, edited by Dr. F. W. Stapel, pp. 433–436.

19 The instructions given by the directors to Warwijck and his vice-admiral, Sebald de Weerd, are to be found in P. van Dam, *Beschryvinge*, Vol. I, part I (The Hague, 1927), pp. 22–29.

20 J. K. J. De Jonge, *De opkomst*, Vol. III, pp. 20–26.

21 Namely, Leitimor. See J. K. J. De Jonge, *De opkomst*, Vol. III, pp. 26–46. Pieter van Dam (Vol. I, Part I, p. 224) says that the fleet consisted of eleven ships, but this happened merely because one of the vessels he considered too small to be counted. However, on p. 213 of the same volume he gives the number 12.

22 See H. T. Colenbrander, *Jan Pietersz. Coen*, Vol. VI, pp. 34–35.

23 P. van Dam, *Beschryvinge*, Vol. I, Part I, pp. 163–164, 224; J. K. J. De Jonge, *De opkomst*, Vol. III, pp. 46–65.

24 P. van Dam, *l.c.*, Vol. I, Part I, p. 506; De Jonge, *l.c.*, Vol. III, pp. 70–71.

25 See below, Ch. VII.

26 De Jonge, *l.c.*, Vol. III, pp. 68–85, 91–98, 276–354; Van Dam, *l.c.*, Vol. I, Part I, p. 568; H. T. Colenbrander, *l.c.*, Vol. VI, p. 37; P. Gonnaud, *La colonisation à Java* (Paris, 1905), pp. 218–222, 276–279; *Journal van alle het gene, dat ghezien ende voorghevallen is op de reyse gedaen door P.W.J. Verhoeven naar de Oost Indien, Philipines, enz,* (Amsterdam, 1646).

27 W. Keeling, *Third Voyage of the East India Company in 1607* (Edinburgh, 1813).

28 *Gesch. van Ned. Indië*, Vol. III, pp. 82–85; De Jonge, *l.c.*, Vol. III, pp. 109–131; P. A. Tiele, *Bouwstoffen voor de geschiedenis der Nederlanders in den Maleischen Archipel*, Vol. I (The Hague, 1886), p. VII.

29 H. T. Colenbrander, *Jan Pietersz. Coen*, Vol. VI, pp. 38–39;

De Jonge, *l.c.*, Vol. III, pp. 131–136; J. P. T. Du Bois, *Vies des Gouverneurs Généraux* (The Hague, 1763), p. 11. On the management of the company see S. Van Brakel, *De Hollandsche handelscompagnieën der zeventiende eeuw* (The Hague, 1908), pp. 71–83.

30 An excellent discussion of the founding of Batavia is to be found in H. T. Colenbrander, *l.c.*, Vol. VI, pp. 177–230.

NOTES FOR CHAPTER III

1 In 1636 there followed another Dutch edition published in Haarlem, while in 1639 and 1641 two other Dutch editions were published in the same city. An excellent English translation was published in 1916 by the Oxford University Press.

2 In the interval between August, 1608, and the signing of the truce in Antwerp in April, 1609, a tortuous policy was followed by the French government under King Henry IV, in its negotiations with the heads of the Dutch government. At this time the king of France sought to found an East India Company of his own. While posing as a friend of the Dutch, he, as well as the king of England, looked with envy on their rapidly expanding trade in the Malay Archipelago, on the coast of the mainland of India, on the island of Ceylon, and on the coasts of China and Japan. The French monarch secretly negotiated with a number of Dutch merchants who were dissatisfied with the course adopted by the directors of the Dutch East India Company.

A great many writers have taken for granted that it was the policy of Henry IV of France to weaken the power of the house of Hapsburg. This has seemed so logical and so natural that few historians have asked themselves whether Henry IV was sincere in his efforts to maintain peace with Spain since the treaty of 1598. For example, H. O. Wakeman in his well-known work, entitled, *The Ascendancy of France, 1598–1715,* made the following statement which has been copied by numerous writers in Europe and in this country: "Thus Henry IV laid the foundations of the policy afterwards so successfully pursued in Italy by Richelieu. In fact, to both of these great Statesmen the end to be attained was the same. The abasement of the Austro-Spanish House in the interests of France was the beginning and end of their foreign policy. But Henry had not the same opportunities of putting his designs into execution which were enjoyed by his successor." Even the more scholarly book by David Ogg, *Europe in the Seventeenth Century*, does not reveal a proper understanding of the foreign policy pursued by Henry IV in the last five years of his reign. Mr. Ogg, like most English writers before him, assumed that the assassination of Henry IV, in 1610, suddenly ushered in a new period in the foreign affairs of the French government. But such was far from true. Long before Henry IV died, it was his sincere hope that his son, later known as Louis XIII, would eventually marry the daughter of the king of Spain. This he eventually did, in the year 1615. If Henry IV had lived until that year, there is no doubt that the marriage would have taken place at that same time.

In the opinion of David Ogg, the old rivalry between France and the house of Hapsburg continued throughout the reign of Henry IV. He informs his reader that the Protestant Union, founded in 1608 by several German princes, considered Henry IV as its patron, and expected his aid in the coming struggle with the Catholic princes. But so little assistance did the Protestants in Germany expect from the king of France, that when they founded this union they did not even notify him of it.

This has been ably demonstrated by G. Pagès in his interesting work entitled *La Monarchie d'Ancien Régime en France* (Paris, 1928), pp. 51–59. Very cautious and rather inconclusive is the verdict of Quentin Hurst as expressed in his book, *Henry of Navarre* (London, 1938), pp. 280–285. He depicts Henry IV as a bit more hostile to Spain than he actually was. However, Henry IV was such an opportunist that he maintained alliances both with Spain and with some of its enemies, such as the Dutch Republic and the duke of Savoy. In 1598, he deserted the English and the Dutch in signing a separate treaty with Spain (of Vervins). But on July 30, 1603, he joined James I of England in completing a treaty of confederation for the defense of the Dutch Republic. In 1604, James I allied himself with Philip III of Spain, while in October, 1604, Henry IV and Philip III signed a treaty in which they professed friendship for each other. Although on February II, 1610, Henry IV took active steps in preventing the duchy of Cleves from falling into the hands of the Hapsburgs, and although on April 25, 1610, he signed two alliances with Savoy against Spain, only two years later his daughter, Elizabeth, became engaged to Philip, son of Philip III of Spain. In the treaty the monarchs of France and Spain promised "de fortifier et tellement étraindre les liens de l'amitié fraternelle et bonne paix contractée par Henri IV et Philippe II . . . laquelle a esté depuis observée et entretenue sincèrement par leurs dites majestés." See *Receuil des traitez de paix*, Vol. III (Amsterdam, 1700, p. 99).

As early as 1865 it was demonstrated by the able Dutch archivist, Mr. J. K. J. De Jonge, that Henry IV was not nearly so friendly to the Dutch and the Protestants in general as had been assumed before 1865. In the third volume of his great work on the rise of Dutch power in the East Indies, he indicates that there are to be found in the national archives in The Hague several valuable documents that throw much light on the negotiations carried on between the representatives of the Spanish and the Dutch governments. Much of this material was published by M. L. Van Deventer in his great work on Van Oldenbarnevelt. (The title of this work is *Gedenkstukken van J. van Oldenbarnevelt 1860–1865*). See Vol. III, pp. 71–312. Not only was Henry IV of the opinion that the Dutch should change their form of government and establish a monarchy, but he also carried on active negotiations with the Spanish party in his own royal council. He was highly pleased with the idea of a royal marriage that would cement the ties between the French and the Spaniards. He issued urgent requests to the members of the Dutch government, suggesting that they become more reasonable in their demands for a share of the trade in the Far East. Even the English decided to take sides with the French and the Spaniards in insisting that the Dutch must come to terms with the Spaniards.

[3] The negotiations for the truce as well as the document itself have been discussed by Miss Frances G. Davenport in her work entitled *European Treaties Bearing on the History of the United States and Its Dependencies to 1648* (Washington, D.C., 1917), pp. 258–269. It should be noted, however, that Miss Davenport published only five of the thirty-eight articles in the truce in question. She makes no distinction between the original editions in the French language published respectively at The Hague and Brussels. Furthermore, in mentioning the publishers in The Hague, she gives only the part of the name that is of lesser importance, while omitting entirely the real name of the publishing house. That name was Hillebrant, while the rest of the name, Iacobssz., which was wrongly spelled by Miss Davenport, merely indicates that this particular member of the family was the son of Jacob Hillebrant. The edition published in The Hague contained merely the thirty-eight articles of the truce, while that published in Brussels was longer, since it included two important documents issued respectively by King Philip III of Spain and published in the Spanish language, and by Albert, archduke of Austria, and his wife Isabella, drawn up in the French language. They were followed by the ratification of the States-General, dated March 22, 1609. Moreover, Miss Davenport makes no mention of the Dutch edition of the Truce which was published by the same publishing house in The Hague that published the first French edition for the States-General of the Dutch Republic. This Dutch edition appeared in the year 1609. In addition to the thirty-eight articles, it concludes with a note that was also published by Miss Davenport immediately at the end of the fifth article of the truce. Another important Dutch edition of the Truce which was also ignored by Miss Davenport, was that which appeared in Antwerp in 1609, and published by Ioachim Trognesius. This edition also contains the ratification by the Dutch government.

According to several British and American writers, the representatives of the Spanish government also signed with the delegates of the States-General of the Dutch Republic a secret treaty, which was reproduced by the Carnegie Endowment in Washington, D.C. It should be noted, however, that contemporary Dutch authorities do not refer at all to this so-called secret treaty. Moreover, the five persons who signed the document were all representatives of the Spanish Netherlands. Not a single person representing the Dutch government signed it. For that reason it can scarcely be called a secret treaty. It was merely an agreement among some Spanish officials at Antwerp, and for that reason it should be called merely an agreement, rather than a treaty.

See F. G. Davenport, *op. cit.,* pp. 267–268. In the footnote at the bottom of page 267, the editor admits that no copy of this secret treaty could be found in the government archives in The Hague. Miss Davenport copied the text from the edition first published in 1656 in the work entitled P. Jeannin, *Négociations,* pp. 638–639. An English translation of the document was published in *British Guiana Boundary, Arbitration with the United States of Venezuela: Appendix to the Counter-case on behalf of Her Britannic Majesty,* Foreign Office Print (1898), pp. 323–324.

4 *Werken uitgegeven door de Linschoten-Vereeniging,* Vols. XIV and XV (1917).

5 G. M. Asher, *Henry Hudson the Navigator. The Original Documents in which his career is recorded collected, partly translated, and annotated* (London: The Hakluyt Society, 1860), pp. 1–44.

6 The contract in the original language, together with an English translation, was published in *Henry Hudson in Holland,* edited by H. C. Murphy, together with notes, documents and a bibliography by Wouter Nijhoff (The Hague: Martinus Nijhoff, 1909), pp. 32–34, 110–111. The original contract was also published in P. van Dam, *Beschryvinge van de Oostindische Compagnie,* ed. by F. W. Stapel, Book I, Vol. I (The Hague: Martinus Nijhoff, 1927), pp. 38–39. It should be noted that Hudson's name is not given as Hendrik (the Dutch for Henry), but as Henry. There is some difference in punctuation between the two editions of the original contract.

7 Published in the volume of the Hakluyt Society dealing with Henry Hudson, pp. 45–93. More important is the edition in Vol. XIX of the works published by the Linschoten-Vereeniging: *Henry Hudson's Reize onder Nederlandsche vlag van Amsterdam naar Nova Zembla, Amerika en terug naar Dartmouth in Engeland,* 1609.

8 P. van Dam, *Beschryvinge,* Book I, Vol. I (1927), pp. 32–33.

9 See H. C. Murphy, *Henry Hudson in Holland* (edition of 1909), pp. 41–54. Mr. Murphy also published an English translation of the important account published in the Dutch language by E. van Meteren in his famous book, *Belgische oorlogen.* A short passage follows here: "The Directors of the East India Company had sent a brave English pilot named Henry Hudson with about 18 or 20 men, in order to seek a passage to China by the northwest or northeast. . . . He found the sea near Nova Zembla as full of ice as he had found it in the preceding year. Thereupon, owing to the cold weather which some who had been in the East Indies could not bear, the English and Dutch began to dispute among themselves. Consequently, Master Hudson offered them a choice between two alternatives, either to sail to the coast of America at a latitude of about 40 degrees (mostly as a result of letters and maps which a certain Captain Smith had sent him from Virginia, and on which he

showed him a sea wherein he might circumnavigate their southern colony from the north and thence pass into the western sea), or to search for the passage by way of the Davis' Straits. To this the men generally agreed."

¹⁰ See Edgar Mayhew Bacon, *Henry Hudson: His Times and His Voyages,* (New York and London: G. P. Putnam's Sons, 1907), p. 175.

¹¹ See Clifford Smyth, *Henry Hudson and the Dutch Founding of New York* (New York and London: Funk & Wagnalls Company, 1931), pp. 86–87.

NOTES FOR CHAPTER IV

¹ Several contracts were actually signed between native kings and the representatives of the Dutch East India Company, in which the latter received a monopoly of the purchase and sale of spices. These have been published in J. K. J. de Jonge, *De opkomst,* Vol. III, pp. 328–330, 345–347, 315–316, and 348–349.

² The English East India Company.

³ A summary of this document is to be found in the *Calendar of State Papers,* Colonial Series, 1513–1616, No. 591. The extracts given above, however, are from the original document, *State Papers,* C.C. 77/1, No. 34.

⁴ *State Papers,* 84/68, fol. 228–232. Summary in *Calendar of State Papers,* Col. Series, 1513–1616, No. 601.

⁵ See No. 53 of the colonial acquisitions in the Algemeen Rijksarchief, The Hague, fol. 227 recto to 228 recto.

⁶ *Resolutions of the States-General,* February 2, March 15, 1612; *Dutch Dispatch Book,* England, 1602–14, pp. 540 ff.; *Calendar of State Papers,* Colonial Series, 606; the original is S. P. 84/68, fol. 250–251.

⁷ The instruction of August 28, 1612, is mentioned by P. C. Molhuysen in the Correspondence of Grotius, I, 229, note 2.

⁸ H. C. Rogge, "De Resolutie der Staten van Holland tot Vrede der Kerk," in *Bijdragen voor Vaderlandsche Geschiedenis en Oudheidkunde,* New Series, VIII (1875), 79–122.

⁹ See fol. 136 recto to verso. See also the excellent description of the separate documents in *Inventarissen van Rijks-en andere Archieven,* vol. I (The Hague, 1928), pp. 73ff.

¹⁰ *Winwood Memorials of Affairs of State,* ed. E. Sawyer, Vol. III (London, 1725), p. 320.

¹¹ See Professor G. N. Clark's admirable article mentioned in a previous chapter, "Grotius's East India mission to England," in *Transactions of the Grotius Society,* XX (1935), pp. 54–55, 63–81.

¹² Cf. *Mare Liberum,* Chap. VIII.

¹³ The English referred to the voyages of Sir Francis Drake and Sir James Lancaster.

¹⁴ Digest VIII. 4. 13, concerning a fishing case.

[15] See H. T. Colenbrander, *Jan Pietersz*, IV, 289; VI, 71.

[16] H. T. Colenbrander, *Jan Pietersz, Coen*, I, 158; VI, 71.

[17] *State Papers* 103/37, fol. 229 recto to 230 recto. Summary in *Calendar*, No. 860.

[18] *State Papers*, 103/37, fol. 233 recto. (Summary in *Calendar of State Papers*. Col. Series, No. 900.)

[19] Professor G. N. Clark says on p. 82 of his article that new negotiations were held in 1614 and 1619. The second date is correct, but the first is erroneous, partly perhaps because the English did not start the new year until March 25th.

[20] See *State Papers*, 103/37, fol. 231 recto. (Summary in *Calendar*, Col. Ser. No. 874.) See also *S.P.* 84/71, fol. 287 recto. (*Calendar*, No. 893.)

[21] See their first brief, dated February 6, 1614 (1615), *State Papers* 103/37, fol. 26 recto—27 recto (pp. 217–219), and *Calendar*, Col. Series, No. 894. See also their second document, dated February 14, 1614 (1615), *State Papers* 103/37, fol. 34 recto—35 recto (pp. 223–225), and *Calendar*, No. 901. Mr. J. K. J. de Jonge, who cannot be accused of having made many errors in his accounts of the three Anglo-Dutch conferences of 1613, 1615 and 1615, does err in believing that the negotiations of 1615 were entirely in writing, as he says on p. LXXVI of his fourth volume: "De Engelschen bragten daarom de onderhandeling, welke alleen schriftelijk gevoerd werd, liever op het terrein van het natuur- en volkenregt." He calls Grotius the chief "penvoerder" of the Dutch commission, but the English in one of their reports referred to him as the "prolocutor" of the Dutch commission. (See *State Papers* 84/71, p. 249.) On April 30, 1615, the Board of Seventeen sent a letter to the headquarters of the East Indies in which it was stated that three oral conferences were held by the two commissions, and that also written statements were presented by both. (See H. T. Colenbrander, *Jan Pietersz. Coen*, Vol. IV, p. 299.)

[22] *State Papers* 84/71, fol. 109 recto (p. 139); *Calendar of State Papers*, Colonial Series, No. 961.

[23] See the report of the English commissioners, signed by the four members of the commission and dated February 22, 1614 (1615), in *State Papers* 84/71, fol. 29 recto-verso (pp. 249–250). *Calendar*, No. 911.

[24] See the *Dutch Dispatch Book* under England for the period 1602–1614 (national archives, The Hague); *Report and Appendices Concerning the Conferences with the English*, a manuscript in the national archives (Rijksarchief) in The Hague; *State Papers*, Public Record Office, London, 103/37, fol. 28 recto—29 recto, which contains the first Dutch reply to the English, in English translation (*Calendar*, No. 896) ; and fol. 36 recto–43 recto, or the second Dutch reply (*Calendar*, No. 905.)

[25] *State Papers* 103/37, fol. 239 recto—243 recto.

[26] *State Papers* 84/71, fol. 111 verso (p. 144). The French text may be found in *S.P.* 103/37, p. 195. The summaries of these documents are in the *Calendar of State Papers*, Colonial Series, No. 961 and No. 975.

NOTES FOR CHAPTER V

[1] J. E. Elias, *Het voorspel van den eersten Engelschen oorlog*, Vol. II (The Hague, 1920), p. 20.

[2] H. T. Colenbrander, *op. cit.*, Vol. VI, pp. 40–41; A. D. Innes, *The Maritime and Colonial Expansion of England under the Stuarts* (London, 1931), p. 55; De Jonge, *op. cit.*, Vol. IV, p. 25; W. W. Hunter, *A History of British India* (London, 1899), Vol. I, pp. 306–382; P. Floris, *His Voyage to the East Indies in the Globe, 1611–1615* (London, 1934); W. Foster, *Voyage of Thomas Best to the East Indies, 1612–1614* (London, 1934).

[3] How skeptical the leaders in the House of Commons were of the king's wisdom may be seen in the words of Sir James Perrot and Sir Richard Weston spoken in Parliament on December 3, 1621. See *Commons Debates 1621*, ed. W. Notestein, F. H. Relf, and H. Simpson, Vol. II (New Haven, Conn., 1935), pp. 488–489. See also E. Sawyer, *Memorials of Affairs of State in the Reigns of Queen Elizabeth and King James I*, Vol. III (London, 1725).

[4] H. T. Colenbrander, *Jan Pietersz. Coen*, Vol. IV, pp. 311–312, Vol. VI, p. 57; J. K. J. de Jonge, *De opkomst*, Vol. IV, pp. XXXII–XXXIII; P. A. Tiele, *Bouwstoffen*, Vol. I, pp. XIV–XXVI, 109–117; *Calendar of State Papers*, East Indies, Vol. II, Nos. 5, 29, 245, 257, 425, 499, 623; *Richard Cocks, Diary*, ed. E. M. Thompson, Hakluyt Society, No. 67 (London, 1888), p. 316. In the year 1624, the English made formal complaints to the Dutch at Batavia over the capture of the *Swan* and the *Defense*. See *Dagh-Register*, 1624–1629 (Batavia and The Hague, 1882), pp. 109–110.

[5] J. K. J. de Jonge, *De opkomst*, Vol IV, pp. XXXVI, 67–71; *Calendar of State Papers*, East Indies, Vol. II, Nos. 424, 425, 500.

[6] See the excellent biography of Coen in H. T. Colenbrander, *Jan Pietersz. Coen*, Vol. VI (The Hague, 1934).

[7] But there was to be no open war between the English and the Dutch, in spite of all the efforts Coen ever made. See J. K. J. de Jonge, *De opkomst*, Vol. IV, pp. XXXVI–XXXVII, 72; H. T. Colenbrander, *Jan Pietersz. Coen*, Vol. I, pp. 301–305.

[8] Th. Rymer, *Foedera*, Vol. XVII (London, 1717), p. 57.

[9] H. T. Colenbrander, *op. cit.*, Vol. I, pp. 421–425, 434; *Calendar of State Papers*, Colonial Series, East Indies, ed. by W. N. Sainsbury, Vol. II (London, 1870), Nos. 500, 511, 547, 601, 609, 763, 814.

[10] H. T. Colenbrander, *op. cit.*, Vol. VI, p. 153; P. A. Tiele, *Bouwstoffen*, Vol. I, pp. XXXVI–XXXVII; J. P. T. du Bois, *Vies des Gouverneurs Généraux*, pp. 38–41.

[11] J. K. J. de Jonge, *De opkomst*, Vol. IV, pp. XCI–XCIII, 132–134; H. T. Colenbrander, *Jan Pietersz. Coen*, Vol. I, pp. 431–439, Vol. VI, pp. 154–157; P. A. Tiele, *Bouwstoffen*, Vol. I, pp. XXXVII–XLII.

[12] J. K. J. de Jonge, *De opkomst*, Vol. IV, p. XCV; H. T. Colenbrander, *Jan Pietersz. Coen*, Vol. VI, pp. 163–165; J. E. Heeres, *Corpus Diplomaticum* (The Hague, 1907), Vol. I, pp. 147–149; P. A. Tiele, *De Europeërs in den Maleischen Archipel*, Vol. IX (The Hague, 1887), pp. 217–218; *Calendar of State Papers*, Colonial Series, 1617–1621, No. 529.

[13] H. T. Colenbrander, *op. cit.*, Vol. VI, p. 169; "A Short Account of the Siege of Bantam," in *Harleian Miscellany*, Vol. V (London, 1745), pp. 271–273.

[14] J. A. van der Chijs, *De Nederlanders te Jakatra* (Amsterdam, 1860); P. Gonnaud, *La colonisation Hollandaise à Java*, pp. 280–304. During the past fifteen years there has been a tendency to remove certain important offices to Bandoeng, which is situated on a plateau to the southeast and is much pleasanter and far more healthful. In 1940, for example, the publication offices of the important daily newspaper, *Java-Bode*, were transferred from Batavia to Bandoeng.

[15] In the second half of 1618 and in 1619 Prince Maurice, the *stadhouder* (governor, or president) of the Dutch Republic, was extremely anxious to please the English government, for he faced strong opposition offered by Oldenbarnevelt's friends, and so he forced the Dutch commissioners to accept disadvantageous terms.

[16] See *Codex diplomaticus Neerlandicus*, published by Het Historisch Genootschap te Utrecht, 2nd Series, Vol. III (1856), pp. 135–136.

[17] *Codex dipl.*, pp. 138–248.

[18] The treaty was published in *Historisch verhaal van het begin, de voortgang en den tegenwoordigen staat des koophandels van de . . . Compagnie*, Vol. II (Arnhem, 1772), pp. 289 ff. Another copy is to be found in Jacqpes Bernard, *Recueil des traités de paix, de trève, de neutralité, de suspension d'armes, de confédération, d'alliance, de commerce . . .*, Vol. III (Amsterdam and The Hague, 1700), pp. 153–156. It is made to appear as if the treaty contains thirty-one articles, instead of thirty, because a separate paragraph follows the article XXX, and this paragraph is introduced by the number XXXI. But it is not a separate article, constituting merely an explanatory note. The treaty is followed here by another document, which is almost as important. It is dated July 15, 1619, old style, hence July 25; and it is signed by thirteen of the commissioners, who explain how the terms of the treaty are to be executed, espcially those in Articles IV, V, VII, VIII, X, XIII, XXVIII, and XXX. How pleased James I was with the treaty may be gathered from the fact that he immediately knighted three of the Dutch commissioners. See *Calendar of State Papers*, Colonial Series, 1617–1621 (London, 1870), No. 707. The treaty itself is mentioned here under No. 706, indicating that the Public Record Office contains a copy listed under this num-

ber (p. 284). A copy of the treaty of 1619 in the French language was published in L. van Aitzema, *Historie of verhael van saken en staet en oorlogh, in, ende omtrent de Vereenigde Nederlanden,* Vol. I (The Hague, 1657), pp. 44–51. A Dutch translation of the treaty and the regulations that follow it in the *Recueil* appears in the same volume (pp. 503–517).

[19] Even the English soon began to complain about the treaty of 1619. For example, the merchants of the East India company presented their grievances to the government as summarized in *Calendar of State Papers,* Colonial Series, East Indies, China and Japan, 1622–1624 (London, 1878), Nos. 511, 518, 527, 541, and 543 (see pp. 324–325, 330, 334–335, 350, and 351). On July 22, 1624, they wrote: "We know ourselves too weak by the start the Dutch have got on us, let us join with the Portugals and root the bloody Dutch out of the Indies." In 1629, they were still complaining and hoping that soon another treaty would be signed. The original treaty was permitted to run its whole course of twenty years, as appears in the treaty signed in 1654 between the English and Dutch commissioners who had been appointed to settle the claims of the two East India companies. The Dutch said that the English company had failed during a period of seventeen years (1622–1639) to contribute its share to the defense of the East Indies. Referring to the year 1639 they said: "jam cessante Tractatu anni 1619." See *Recueil des traités de paix,* Vol. III, p. 661. Aitzema reports that in 1623 James I did not wish to press the Dutch too hard for damages, because he expected them to help him in recovering from his son-in-law, Frederick V of the Palatinate, his lost country. A few years later Cats and Brassert were sent to England to see what they could do about the treaty of 1619, but little was accomplished. (See Aitzema's first volume, p. 504.)

NOTES FOR CHAPTER VI

[1] Wm. Campbell, *Formosa under the Dutch* (London, 1903), pp. 1–9; F. Valentyn, *Oud en Nieuw,* Vol. IV, pt. II, Formosa, pp. 33–37; P. van Dam, *Beschryvinge,* Vol. II, pt. I, p. 710.

[2] W. P. Groeneveldt, *De Nederlanders in China,* Vol. I (The Hague, 1898), pp. 22–23; P. van Dam, *Beschryvinge,* Vol. II, pt. I, p. 671; J. K. J. de Jonge, *De opkomst,* Vol. III, pp. 148–149.

[3] P. van Dam, *Beschryvinge,* Vol. II, pt. I, p. 672; Vol. I, pt. II, pp. 485, 499, 517; Hugo Grotius, *De Jure Praedae* (The Hague, 1868), p. 314; R. Fruin, *Verspreide Geschriften,* Vol. III (The Hague, 1901), p. 378; Hugo Grotius, *Annales et Historiae,* lib. X, p. 428 of the 8th ed.; J. Wagenaar, *Vaderlandsche historie,* Vol. IX (Amsterdam, 1753), p. 146.

[4] R. Fruin, *Verspreide Geschriften,* Vol. III, p. 394; H. Grotius, *De Jure Praedae,* pp. 318, 201.

[5] *Gesch. van Ned. Indië,* Vol. III, p. 220; J. Burney, *Chron. History of Discoveries,* Vol. III, pp. 45–46; F. Valentyn, *Oud en Nieuw,* Vol. IV, pt. II, Formosa, p. 46.

⁶ *Dagh-Register*, 1624–1629, p. 7.

⁷ Richard Cocks, *Diary*, Vol. II, December 31, 1622, p. 339.

⁸ P. van Dam, *Beschryvinge*, Vol. II, pt. I, p. 689; *Gesch. van Ned. Indië*, Vol. III, p. 221; P. Auber, *China* (London, 1834), p. 86. On December 9, 1624, Sonck's information reached Batavia. See *Dagh-Register*, 1624–1629, p. 141.

⁹ P. van Dam, *Beschryvinge*, Vol. II, pt. I, p. 370; *Calendar of State Papers*, Colonial Series, East Indies, Vol. IV, No. 255; Vol. III, No. 415.

¹⁰ F. Valentyn, *Oud en Nieuw*, Vol. IV, pt. II, Formosa, p. 49; *Dagh-Register*, 1624–1629, p. 144; *Gesch. van Ned. Indië*, Vol. III, p. 221; S. Kalff, "De Val van Formosa," *De Gids* (1897, pt. II), p. 106; L. Knappert, "Hollandsche Pioniers op Formosa," *Ned Arch. Kerkgesch.* Vol. XIX (1926), p. 98; H. E. Hobson, "Fort Zeelandia," *Journal of North-China Branch R.A.S.*, Vol. XI (1877), p. 33.

¹¹ *Dagh-Register*, 1624–1629, p. 225; J. Burney, *Chron. History of Discoveries*, Vol. III, p. 49; A. Montanus, *Ambassades mémorables de la Compagnie des Indes Orientales des Provinces Unies* (Amsterdam, 1680), p. 37; F. Valentyn, *Oud en Nieuw*, Vol. IV, pt. II, Formosa, p. 65.

¹² O. Nachod, the author of an excellent work on the relations between the Dutch East India Company and Japan, was mistaken in his belief that Van Linschoten was the first Hollander to visit Japan. As a matter of fact, he never saw this country at all. Nachod bases his opinion upon unreliable contemporary accounts. See his work, *Die Beziehungen der Niederlaendischen Ostindischen Kompagnie zu Japan im siebzehnten Jahrhundert* (Leipzig, 1897), p. 91. See also F. Valentyn, *Oud en Nieuw*, Vol. V, pt. II, Japan, p. 25.

¹³ J. W. IJzerman, *Dirck Gerritsz Pomp alias Dirck Gerritsz China de eerste Nederlander die China en Japan bezocht (1544–1604)*, Vol. IX, Linschoten-Vereeniging (The Hague, 1915), pp. 1–2, 5–7; A. Wichmann, *Dirck Gerritsz. Ein Beitrag zur Entdeckungsgeschichte des 16ten und 17ten Jahrhunderts* (Groningen, 1899); F. C. Wieder, *De reis van Mahu en de Cordes door de Straat van Magalliaes naar Zuid-Amerika en Japan, 1598–1600*, pt. III, Linschoten-Vereeniging, Vol. XXIV (The Hague, 1925), p. 3.

¹⁴ J. W. IJzerman, *Dirck Gerritsz Pomp*, pp. 7, 13, 14; *Het Itinerario van Jan Huygen van Linschoten*, pt. I, Linschoten-Vereeniging, Vol. II (The Hague, 1910), pp. 99–103; C. A. Montalto de Jesus, *Historic Macao* (Hongkong, 1902), p. 53.

¹⁵ J. W. IJzerman, *Dirck Gerritsz Pomp*, p. 14.

¹⁶ Pomp left Japan on March 20, 1586: J. W. IJzerman, *Dirck Gerritsz Pomp*, pp. 15–17.

¹⁷ J. W. IJzerman, *Dirck Gerritsz Pomp*, pp. 18–22.

¹⁸ Van Linschoten, *Itinerario*, Vol. I, pp. 103–107; A. C. Burnell, *The Voyage of John Huygen van Linschoten to the East Indies*, Hakluyt Society, No. 70 (London, 1885), pp. 151–165.

¹⁹ Rev. Petrus Plancius was famous for his work on sea maps

(*portolani*). See Hugo Grotius' *Correspondence*, ed. P. C. Molhuysen, Vol. I (The Hague, 1928), No. 53, pp. 44–45. See also Van Linschoten, *Itinerario*, Vol. I, pp. 30, 70; J. K. J. de Jonge, *De opkomst*, Vol. I, pp. 184–200.

[20] F. C. Wieder, *De reis van Mahu en de Cordes door de Straat van Magalhaes naar Zuid-Amerika en Japan* (*1598–1600*) , Vol. III, p. 5; E. M. Satow, *The Voyage of Captain John Saris to Japan 1613*, Hakluyt Society, 2nd Series, No. 5 (London, 1900), p. 188.

[21] F. C. Wieder, *De reis van Mahu en de Cordes*, Vol. III, pp. 4–8.

[22] O. Nachod says on p. 92 of his book, *Japan*, that the trip was sponsored by the States-General, but in the footnote he refers to resolutions of the provincial estates of Holland on June 16, 1595. Nachod was mistaken in his reference to the resolutions of the provincial estates in respect to this matter. The resolutions were the action of the States-General. See N. Japikse, *Resolutiën der Staten-Generaal van 1576 tot 1609*, Vol. VIII, 1593–1595 (The Hague, 1925), pp. 632–633. For the complete instructions given by the States-General to Willem Barents, who was to be in command of the expedition and to Brant Ysbrantsz. of Enkhuizen, the chief pilot, see *Kronijk van het Historisch Genootschap Gevestigd te Utrecht*, Vol. XXI (Utrecht, 1865), pp. 293–301.

[23] This company was called .the "Compagnie der Zuidnederlanders te Rotterdam." See *Gesch. van Ned. Indië*, Vol. II, pp. 397–407, Vol. III, pp. 7–8.

[24] F. C. Wieder, *De reis van Mahu en de Cordes*, Vol. I (The Hague, 1923), pp. 30–31, 89–90; Vol. III, pp. 3–49; O. Nachod, *Japan*, p. 93; P. Auber, *China* (London, 1834), p. 372; T. Rundall, *Memorials of the Empire of Japan in the Sixteenth and Seventeenth Centuries*, Hakluyt Society, No. 8 (London, 1850), pp. 18–24; Peter Pratt, *History of Japan*, ed. M. Paske-Smith, Vol. I (Kobe, Japan, 1931), p. 2; J. K. J. de Jonge, *De opkomst*, Vol. II, pp. 218–220; F. Valentyn, *Oud en Nieuw*, Vol. V, pt. II, Japan, p. 25. In the Nagasaki record there is this entry: "In the 5th year of Keicho 1600 a large vessel arrived at Sakai-ura, which on inquiry was found to be a Dutch ship come to trade. She was ordered to proceed to Edo. On her voyage there, she was overtaken by a gale at Uraga and wrecked. The crew proceeded to Edo by land, where they resided for some time, having no vessel in which to return to their native land. Among the crew were two men called Yayosu and William Adams." See Yamagata, *The Political Relations of Japan and Holland under the Tokugawa Regime, in Notulen van de Algemeene en Bestuursvergaderingen van het Bataviaasch Genootschap*, Vol. XXX (Batavia, 1892), p. LXXX. The greater part of Yamagata's book has been incorporated into J. Murdoch and J. Yamagata, *History of Japan during the Century of early Foreign Intercourse, 1542–1651* (Kobe, Japan, 1903). This in turn has been included in J. Murdoch, *History of Japan*, 3 vols. (London, 1925).

[25] For William Adams' Letters see *Transactions of the Asiatic So-*

ciety of Japan, Vol. XXVI (1898), Appendix II, pp. 194–211; T. Rundall, *Memorials of the Empire of Japan*, pp. 19–24, 35–38 (F. C. Wieder, *De reis van Mahu en de Cordes*, Vol. III, pp. 54–68 gives Adams' letter of October 22, 1611); *Calendar of State Papers*, Colonial Series, East Indies, Vol. I, No. 585. For Adams' letter see also F. C. Danvers and W. Foster, *Letters Received by the East India Company from Its Servants in the East, 1602–1617*, Vol. I (London, 1896), pp. 142–152.

[26] F. C. Wieder, *De reis van Mahu en de Cordes*, Vol. III, pp. 17–18.

[27] F. C. Wieder, *De reis van Mahu en de Cordes*, Vol. III, pp. 21–22; P. Auber, *China, pp.* 380–382; O. Nachod, *Japan*, p. XXXIX.

[28] This was the fleet commanded by Matelief de Jonge: De Jonge, *De opkomst*, Vol. II, pp. 235–236; O. Nachod, *Japan*, p. 105. Some of the ships were to go to China, and if they were successful in their attempt to open commercial relations with this country, the commander would dispatch one ship from Japan to China.

[29] F. C. Wieder, *De reis van Mahu en de Cordes*, Vol. III, pp. 42–43.

[30] O. Nachod, *Japan*, pp. 99–115; J. K. J. de Jonge, *De opkomst*, Vol. III, pp. 84–87; P. Pratt, *History of Japan*, Vol. II, p. 222; Heeres, *Corpus*, Vol. I, pp. 69–70; P. Auber, *China*, p. 383; F. Valentyn, *Oud en Nieuw*, Vol. V, pt. II, Japan, p. 26; P. van Dam, *Beschryvinge*, Vol. II, pt. I, p. 366.

[31] J. K. J. de Jonge, *De opkomst*, Vol. III, p. 86.

[32] See J. K. J. de Jonge, *De opkomst*, Vol. III, pp. 86–87, 296–301; L. C. D. Van Dijck, *Iets over onze vroegste betrekkingen met Japan*, pp. 15–35; P. Pratt, *History of Japan*, Vol. II (Kobe, Japan, 1931), pp. 222–223; O. Nachod, *Japan*, pp. IX–XIX, 110–116; G. Lauts, *Japan in zijn staatkundige en burgerlijke inrigtingen en het verkeer met Europesche natiën* (Amsterdam, 1847), p. 171; *Gesch. van Ned. Indië*, Vol. III, p. 224; H. T. Colenbrander, *Coen*, Vol. VI. p. 36; F. Valentyn, *Oud en Nieuw*, Vol. V, pt. II, Japan, p. 26. For the pass of the emperor see Samuel Purchas, *Hakluytus posthumus or Purchas his Pilgrimes*, Vol. III (Glasgow, 1905), pp. 548–550; Heeres, *Corpus*, Vol. I, p. 70; J. K. J. de Jonge, *De opkomst*, Vol. III, p. 301; Shozo Yamagata, *The Political Relations of Japan and Holland under the Tokugawa Regime*, pp. LXXX–LXXXI; *Gesch. van Ned. Indië*, Vol. III, pp. 76–78. The Spanish attempted but without success to induce Ieyasu not to grant trading permission to the Dutch. See J. Murdoch, *History of Japan*, Vol. II, p. 479; Yosohuro Takekoshi, *Economic Aspects of Japan*, Vol. II, pp. 107–108.

[33] Van Dijk, *Iets over onze vroegste betrekkingen met Japan*, pp. 24, 34; O. Nachod, *Japan*, pp. XXI–XXIV.

[34] E. Kaempfer, *History of Japan*, Vol. II, p. 170–171. For the terms of the pass granted on August 30, 1611, see E. Kaempfer, *op. cit.*, p. 259 or Plate XX; Heeres, *Corpus*, Vol. I, pp. 94–95. It is curious that this pass was not published by Nachod. He makes much of the pass of 1609, and he also publishes that of 1617. For further informa-

tion about the pass of 1611 see A. Montanus, *Ambassades mémorables*, p. 195; Kaempfer, *op. cit.*, Table or Plate XX. These two copies given by the two different writers have the same meaning, but that by Kaempfer is much longer. The Japanese pass in the original consisted of only six lines.

35 O. Nachod, *Japan, p.* XXXI–XXXVI.

36 O. Nachod, *Japan,* pp. XXXVIII–XXXIX.

37 *Gesch. van Ned. Indië,* Vol. III, p. 228; O. Nachod, *Japan,* p. 169; *Calendar of State Papers,* Colonial Series, East Indies, Vol. II, No. 221; P. Pratt, *History of Japan,* Vol. II, p. 231.

38 O. Nachod, *Japan,* p. 117; P. Pratt, *History of Japkan,* Vol. I, p. 186; Vol. II, p. 225. Cocks complained that the King of Hirado "was going to ask the emperor to have the Hollanders and us to goe to som other place, for that he was awery of us and of our proceadinges." See Cocks, *Diary,* Vol. I, p. 246. Adams sought for larger privileges for the English, but the Emperor refused. See Cocks, *Diary,* Vol. I, pp. 312–313; P. Pratt, *op. cit.,* Vol. I, p. 241.

39 For the pass given to the Dutch in 1617 see E. Kaempfer, *History of Japan,* Vol. II, pp. 259–260, 263; O. Nachod, *Japan,* pp. 170–171, XLIX–L; Heeres, *Corpus,* Vol. I, p. 133. The Dutch were granted a rather remarkable permission in that their ships were permitted to enter all ports of Japan when necessity demanded, while at the same time all other foreigners were confined to Hirado and Nagasaki. See Heeres, *l. c.,* Vol. I, p. 133.

40 Van Dam's figures of trade are very sketchy until the year 1649. See P. van Dam, *Beschryvinge,* Vol. II, pt. I, pp. 556–557.

41 *Dagh-Register,* 1624–1629, p. 41; O. Nachod, *Japan,* pp. 186–187.

42 O. Nachod, *Japan,* p. 187.

43 J. Murdoch, *History of Japan,* Vol. II, p. 626; O. Nachod, *Japan,* p. 188. At the same time no Japanese Christians may leave Japan, and no Japanese may go to Manila. See *Dagh Register,* 1624–1629, p. 13; R. H. Akagi, *Japan's Foreign Relations* (Tokyo, 1936), p. 6.

44 O. Nachod, *Japan,* p. CXXII.

45 O. Nachod, *Japan,* pp. 224–226; Akagi, *Japan's Foreign Relations,* pp. 6–7; P. van Dam, *Beschryvinge,* Vol. II, pt. I, p. 371.

46 All attempts to secure a restoration of the old trading rights were in vain: Heeres, *Corpus,* Vol. I, pp. 213, 338. See also O. Nachod, *Japan, pp.* 226–227.

47 E. Kaempfer, *History of Japan,* Vol. I, p. 328; O. Nachod, *Japan,* pp. 230–234. This revolt started as an economic rebellion and then became a Christian revolt according to the Dutch commander Couckebacker. See J. Murdoch, *History of Japan,* Vol. II, pp. 650–652. See also L. Pagès, *Histoire de la religion Chrétienne en Japon, 1598–1651* (Paris, 1869–1870); P. F. X. de Charlevoix, *Histoire de l'établissement, des progrès et de la décadence du Christianisme dans l'Empire du Japon,* 3 vols. (Rouen, 1751).

[48] P. van Dam, *Beschryvinge*, Vol. II, pt. I, p. 366; O. Nachod, *Japan*, pp. 163–165, 259–267; J. Murdoch, *History of Japan*, Vol. II, p. 657; Yamagata, *Political Relations of Japan and Holland*, p. LXXXVII; E. Kaempfer, *History of Japan*, Vol. II, p. 172.

[49] E. Kaempfer, *History of Japan*, Vol. II, pp. 158–162, 165–166; J. K. J. de Jonge, *De opkomst*, Vol. II, p. 106; J. Murdoch, *History of Japan*, Vol. II, pp. 663–664, 672–673.

[50] The measure which had put the Portuguese out of Japan was greeted by the Dutch with great joy but it proved to be a two-edged sword that could cut and hurt them; as the Day Book in Batavia said "want hadde d'ervarentheyt altyt geleert, dat, wanneer 't op de Portugesen regent, op de Compe gemeenelyck mede al druppen will." See *Dagh-Register*, 1640–1641, p. 149; Heeres, *Corpus*, Vol. I, p. 338. In May, 1641, the Dutch were confined to the small island of Deshima in Nagasaki harbor. See F. Valentyn, *Oud en Nieuw*, Vol. V, pt. II, Japan, pp. 36–37; O. Nachod, *Japan*, pp. 245–246; 296–298; Heeres, *Corpus*, Vol. I, pp. 344, 356–358; *Dagh-Register*, 1641–1642, pp. 65–67.

[51] E. Kaempfer, *History of Japan*, Vol. II, p. 171; O. Nachod, *Japan*, pp. 280–281; A. Montanus, *Ambassades mémorables*, p. 24; J. Murdoch, *History of Japan*, Vol. II, pp. 675–676; Takes Itazawa, *Development of the Dutch Studies* (Tokyo, 1933), p. 9; Yamagata, *Political Relations of Japan and Holland*, p. LXXXVI; F. Valentyn, *Oud en Nieuw*, Vol. V, pt. II, Japan, p. 101. How badly the Dutch were treated in 1671 can be gathered from the instructions which the British agent at Batavia gave to the crews of the ships the *Crown* and the *Bantam* when they set out for Japan in order to resume negotiations with the Japanese government. See P. Pratt, *History of Japan*, Vol. II, pp. 154, 259. See also F. Caron's own story of Japan in *Beschrijvinghe van het machtigh Koningkrijcke Japan* (Amsterdam, 1648).

[52] J. Feenstra-Kuiper, *Japan en de bruitenwereld in de achttiende eeuw* (The Hague, 1921), pp. 176–182.

[53] For a list of the Dutch imports see E. Kaempfer, *History of Japan*, Vol. II, p. 214.

[54] In 1649 the Dutch made a profit of 200 per cent from the trade with Japan. See P. van Dam, *Beschryvinge*, Vol. II, pt. I, p. 283.

[55] F. Valentyn, *Oud en Nieuw*, Vol. V, pt. II, Japan, pp. 36–37; P. van Dam, *Beschryvinge*, Vol. II, pt. I, pp. 366–367; O. Nachod, *Japan*, pp. 245–246, 295–298. The island of Deshima was six hundred feet long and two hundred forty feet wide. See E. Kaempfer, *History of Japan*, Vol. II, p. 173; See also Yamagata, *Political Relations of Japan and Holland*, p. LXXXVIII.

[56] In November, 1640, the Japanese issued regulations to the Dutch. See Heeres, *Corpus*, Vol. I, pp. 338–339; *Dagh-Register*, 1640–1641, p. 156; F. Valentyn, *Oud en Nieuw*, Vol. V, pt. II, Japan, p. 101; O. Nachod, *Japan*, p. 199.

⁵⁷ For the ordinances of 1641 see Heeres, *Corpus*, Vol. I, pp. 356–358. See also *Dagh-Register*, 1641–1642, pp. 68–69.

⁵⁸ P. van Dam, *Beschryvinge*, Vol. II, pt. I, p. 372; R. H. Akagi, *Japan's Foreign Relations*, p. 7.

⁵⁹ P. van Dam, *Beschryvinge*, Vol. II, pt. I, p. 373.

⁶⁰ The regulations were given by the Emperor to Jan van Elserack in December, 1643. See Heeres, *Corpus*, Vol. I, pp. 419–422; *Dagh-Register*, 1644–1645, pp. 177, 195–196, 198, 209; O. Nachod, *Japan*, p. 310.

⁶¹ P. van Dam, *Beschryvinge*, Vol. II, pt. I, p. 380; O. Nachod, *Japan*, p. 306; *Dagh-Register*, 1643–1644, pp. 1–4; *Dagh-Register*, 1644–1645, pp. 175–197; F. Valentyn, *Oud en Nieuw*, Vol. V, pt. II, Japan, pp. 101–103. One Japanese authority accounts for the sparing of the lives of the Hollanders by the fact that three of them were made gunnery instructors, who at that time were very greatly in demand, and two others practised surgery. See Yamagata, *Political Relations of Japan and Holland*, pp. LXXXIX–XC.

⁶² P. Van Dam, *Beschryvinge*, Vol. II, pt. I, pp. 376–377: "Want die, volgens het spreeckwoort, het al soeckt, dat die veel off al verliest." Van Dam, *op cit.*, p. 377. See also the letter of the Seventeen of September 21, 1644.

⁶³ P. van Dam, *Beschryvinge*, Vol. II, pt. I, pp. 405, 423. The Dutch were still cautioned about their religion and the bringing in of Christian books. See Van Dam, *l. c.*, pp. 409–410; F. Valentyn, *Oud en Nieuw*, Vol. V, pt. I, Japan, pp. 91, 100, 165–166; O. Nachod, *Japan*, pp. 285, 302, 338.

⁶⁴ P. van Dam, *Beschryvinge*, Vol. II, pt. I, p. 428; *Dagh-Register*, 1663, pp. 650–653; *Dagh-Register*, 1664, pp. 501–510; P. Pratt, *History of Japan*, Vol. II, p. 254.

⁶⁵ P. van Dam in his work *Beschryvinge*, Vol. II, pt. I, gives figures for the Dutch trade after 1649. The percentages of profit to the Dutch each year were as follows:

1649	200%
1650	40%, much bad weather and storms encountered
1651	80%
1652	65%
1653	103%
1654	80%
1656	65%
1657	40%
1658	100%
1659	80%
1660	68%
1661	79%
1662	52%
1662	over 5 tons of gold (no figures given)

No profits are given for the years 1655, 1663, 1664. The average profit for the years 1649–1662 was 81 per cent. Van Dam states that the profits for the years 1642–1660 were 12,369,824 guilders.

[66] See J. Schouten, *A True Description of the Mighty Kingdoms of Japan and Siam* (London, 1663); G. F. Meylan, *Japan* (Amsterdam, 1830); A. F. Cardim, *Relation de ce qui s'est passée au Japon* (Paris, 1646); J. H. Longford, *The Tokugawa Epoch, 1652–1868* (London, 1926).

NOTES FOR CHAPTER VII

[1] See his excellent book, *The Anglo-Dutch Alliance and the War Against Dutch Trade* (Manchester, 1923). Clark points out that "strictly speaking, the alliance existed before 1688." The defensive alliance of 1667–1668 was confirmed upon the accession of James II. See pp. 1–5.

[2] G. N. Clark, *op. cit.*, pp. 12–38, 43. See also H. Sée, "Que fait-il penser de l'oeuvre économique de Colbert?" in *Revue Historique*, Vol. CLII (1926), pp. 181–197. Sée shows that Colbert was more interested in ruining the European trade of the Hollanders than in expanding French colonial gains in America or India. See p. 192.

[3] An excellent account of the fall of Formosa is to be found in the doctoral dissertation by my student, Dr. Paul B. Cares, who based his study very largely on the Dutch sources. Those left by the Chinese have been used with marked success by Dr. Earl Swisher, Assistant Professor at the University of Colorado. But he is mistaken in his opinion that according to the Dutch sources the local fort and garrison surrendered on April 31, 1662.

[4] Yosoburo Takekoshi, *The Economic Aspects of the History of the Civilization of Japan*, Vol. III (New York, 1930), p. 200.

[5] Y. Takekoshi, *op. cit.*, III, 199–202.

[6] Takekoshi remarks that "the chief reason for the decline in Dutch trade in Japan was the development of home industries brought about as a result of the Japanese intercourse with foreign countries, by which Japan became a self-supporting country." There is much truth in this remark.

[7] An interesting discussion of the Dutch in Australia may be found in a series of three articles published by F. Dekker in the Dutch periodical *Neerlandia* for January, February, and March, 1938.

[8] H. E. Wildes, *Aliens in the East* (Philadelphia, 1937), pp. 45–60, 165–173.

[9] H. E. Wildes, *op. cit.*, p. V. It should be noted, however, that Wildes himself is not aware of the scientific work done by the Dutch in Japan. He is of the opinion that the Dutch knew very little about the country and the people. His opinion is refuted in the writings of Engelbert Kaempfer, Charles Peter Thunberg, and Izaac Titsingh.

[10] Amry Vandenbosch, *The Dutch East Indies* (Berkeley and Los Angeles, 1941).

[11] C. R. Boxer, *Jan Compagnie in Japan* (The Hague, 1936). The only reference made by Vandenbosch to the Dutch in Japan is a brief repetition of a few remarks made by Boxer and one made by E. N. van Kleffens (in his work, *De internationaal rechtelijke betrekkingen tusschen Nederland en Japan, 1605–heden*, Leyden, 1919). To the whole history of the Dutch in Japan Vandenbosch devotes less than four pages.

[12] The title of this book is *Kwai-Tsusho-ko.*

[13] See the interesting series of three articles on the Dutch in Japan by F. Dekker in *Neerlandia* for February, March, and April, 1941. See also H. E. Wildes, *Aliens in the East*, pp. 197–224.

[14] H. E. Wildes, *Aliens in East*, pp. 211–224; E. N. van Kleffens, *De internationaal rechtelijke betrekkingen tusschen Nederland en Japan*, p. 37. On the services rendered by the Dutch prior to 1853 see R. H. Akagi, *Japan's Foreign Relations*, pp. 16–18. See also J. H. Gubbins, *The Progress of Japan 1853–1871* (Oxford, 1911), pp. 40–64.

[15] E. S. de Klerck, *History of the Netherlands East Indies*, Vol. II, pp. 110–119.

[16] J. S. Furnivall, *Netherlands India*, p. 206.

[17] Many of the figures given above may be found in J. S. Furnivall, *Netherlands India* (Cambridge, 1939), pp. 303–345.

NOTES FOR CHAPTER IX

[1] *Ten Years of Japanese Burrowing in the Netherlands East Indies*, New York: The Netherlands Information Bureau, no date given, pp. 93–94.

[2] C. C. Tansill, *Back Door to War: The Roosevelt Foreign Policy*, Chicago, Ill., 1952, p. 645.

[3] *Idem, Ib.*

[4] C. E. L. Helfrich, *Mémoires*, 2 vols., Amsterdam 1950.

[5] P. S. Gerbrandy, *Indonesia*, London, New York, 1951, p. 42.

[6] C. Smit, *De Indonesische quaestie*, Leiden, 1952, pp. 2–11.

INDEX[1]

---

[1] Since the present work does not contain a formal bibliography which is made up of a mere list of books, alphabetically arranged, but rather an extensive bibliographical discussion giving the complete titles of all the important books mentioned, the names of the authors most frequently discussed are included in this index, each being marked with an asterisk.